SIXTEEN SYMPHONIES

SIXTEEN SYMPHONIES

By

BERNARD SHORE

With a Foreword by
SIR ADRIAN BOULT

WITH 16 PORTRAITS

1724

LONGMANS, GREEN AND CO
LONDON ♦ NEW YORK ♦ TORONTO

LONGMANS, GREEN AND CO. LTD
6 & 7 CLIFFORD STREET, LONDON W.1

LONGMANS, GREEN AND CO. INC.
55 FIFTH AVENUE, NEW YORK 3

LONGMANS, GREEN AND CO.
215 VICTORIA STREET, TORONTO 1

ALSO AT MELBOURNE AND CAPE TOWN

ORIENT LONGMANS LTD
BOMBAY, CALCUTTA, MADRAS

First published 1949

DEDICATED

TO

SIR ADRIAN BOULT

FOREWORD

IT IS rather sad that popular taste is apt to magnify the importance of the reproducing artist and to forget that he is the servant
of the creator—the composer, the playwright, the poet. It is
natural perhaps that the man who stands before us, whose efforts
we see, whose emotion we share, grows in importance in our
minds, and we think less of the creative genius who has toiled for
us and maybe suffered for us in a measure which performers can
themselves easily forget.

I remember seeing Toscanini open the score of Beethoven's
Mass and turn to that noble Praeludium (between the Sanctus and
the Benedictus), which, in the service of the Mass, goes with the
elevation of the Host. He seemed to prostrate himself before it
as if he could hardly bear to contemplate its beauty. "I close my
eyes," he said, "when I come to this, and it seems to overwhelm
me." Anyone who has had any contact with that great man will
have been struck with his sense of service to the composer and to
his music.

Many readers have told me how much they enjoyed Mr.
Bernard Shore's earlier book, *The Orchestra Speaks*, with its
stories of interpreters and interpretation. I think the present book
will be even more welcome, for he now turns to the root of the
matter, and gives us a penetrating study of most of the greatest
symphonic masterpieces and their composers. He adorns, alas, no
longer the grand vantage point in the front of the orchestra, from
which he was able to observe, while devoting himself to the
cause of great music. This book embodies his 'recollections
in tranquillity,' if indeed the word 'tranquillity' can be used of
the ever more important and stimulating work that he is now
doing: whilst still a soloist he brings inspiration to the art of
music teaching throughout the land.

I feel sure that this book will be warmly welcomed wherever
music is heard and loved.

ADRIAN C. BOULT.

AUTHOR'S NOTE

Like *The Orchestra Speaks*, this book owes not a little to the urging and the suggestions of my friend Richard Capell. I have made use of a good many of his promptings and even, at times, of his actual turns of phrase.

B. S.

ERRATUM

p. ix   *For* Dvořák : Symphony No. 1 to Messrs. Alfred Lengnick & Co., Ltd., copyright owners for the British Empire
Read Dvořák : Symphony in G to Messrs. Novello & Co., Ltd.

CONTENTS

PART ONE

PART TWO

PART THREE

ACKNOWLEDGMENTS

For permission to include passages from Bax's Th
phony we are indebted to Sir Arnold Bax and Messrs. C
Co. Ltd.; for passages from Walton's Symphony to Dr.
Walton and the Oxford University Press, who publis
orchestral score in a music octavo edition; for passa
Holst: The Planets, Edition No. 90725 to Messrs. J. (
Sons Ltd.; for passages from Elgar: Symphony No. 2
Novello & Co. Ltd.; for passages from Dvořák: Symph
to Messrs. Alfred Lengnick & Co. Ltd., copyright own
British Empire; for passages from Schubert: Sympho
(Hawkes' Miniature Score) to Messrs. Boosey & Hav

Passages from Vaughan Williams's London Sym|
printed by permission of Messrs. Stainer & Bell Ltd.

Passages from Sibelius, Symphony No. 2, are repr
courtesy of the original publishers, Breitkopf & Haertel,
Passages from Schumann: Symphony No. 4, Haydn:
No. 88, Mozart: Symphony No. 40, Beethoven:
No. 6, and Berlioz: Symphonie Fantastique, are repr
permission of Messrs. Breitkopf & Haertel, in Leip
scores have been used.

PORTRAITS

With a few exceptions the portraits have been chosen to show the composers at the ages at which their symphonies were written

HAYDN
(1732–1809)

HAYDN—this is a name never to be mentioned without reverence. It is, by those who know what it represents, never mentioned without love.

Let us not be guilty of the old impertinence of calling this great master, the first of the four great masters of the classical symphony, 'Papa Haydn.' It was the familiar word that his orchestra had for him in the old days at Esterház, but on the lips of posterity it has a patronizing sound, an inappropriate sound, misrepresenting to the outside world a man who, although he was modest, urbane and good-natured, was one of the world's supremely great artists.

And let us never again hear Haydn called 'the father of the symphony.' The phrase is hackneyed and it does not tell the truth.

Mine is not an historian's but an orchestral musician's book, and is not the place for a history of the symphony. This paragraph, then, must be only summary. Only by chance has the word 'symphony' come to have its present-day sense. It is only by chance that we do not use the word 'harmony' for music in general and 'symphony' for what we know as harmony. This book is concerned with classical and post-classical symphonies; but there was also the pre-classical symphony which—and not Haydn—was the father of the symphony known to present-day audiences.

Or rather—as in a human generalization—the symphony had a couple of progenitors, not to speak of ancestors. The progenitors were the opera overture and the orchestral suite. An opera overture at the end of the seventeenth century consisted of a slow movement, a quick one and a minuet, or—a particularly Italian form—of two quick movements with a slower one between. Before the middle of the eighteenth century such overtures were composed and performed independently of operas, and—now called symphonies—were a characteristic musical diversion of the rococo age, an age when the arts reflected an exquisitely refined society, elegantly frivolous.

The symphony, the musical form of seriousness, above all, as we think of it, of tragic passions and great spiritual adventures, began as a diversion of that society. The style of this mid-eighteenth-century social music which I term 'rococo' is known in Europe as the 'galant' style, and it was distinguished from the contemporary 'learned' style of the church musicians and from the grand manner, gradually falling out of fashion, of the composers of baroque tragic operas. How suddenly the 'learned' style fell out of fashion is seen by the fact that two gifted sons of the great Bach, K. P. E. and J. C. Bach, turned their backs on their father's style and both, the one in Germany and the other in London, shone as rococo composers pure and simple.

Why is Haydn something more than a mere rococo composer? It is because of the largeness and depth of his nature—because of the poetry that was in him. All his earlier work was rococo—and that word must not be understood too disparagingly. Rococo music is, at its best—for instance, in the works of the young Mozart's rococo period, some of which are still in the repertory—delightful; and even at its flimsiest it is well-bred. Haydn was not a precocious and not a facile composer. He developed late. But as he developed he found in his heart a depth of feeling and also an exuberance not to be expressed by the rococo formulas. He drew on his technique as a contrapuntist to an extent that a typical rococo composer would have considered excessive for polite society. The slow movements of the rococo symphonies were lightly sentimental. In his slow movements Haydn touched deeper chords. And into his final rondos there entered a spirit that was not that of the drawing-rooms of the seventeen-fifties and seventeen-sixties—a bucolic spirit which, though it minded its manners, since after all Haydn belonged to a polite century, reminds us that Haydn was a sturdy peasant.

Haydn, in a word, brought new humanity into music, and the time was ripe for it. Prodigious was his vogue throughout Europe in the last quarter of the century, and the evidence of this survives in the immense number of contemporary editions of his symphonies and quartets. Long before his two famous visits to England in the seventeen-nineties, he had been admiringly known, and when at last he came to London he was given a more than princely welcome.* Those visits are memorable for the production of his twelve last and finest symphonies, as well as for the inspiration he found in our choral concerts for the two great choral works of his last period, 'The Creation' and 'The Seasons.'

This is not a biography of Haydn. The one circumstance of his life which must be mentioned, as vital to his musical achievements, is the security he enjoyed as master of the music of a princely household, that of the Hungarian Esterházys. Such a position was, in that age, the only one satisfactory for a composer who was not a virtuoso and not primarily a musician either of the church or of the theatre. Haydn made the most of it. His genius, I have said, matured slowly. We do an injustice to that bygone social system if we do not acknowledge that to it, in good part, we owe our heritage of Haydn's music. He himself left this testimony:

"My Prince was always satisfied with my works, and I both had the encouragement of constant approval and could, as conductor of an orchestra, make experiments—observe what produced an effect and what weakened it—and was then in a position to improve, alter, and make additions and omissions, and be as bold as I pleased. I was cut off from the world; there was not one to confuse or torment me; and I was forced to become original."

There is another thing to be said about Haydn and his age. It

* Dr. Burney greeted him with a set of verses beginning:
 "Welcome, great master, to our land and isle,
 Already partial to thy name and style!"
Miss Marion Scott, in a study of Haydn in London, has said: "For cultivation, quick understanding, good taste and enthusiasm, those London audiences of the late eighteenth century were unsurpassed."

was a century of belief in reason and moderation, and a sanguine age. This prevailing spirit, as well as his comfortable economic position, was a check upon a certain moodiness which appears to have been a factor in Haydn's temperament, philosophically cheerful though he predominantly was. A pessimistic age, whose own music is so often grim and desperate, may overlook some of the shadows which cross and enrich the radiant land-scapes in Haydn's symphonies; and it may not appreciate that Haydn's cheerfulness was not altogether facile or lightly won. Here is a letter, written in his latter time, which illustrates the character of this great man:

"Often, when struggling with the difficulties of all kinds which have arisen in the way of my labours—when my strength of body and spirit sank low and it was hard to persist along the path—a voice whispered thus to my inner ear: 'Here on earth where few there are of the joyous and contented of heart, on this earth oppressed by care and tribulation, it may be that thy work will sometimes be a fountain at which careworn and burdened man will find repose and refreshment.' Herein lay a mighty incentive to struggle forwards, and herein is the reason why to-day I can look back with gladness of spirit over the labour I have, so many and many a year, with incessant pains and effort, devoted to my art."

Where is the place of a Haydn symphony in a present-day programme? It must come first if there is Mozart in the pro-gramme or Beethoven—Mozart with his more exquisite wit and grace, or Beethoven with his tragic energy—or a piece of romantic music. But in an evening in which such a composer as Hindemith or Stravinsky figures largely, Haydn may well come at the end, to restore our faith in humanity and remind us of the qualities of a heart of goodness. At the beginning of a programme Haydn shows at once what an orchestra is made of, and establishes its relation with the audience. Whatever music comes later, the cord between the two has been firmly tied, and it is not Haydn's fault if any later violence should break it. True, some of those playing inner parts may lose enthusiasm during a long-drawn-out slow movement, but there is not one of the great symphonies that has not moments in which Haydn irresistibly brings a smile to a dejected second violin or viola. And he could never be dull in a quick tempo. In any case, it is only the inner parts that have cause for complaint. In 104 symphonies and 84 quartets Homer himself would have nodded, but it is characteristic of Haydn that as he grew older such moments become more and more rare.

The later symphonies, and above all the twelve 'London' ones, are all masterpieces. They need the most careful and accomplished playing. Beethoven is the conductor's business, but Haydn is essentially the orchestra's; and technical passages, ensemble, intonation between woodwind, horn and strings, though seeming simple to the listener, need a flawless style. A blot in the slow introduction, imperfect attack on an innocuous chord, the slightest discrepancy in pitch between flute and first violins, heavy and dull accompanying by the disgruntled inner parts, or any slackness in the rhythm—any of these things will show up flagrantly. Since Haydn generally comes at the opening of a programme, the orchestra's duty is to set the standard of the evening in his very first bar.

The orchestra must possess the intimate Haydn spirit, and the conductor, if he knows his art, will enhance this and not seek to clothe the players in wrong costumes, to use Haydn for his own honour and glory. The humour and wit in the symphonies need no emphasis. Tact is required in the vexing lack of crescendos and diminuendos in the old scores. Let the music sound natural, like the normal inflections of a voice ! Then there will be no need for those heavily edited later publications, where crescendos, diminuendos, *ff*, *pp*, fill the page. The style of the orchestra should be such that the music becomes full of inspiration and lovely playing. It is not enough—it is, indeed, deadening—stolidly to obey the rigid 'piano' and 'forte' of the original scores.

Toscanini, conducting Haydn, expects the orchestra to be imbued with the spirit of the music, and as long as he gets this response and the players sing their phrases with warmth and delight he is happy and the rehearsal flows on uninterrupted. But if some luckless player forgets himself, there is catastrophe, and the score goes flying into the stalls, with curses hurled at the offender, and general vituperations of all who play notes and nothing behind them.

"Ah, why don't you sing?—ben cantando! Ben cantando! Sempre cantando! You must sing every note you play—sing even through your rests!"

The twelve London symphonies are Haydn's greatest orchestral works, but the previous eleven, called the 'Paris' symphonies from their having been composed for the Paris 'Concert Spirituel,' are all delightful and characteristic works. I choose for particular discussion the seventh of this set, in G, composed in 1787, that is to say, in the decade in which Haydn had been profoundly influenced by his young contemporary, Wolfgang Amadeus Mozart. The slow movement, with its rare scoring of solo violoncello and solo oboe, has a depth of feeling that is very near Mozart, whilst the first and last movements are full of the dance of Haydn's countryside. As in Mozart and Beethoven, every note carries its full weight, and this G major symphony gives a very clear picture of the art and the character of the beloved Haydn.

II

HAYDN'S EIGHTY-EIGHTH
SYMPHONY

THERE are 104 symphonies by Haydn in the thematic list published in *Grove's Dictionary*, and of these the Paris symphony in G is the 88th. It is a fact, strange but true, that no collected edition exists of Haydn's works, and the symphonies of his middle years, Nos. 50 to 81, are inaccessible. Breitkopf and Haertel long ago projected an edition, and the symphonies down to No. 49 were published. There the enterprise halted. Alone among the great composers Haydn has been badly treated by critics and biographers, editors and publishers. In the autumn of 1946 some of the forgotten symphonies were brought back to light by Miss Marion Scott, the first authority on Haydn in England, and were broadcast by the B.B.C. It is to this day impossible for the ordinary student to follow, step by step, the development of Haydn's symphonic style as he can the composer's chamber music, in the always accessible editions of the eighty-four string quartets. The list of the symphonies in *Grove* must be our stand-by, pending the time when someone does for Haydn what Koechel and Einstein have done for Mozart, in establishing a complete chronological catalogue. Programme-makers still refer sometimes to a Haydn symphony by the number given to it in some publisher's selected list, but the sensible thing is to give it the number allotted to it in *Grove*.

To illustrate Haydn's immense contemporary popularity be it said that in the eighteenth century a London publisher, William Forster, published 129 of his works, including eighty-two symphonies. Of the eleven written for Paris between 1784 and 1790, this in G major is the seventh. It dates from 1787, when Haydn was fifty. Its scoring is for his usual orchestra—two flutes, two

oboes, two bassoons, two horns, two trumpets, strings and kettledrums. The work opens with a slow and stately introduction,
with two ideas, the one of broad, strong chords, and the other
more feminine in character:

Fig.1 *Adagio*

This form of introduction was usual with Haydn in his later
works. These opening bars look simple on paper; but how many
orchestras rehearsing on cold Sunday mornings have run into
heavy conductorial storms because that easy-looking first note is
ragged or the held chords insufficiently sustained by players not
yet awake! Haydn's slow introductions are not always what they
seem to a casual glance, and even in a heated hall, with an audience
not too frigid, they demand steady nerves. This introduction is a
mystification of Haydn's which, often though it is repeated,
never fails in effect. It is Haydn indulging in his love of surprise
and delight in leading his listener up the garden. Such solemnity!
Surely it is a preparation for some highly serious pronouncement.
But then he disappears over his garden wall and we are suddenly
caught up in a spritely dance tune—the beginning of the Allegro,
or first movement proper:

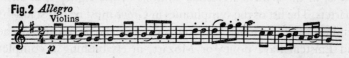

Fig.2 *Allegro*

First and 2nd violins trip away with the tune, and then the whole
orchestra gets merrily to work. Bassoons, violas and cellos join
in with another idea:

Fig.3 Cello & Viola

But the basis of the movement is all in the first bar of the Allegro.
Everything else grows out of this little germ. Variants, modulations and high spirits take us to the end of the first section almost

before we know we are there. Two ideas in contrast to the general
character should be noted. The one is the 'second subject,' as its
new key indicates, though it is a very little subject for so portentous a name:

The other is the plaintive piping of the two oboes on the basic
rhythm of the principal tune, but in a falling chromatic scale.

To this the violins give a sympathetic word, but then quickly
make off again to a dance still merrier than before. The first section of the movement ends suddenly with everyone playing C,
and in an attitude which was to be a favourite with Beethoven
Haydn hesitates for a moment with a little figure on the 1st and
2nd violins, before he abruptly sets them off again in the distant
key of A flat, to the accompaniment of the lower strings.

This is the beginning of the development, a section of intricate
counterpoint and brilliant orchestration. In short space much
takes place, and the total effect of crowded movement and complicated dance figures is a riot of lovely sound. A landmark
appears after the second violins have been observed doing their
utmost to be heard in a semiquaver passage of this character:

against a pounding on the basic rhythm by the rest of the orchestra. Haydn in this way brings us, after the many adventures, to
the dominant chord of G, and the development ends with an
abrupt pause. The recapitulation opens like the original Allegro,
with 1st and 2nd violins playing the tune. This time, however,

I*

Haydn gives the flute an enchanting improvisation, performed, as it were, in a sudden flash of spotlight:

The music then dances through much the same countryside as before. The flutes this time join the plaintive oboes in the appointed place; and if sparks ever flash from such lower orders as violas, cellos and basses, then these players should be particularly observed a few bars before the end of the movement, for what they can do with the figure already quoted (Fig. 3) at the beginning of the Allegro.

The slow movement might well be called a Romance. It is among the loveliest of Haydn's slow movements. There is a particular interest in the scoring, in that it is one of the rare occasions in a classical symphony when the first cellist is directed to play solo with the oboe. This was a discovery made in the 1930s when the British Museum produced a manuscript score showing unmistakably that Haydn had desired this effect.* The peculiar colour of the cello solo blended with oboe entirely suits the lovely and divinely simple melody, which is one that Beethoven might have written—it is curiously akin to the music of Beethoven's earlier slow movements.

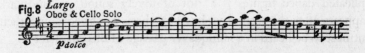

The first section of this deeply contemplative movement entirely rests on this tune. Haydn brings it to an end, and there is silence for the best part of a bar; then suddenly, with a true master's release of husbanded resources, Haydn brings in for the first time the sound of trumpets and percussion, in a complete contrast of mood. Whilst forceful chords are held by the wind,

* British Museum Additional MS. Score 31, 710; late eighteenth-century parts published by Longman and Broadrip.

the strings fill up the chords with violently reiterated notes. The sounds abruptly cease and the lonely oboes utter two plaintive notes:

Fig. 9

Twice the chords break out. Then Haydn invents a most moving episode growing out of the oboe's cry, full of lovely and striking harmonies. The chords have shattered the quiet mood of the Romance, but Haydn now gives us seven bars of this lovely harmony to restore the contemplation which he now resumes with increased orchestration and material. Two enchanting scales on the first violins lighten the sombre mood. The dramatic chords again break in with added intensity, in D minor, and by sheer brute force drag the music into F major. The violin and cello, this time without the oboe, nobly attempt the tune, but are not able to sustain it, as if the pitch were too high, and they give it up in A major. The chords now have more approval in their sounds and set the key fast in a series of resolutions to A major, the dominant of the basic key. Finally the cello soloist once more joins the oboe and they play the whole tune through with much new interest in the accompaniment; the movement draws to a close, inevitably punctuated by the chords. It is not an easy movement to play, for the tendency is to drag. The orchestral balance is difficult, and the accompanying has to be extremely alive and sensitive without ever obscuring the great melody.

Haydn was never more himself than in his minuets. Into the old courtly dance he introduced a countryman's vigour, and one of the wonders of music is the variety of invention to be found in the hundreds of minuets comprised in his work. The minuet of this Paris symphony is a grand movement. Immense is the great striding tune. Haydn knew the capabilities of his strings and what brilliant sounds could be made by sweeping strokes of the bows. The fine little turn, so characteristic of the tune, gives it verve and

dash—a decoration very different from the rococo ornaments of
the fashionable music of Haydn's youth.

Haydn's fondness for contrast is much in evidence throughout
the first part of this grandly swung movement. Vigorous fortes
regularly alternate with delicate soft tones. The Trio is delicious
in its complete change of character. It is formed upon a drone
bass—not the drone and wail of a bagpipe, but the quiet and
living rhythm of the lower strings. The tune is beautifully scored
and it demands skill in phrasing from the soloists—oboe and the
leaders of the 1st and 2nd violins.

In this Trio Haydn enjoys himself by subtly changing accents in
the rhythmic line, and changing also its actual character. First the
line is smooth and gently stroked, then picked out in the shortest
pin-points of notes. The movement is the finest example of what
Haydn could do with his 'new style' minuet; and the intimate
scoring of the Trio sounds like chamber music in contrast to the
orchestral brilliance of the principal section.

If Haydn transformed the minuet, he invented his own particular finale. Each one was, in conformity with the spirit of the
age, a happy ending. Even Mozart wrote no tragic symphonies,
though at times his symphonies, concertos and chamber music
were pathetic and elegiac, with finales that occasionally did
nothing to lighten the pathos. Haydn was less romantic. But
within their convention of the happy ending, what audacity,
what irregularities and surprises! None of the masters has written
more entrancing last movements. True, the Haydn finale is on no
great scale, but in its own inimitable way it completes the symphony to perfection. There is always something in these last
movements to make us chuckle. Good humour, lively tunes,

masterly orchestration have free play, and even though some departments of the orchestra may have felt their parts tedious in a preceding movement, one is always aware of the tightening of their interest in the Finale.

This particular Finale is a gem of gems. Though it is in rondo form its mood is similar to the first movement. The music springs from the one source—a dance motive of the countryside, made altogether irresistible by Haydn's genius for invention and humour. Note the scoring of violins and bassoon, which at once stimulates a smile.

Fig.12 FINALE. *Allegro con spirito*
Violins and Bassoons

A well-known conductor once put words to this tune for the benefit of children, but though I now find them inseparable from the music, I will not infect the reader's mind with them. Let me warn him that it is too dangerous a tune to play with. It is made of the stuff from which spells are woven. With its tripping, trotting rhythm, this little motive never ceases; nor does the pace slacken, though many new and exciting ideas are introduced, such as this:

Fig.13 Violins

But the spirit of the movement remains and multiplies upon itself until the orchestra suddenly breaks off, leaving first and second violins quietly gossiping on the rhythm above (Fig. 12) without the semiquavers. They are joined by the rest of their family, still talking very much in whispers, and then the first violins suggest a new note, E flat, and with a different accent. Horns now add their popples of approval, and finally flutes and bassoons appear, as if trying to get on the right foot for the dance again. The violins take them in hand, and after one of those invisible but magnetic signs from the conductor, first violins, flutes and bassoons dance off with the tune again. Haydn, lest any feet should start to run away with themselves, now suddenly calls a halt and takes charge of everyone in a few bars of clear chordal remarks. He decides to close the movement in a grand set piece—not an unholy scramble. So after a pause he brings all together in a blaze of colour and movement, all working out to a marvellous pattern. The pace is not varied, but keeps its same speed to the end, which comes all too quickly. Until Haydn clutched the reins the movement had never lost its ceaseless tripping movement, the very music of the legend of dancing slippers. Afterwards the rhythm becomes heavier, but the sound more brilliant than ever.

This symphony as much as any shows Mozart's influence, which had deeply affected the middle-aged Haydn. The unusual depth of feeling in the slow movement, the grandeur and contrast of the minuet and trio, and particularly the fascinating development sections of the first and last movements—all that would have been beyond the Haydn of ten years before. It is a work that orchestras delight in playing, provided the conductor is not too rigid and gives the players a reasonable length of rope. Crescendos and diminuendos of extreme refinement do not belong to the music of the period, but the work must have inspiration and a continuity of line. Beecham's marvellous genius for the essence of music is never more entrancing than in Haydn. Tempos and expression marks will all be particularly his own, and the orchestra will probably agree that they get more delight out of Beecham's Haydn than with any other conductor—and that, after all, would probably have pleased Haydn mightily. It must be said, however, that the more objective leadership of Toscanini or Walter affords a clearer view of Haydn, especially in contrast to the other works on the programme, without any loss of the qualities that are at the heart of the music. A great artist can re-create the heart of the music, even while remaining within the limits of his style.

III

MOZART
(1756–1791)

MOZART! To become engrossed in his music is to feel that here was the most musical being that ever lived, the incarnation of music's self. The wonder of this man's short life has never ceased to dazzle the world. Such different composers as Beethoven, Gounod, Tchaikovsky and Richard Strauss recognized in him the master of masters. It is true that at the height of the romantic movement he was, although admired, rather disparaged beside the tragic Beethoven and the spellbinding Wagner. But we live in the age of a great Mozartian revival. The cult of Mozart, both by artists and scholars, has characterized all civilized countries in the last thirty years or so. England has taken no small part in this movement. One of the first duties the young Beecham undertook was to extend the London public's acquaintance with the less familiar operas and orchestral works; and in the 1930s there came into being, on the Sussex Downs, John Christie's now celebrated opera house, designed for the production of Mozart.

This is no place for a Life of Mozart. His biography has been written over and over again. Two of the best short books about Mozart were the work of Englishmen—Edward Holmes's in the nineteenth century and Eric Blom's in our own. The most comprehensive Life is Abert's revision of Jahn (in German). There exists a catalogue of his works—Koechel's, revised by Alfred Einstein—which is one of the wonders of the world of scholarship. The most extensive and subtle criticism of Mozart is (in French) in the five volumes of Wyzewa and Saint-Foix.

Rather than tell again an oft-repeated tale, I prefer to refer to those factors and circumstances of Mozart's life which most directly bear on his music; and to utter only in passing a word of warning against uncritical acceptance of the usual nineteenth-century accounts of his grievances and woes, according to which these were inexplicably the world's one-sided fault. The romantic biographies of the last century inclined similarly to represent Beethoven and Schubert as victimized by a wicked world. Not all the contemporaries of those great composers were as wise, generous and appreciative as the enlightened later age; but the fact remains that those composers, and Mozart, lived in a time when, somehow or other, they were able to produce a corpus of immortal masterpieces, and it stands to reason that there was in their age, in its culture and facilities, something that favoured that achievement—one may say, that in a measure was a collaborator in it.

To try to explain why Mozart came, economically and physically, to shipwreck would be outside my scope. But it may be roughly suggested that there was something odd about him, something undeveloped and childlike. And childlikeness in a grown man is not endearing. The fecklessness and irresponsibility natural to a child are disconcerting in a man; during the last ten years of Mozart's life these characteristics were too much for his friends. Wagner was misled and misleading in every way when he wrote of Mozart as "childlike in his meekness, shyly contemptuous of ostentation and advantageous proposals, modest to the point of bashfulness, unselfish to the point of self-forgetfulness." Not a word of this is true. Mozart's childlikeness was not that sort at all. His sister, Maria Anna, showed more sense when she said:

> "Outside music he was and remained something of a child, and that was a trait on the seamy side of his character. He always was in need of a father, mother or guardian. He could not cope with money matters, and against his father's will he married a girl most unsuited to him—and hence the great domestic disorder at the time of his death and after."

Mozart was born into a musical world. How many great musicians have been lost to us by the want of such an environment in their earliest years, the environment in which music is as

natural a form of utterance as speech, and the lack of which is
something for which not even genius can compensate fully!
Salzburg, his birthplace, was a very small town, but it was the
seat of a princely archbishopric, and the archbishop's court included, according to the custom of the time, a musical establishment such as Canterbury and York have never known. Mozart's
father was a violinist of this establishment, in which German-
speaking musicians predominated, but which was more Italian
than German in tradition and taste.

The next and all-important factor in the shaping of Mozart's
genius and the direction it took was the character of his remarkable
father, Leopold. Not a man of genius, but as well as an accomplished musician a man with an ambition in him and a force of
will superior to his son's. There is no accounting for genius; but
Mozart would not have been the Mozart we know but for the
instruction and experiences Leopold Mozart put in his son's way.
Not everything was admirable in Leopold's character; nor yet
in Wolfgang's. There was something limited, worldly and even
mean about the father's ambitions. But his balance, his hard
commonsense and his very worldliness were invaluable to the
marvellous boy, who, without such a father's control, might have
frittered away his gifts. We have said that there was something
in our Mozart's character that may be called irresponsible.

Leopold saw a fortune to be made out of the boy's precocious-
ness, together with the charm of his talented sister. But, while
exploiting the children, Leopold saw to it that they should have
solid instruction. Mozart might—while always dazzling—have
become no more than the most brilliant of the rococo composers,
but his father saw to it that he possessed also the accomplishments
of the learned school. A hundred times the tale has been told of
the travels of the Mozart children in France and England and
of the boy Mozart's later visits to Italy. The importance to us of
these travels is the contacts they afforded the boy with all the
schools of composition then flourishing in western Europe. For
the characteristic in the young Mozart which strikes us above all
is his aptitude for assimilating forms and fashions and traits of
style, from here, there and everywhere, and transmuting them

into a finer element—into Mozartian compositions, which still reveal the suggestion that had prompted them.

Italian music was predominant in Mozart's time in all the countries of Europe, and if a national name is to be given to Mozart's art it ought no doubt to be called Italian. But even in that unified Europe there were different strands and currents, and Mozart would adopt now one and then another. In France he took on French characteristics—only to transcend them. There was a time when he made the acquaintance (never very thorough) of Bach and Handel, and those contacts are at once apparent in his compositions. A purely German music can hardly be said to have existed in his time, but when he came to write German dances and German operas popular German elements entered into his scores. The French critic Saint-Foix enumerates thirty-three different periods of Mozart's production. And yet what musician's work appears more consistent and homogeneous? The transmuting factors were Mozart's genius, his technique and his taste.

To Leopold Mozart Haydn said these memorable words:

"I declare to you before God, as a man of honour, that your son is the greatest composer I know, either personally or by reputation. He has taste and, beyond that, a consummate knowledge of the art of composition."

One fallacy I must try to dispel: the belief that the boy Mozart was not merely precocious but miraculously developed—that as a boy he composed as he did as a man. It is true that the boy Mozart wrote with skill and charm, and was almost at once more than a mere imitator; but none of his great works was written until he was a grown man. The development of his adolescent mind was less remarkable than Schubert's. It still seems almost unbelievable that those unsurpassed Goethe songs of Schubert's should have been composed when he was only sixteen or seventeen. There is never a hint that they are anything but the work of a man who has lived and suffered. Of none of Mozart's early music could this be said.

Mozart was both a violinist and pianist of soloist's rank. This again is one of the biographical facts that bear directly upon the man's art. "If you would only do yourself justice," his father once wrote to him, " and play with fire and boldness you would be the first violinist in Europe." But he preferred on the whole the piano, and the incomparable series of piano concertos composed at Vienna in the 1780s—so much greater works than the earlier Salzburg violin concertos—were written for his own performance. In the string quartet he played viola; and though my subject is, strictly speaking, not Mozart in general, nor even one category of his works—for each category really demands a large book, and about the piano concertos alone two big volumes have been written by an English scholar, C. M. Girdlestone—yet as a violist I cannot refrain from mentioning the one work in which he gives the viola a great concertante part. This is the double concerto in E flat for violin and viola. One might easily think it to be a later work, such is the depth of its emotional feeling. The maturity of the lovely melodic line seems to belong to a man in his forties, but Mozart was only twenty-three when he wrote it. A sidelight on his familiarity with the viola and its tendency to elusiveness is revealed by his instructions that the viola player should tune his instrument up a semitone, so that the increased tension of the strings should give its tone more edge and render it the more easily able to cope with its brilliant partner the violin. No work shows more clearly his mastery of orchestral balance.

My subject, strictly speaking, is one symphony; and that which I have chosen is the last but one, in G minor, of the forty-one he composed. Something, however, must be said about the corpus of the symphonies. The earliest, written when Mozart was a mere child, were copies of J. C. Bach. About twenty symphonies were composed at Salzburg, and are in the rococo style as a rule. They are little works compared with the great symphonies that were to come, and it is only in recent years that their charm and lively grace have once again been appreciated. None of them is likely ever to become familiar at our great orchestral series, but the public that attends chamber-orchestra concerts will appreciate this delicious music of the 1770s.

In a different style is the brilliant 'Paris Symphony,' in D, of 1778, composed in Paris with an eye to the contemporary French liking for pomp and circumstance. Mozart has for the time being hidden his tender heart. It is a symphony which Beecham has exhibited in the dazzling light that suits it. In his next symphonies Mozart shows signs of Haydn's influence. One says that; but the proviso must be made that no casual listener will hear in them anything but pure Mozart. What he learned from Haydn was much. Haydn, in fact, pointed to Mozart the way from the formal elegance of the rococo style. In particular, the effect of Haydn's counterpoint and of the relief afforded to the tonal scheme by the rich colour of strange keys in the development of first movements was not lost on Mozart. The younger man, however, never adopted some of his elder's peculiarities. He did not take to Haydn's characteristic metrical irregularities—one of the devices of Haydn's humour. He was, first and last, the more aristocratic mind. He may on occasion mock at rustic music, but that is as far as his interest in it goes— he never cares to idealize it. His suppleness, his grace were at this time far beyond Haydn's, as also his orchestral technique, which was founded on acquaintance with the best orchestras in the world. Haydn was by comparison a provincial. Nothing of its sort is more curious than the interactions between the two musicians in that decade, the 1780s.

Mozart's last six symphonies are all famous. They are the 'Haffner,' the 'Linz' and the 'Prague'; and then the three symphonies composed in the summer of 1788, the E flat, the G minor and the C major. I have mentioned Mr. Girdlestone's great work on the piano concertos. I suppose a weighty book could be written about these symphonies alone. We have been told a thousand times that the last three were composed in the weeks between June 26 and August 10; but the vitality that this fact represents, the incandescence of the artist's mind—this is something at which one can never cease to marvel. Each is an insuperable masterpiece; and the consummate beauty of each is enhanced by the totally different character of the others. They are like a trio of supremely beautiful women—all of the same age, the same height, equal in charm and breeding, but different in type and temperament. The E flat symphony is warmly appealing, gracious, gentle-hearted. The G minor symphony is pathetically wistful, agitated and forlorn. The C major is radiant, vital and triumphant. Its contrapuntal finale is the gayest piece of music in existence—divinely gay, springing from a fount of animation that seems ageless and inexhaustible as the stars.

It is Mozart's last symphony. Little more than three years after its composition he was dead. Mozart—dead at the age of thirty-six! As antiquity mourned the death of Adonis, so must we and the generations after us lament him. Marlowe, Keats and Shelley, Purcell and Schubert—what an unimaginable wealth had been the world's if these men had not been cut off in their prime!

Like Schubert, Mozart helped to kill himself. There is something terrifying about the record of the production of each in his last years. Both seem to have been men possessed; and the mortal frame could not stand the strain. Mozart, like Schubert, was in full process of development. We are left guessing what would have been the effect upon him of Beethoven's turbulent and tragic genius—upon him, so quick to catch at any new sound, so apt to transmute any element into Mozartian gold. What he has left us is the supreme poetry of his age.

I end this chapter with a quotation from the last pages of the Comte de Saint-Foix's great book on Mozart, a book that represents the labours of nearly thirty years. It came out in five volumes, between 1912 and 1946. The last pages were written on the 150th anniversary of Mozart's death, in the terrible winter of 1941; and Saint-Foix then said:

"Despite the accumulation of ruins and sorrow I have sought to proclaim the grandeur, alone inviolable, of the things of the spirit. May Mozart's work more and more bring to its lovers, and in the future to those who as yet know it not, something of the soul of him who made it: a soul filled with love for his fellows, filled with moral greatness, with simple and pure goodness of heart and divine serenity! May his message spread throughout a ravaged world and shed consolation!"

IV

MOZART'S FORTIETH SYMPHONY
IN G MINOR

HOW many persons hearing a performance of the G minor symphony are alive to all the peculiar quality and originality of its opening—those first bars of pulsating accompaniment? Not quite unique in Mozart's work, but very rare, is this launching of a symphonic movement with an accompaniment figure. (The reader may be reminded of the last piano concerto.) To realize the poetry of this apparently simple idea one should read or play the first page as though it immediately began, in the regular eighteenth-century manner, with the first subject. Here is the substance of this opening:

Fig.1 *Allegro molto*

There is a peculiar sound in this, as the violas play it, which will for ever be unique. It is merely the G minor chord broken up, but for anyone who has ever played it and for most who have ever heard the work it has the magic of conjuring up the whole symphony like a vision. Though cellos or violins are able to play these same notes, only the violas can make the magic. To realize how much the idea depends upon the quality of the tone it should be tried on the piano. The clatter set up is quite abominable.

It is difficult to poise the sound to perfection. Tempo, colour, ensemble and style, all must be clear in order that the first and second violins can freely play their tune, which, like its

accompaniment, is quite illimitable in its grace and poetic
delicacy.

Fig.2

There are no other marks in the score, yet many are the ways
in which conductors interpret and phrase this opening. The
accompaniment is generally played in a very light spiccato—a
word string-players use for a pointed and sparkling style of bowing
—while others have it played in smooth, full-length notes, to
make it quieter and less fussy. The latter reading can sound quite
natural, but it involves a risk of heaviness creeping in later on.
The orchestra may one day be rehearsing this first subject for a
pedantic conductor who insists on a strong accent on the first
of each bar and wants the second part of the phrase softer than
the first. The next time the conductor may direct a rhythmic
accent on the first beat of the alternate bars, with both parts of
the phrase equal in strength. Yet another will delight in large
crescendos and diminuendos, and actually encourage a slide up to
the top notes.

Conductors, be it known, are to some extent in the hands of
the orchestra. A well-trained orchestra, worth its salt, will have
developed a certain style of its own in the music of various composers and periods. A Mozartian style is an important part of its
equipment. In these magical opening bars the orchestra should at
once have the right clothes on, and forget that the piece just
played was Beethoven's 'Leonora' overture. Great emotional
crises, full-blooded fortes and shuddering pianissimos are out of
the picture, if Mozart is to be heard aright. What the orchestra
prays for in this symphony is first of all a conductor who, like
Bruno Walter, for instance, has a firm hand but an exquisite
touch. Walter's approach at rehearsal brings Mozart to life. His
incessant cry is, "Più piano! Più piano, gentlemen! This is
Mozart! You know I want you to play so deliciously quietly that

I can hardly believe it, yet everything must be there—colour, life, rhythm. It must be expressive. Nothing of that deadly coldness you have in England! I cannot bear it!"

With Walter, then, there will be great delicacy, and the strings will show their pastel colours. The poise of the phrases will be exquisite, and the whole ensemble of the orchestra intimate as in chamber music. The rhythm will be imperceptible but nevertheless felt. The doleful bump–bump of a heavy-footed orchestra with its unintelligent rhythm and this symphony is murdered—killed stone-dead from the opening bars, and never to be resurrected.

The principal matter all springs from these first four bars. The movement seems to grow with the spontaneity of improvisation. It is as though Mozart had caught the sparks of his theme in his mind and blown it into a marvellous fire. He at once repeats the first four bars with a subtle change a half-tone lower, and then, after a different turn in his mind, he answers the first eight bars with:

Fig. 3

finally rounding off the whole subject matter with an approving phrase from the woodwind.

Fig. 4   W. Wind

Note that there is no crescendo marked for this phrase, but while an artist like Walter or Toscanini imperceptibly encourages the players to sing the phrase with the inflection of a human voice, a lesser man cannot resist the temptation to paint the lily, directing a crescendo that utterly spoils the effect.

In the performance of this opening section we have quickly discerned the style of playing and interpretation we are to enjoy in the rest of the work. Is it to be the pure, unimaginative but scrupulously correct performance of some great authority like Richard Strauss or Weingartner? If so, the bare marks of the score will be faithfully followed and the music left almost to play itself. Or is it to be rather more coloured with emotion and with careful reading between the lines? With the fuller crescendos and diminuendos of a later period, but yet musical and sincere? It will still sound lovely music, if less purely Mozartian. At an extreme one may hear a very vivid performance miles away from Mozart, and the result is merely a reflection of the conductor's personality. All these characteristics may be observed in the playing of the principal subject. Well remembered is a performance under a certain foreign conductor who carefully marked the expression of every bar and had a particular fondness for a heavy accent on the first of the quavers of each pair in the subject, giving syncopated liveliness to the music. Thus is Mozart at the mercy of his performers. Later masters gave fuller directions in their scores. Elgar, for instance, accounts for every nuance.

Another matter to be considered is one over which there is much argument. If a large orchestra is playing, are all its members to be employed in this symphony? Often the strings are reduced to a few desks, and the consequent gain of intimacy between strings and wind sets the stage, to my mind, far more appropriately, for the heart of this symphony, especially in the first three movements, belongs to the realm of chamber music. It is most important in particular that the flutes should sit very near the first violins and the horns, too, somewhere near the front, where they can feel themselves in the midst of the players. Rows and rows of strings tend to thicken this delicately woven tissue into a blanket.

The scoring is transparent and of the lightest—particularly in the first version (without clarinets). In the more familiar version, with clarinets, the colour is richer. It remains a wonder how beautifully Mozart in the first version rendered the quivering sensibility of his ideas in this, his most pathetic music, without the tone of the more sensuous instrument.

Having rounded off this opening section with bold chords over a military rat-a-plan accompaniment on the strings, Mozart now continues with the first subject-matter, only to slip the second

phrase into another key for a new and much contrasted idea, full
of rough liveliness and a vigour as masculine as his lovely initial
theme was feminine.

Fig. 5

f Violins

He concludes this episode solidly in the key of F, the dominant
of B flat, which is the key of his second subject, now at hand.

The strings again are allotted this second subject, which is in a
more tender and quieter mood than the beginning. In its second
bar comes a very Mozartian remark from the wind, which
brings the slightest touch of sunlight into the tune.

Fig. 6 Strings Wind   Strings

The theme, after a momentary darkening of mood, suddenly
cheers up. With great activity we are hurried on to a bright forte
chord of E flat, and suddenly a heavenly little scale for flutes,
bassoons and strings flutters down to the key of B flat, where two
fragments of first and second subjects, with sudden violent reiteration of the former, bring us to the end of the exposition with fine
vigour and dash.

Now heavy chords from the whole orchestra change the key
to the surprising and remote one of F sharp minor. This startling
modulation is all arranged with masterly strategy by the woodwind. The tune is the same, but it now has a new sharpness and
incisiveness, ready for the vigorous development it is to undergo.
A motive derived from Fig. 5, of fugal character, is tacked on to
the first subject and gives the music a glittering vigour.

Fig. 7

from the 1st subject

The lower strings have a great time with their hard, short quavers; keys are changed; the woodwind get a word in when possible. Then a pedal note sounds from the basses, with the violins insisting on this figure:

Fig.8

The mood becomes less tense, while this persistent figure goes about the score. The woodwind strategists take charge of it in another form, and thence lead us back again to the original key and mood of the opening bars of the movement.

In the recapitulation, Mozart makes a great deal of the subsidiary figure of the first subject (see Fig. 5). Not only does he give it great prominence, but the whole orchestra plays with it in every way, while in the background there is continual movement, filling the air with strenuous bustle. The second subject returns again in its place. It is now in G minor, with the scoring much enriched. As before, the many activities and modulations suddenly cease in order to show up the little fluttering scale, which adroitly moves the key to C minor, ready for the final return to the basic key of the movement.

Similar music occurs again in the final section of the movement, when Mozart uses fragments of the first and second subjects, but now, drawing to the end, he screws up the tension semitone by semitone to a climax, only suddenly to cut out all instruments but the woodwind, who poise the music on a thin chord of G minor. There are eight bars of pure string-quartet writing and a heavenly summing up, in which the woodwind has the final word. A very conventional tonic-and-dominant business of great vigour ends the movement.

The slow movement is in E flat, and in its slow, regular motion, deeply thoughtful, it forms a great contrast to the agitation of the first. The main theme is in two parts. The first may be called harmonic, the second melodic. The scoring is for string quartet.

The first part of the theme consists of a building up of harmony in three bars from this line of the viola:

The cellos and basses take the bass line, the 2nd violins enter at the end of the bar and 1st violins complete the chord. The 1st and 2nd violins round off the subject with a graceful eighteenth-century bow.

The second part of the tune is different, and is a lovely answer to the sustained thoughtfulness of the first. The 1st and 2nd violins have it:

A question arises over the first two notes at the beginning of the movement, and similarly, of course, whenever the phrase recurs. An established practice was for the first note to be slurred to the succeeding quaver, and in fact nearly every orchestral part has a slur actually printed, editors having taken it for granted that the composer had left it out in error. Mozart, however, was extremely clear in his string quartet writing, and it is likely he meant what he wrote in his manuscript, which shows no slur. This, when pointed out by Sir Adrian Boult when conducting in Vienna, considerably surprised the Vienna Philharmonic Orchestra.

It is undeniable that the general legato style of this movement certainly seems to suggest that a slur would be natural, and thus it is nearly always played.

The little demisemiquaver figure in the second part of the theme should be noted. It beautifully lights up the sombre colours. Heard incessantly throughout the movement, it refuses to allow the general mood to become too dark and elderly. The core of the movement lies in its wonderfully sustained character, and this is trying for the strings. It taxes their ability to keep the colours warm and never to lose their lustre. This symphony of all needs the chamber-music player, whose every note is played with care and skill. The orchestral player becomes tired of playing accompaniments and harmonic background. The first bar of the slow movement is typical in its reiteration of one note. A movement like this may lose the interest of the inner parts, and once this happens the whole effect flags. It must be looked on as chamber music, in which inner parts are realized as vital as any other. The performance then will be properly poised, and those lovely sounds associated with the string quartet will be made all the more lovely with the added strings of the orchestra. That first bar, then, instead of consisting of the six same dull notes, will have rhythm in them. A touch of left-hand vibration will bring the notes to life, with the bow subtly changing its pressure to allow each of them to breathe.

The woodwind makes its first entry with this cantabile phrase:

Fig. 12

_p_ Woodwind

which is brought to a cadence of the most lovely grace by the whole orchestra.

The first sign of contrast to this thoughtful mood appears in a change of key to B flat, which takes us into affairs of the open air, until flute and 1st violins engage in a beautiful little dialogue on the demisemiquaver figure of the main theme. Between them they gradually restore the mood of contemplation, which now becomes deeper than ever in its flatter key of D flat, though there are high-lights painted in by various instruments.

This ubiquitous little demisemiquaver figure now becomes more purposeful; the colours of the orchestra begin to glow, and a climax wells up in the key of B flat. Mozart, however, having worked up some considerable tension, suddenly tires of it, and after a complete silence, as on the sudden slamming of a door, a new strain of the most tender and touching feeling is whispered by the 1st violins, exquisitely poised over the softest chords:

This phrase comes to an end with the little demisemiquaver figure once more, and its effect is of a most charming smile.

After the woodwind has echoed the strings, apparently carried away by their enchantment, the composer rudely breaks in and harshly drives the orchestra through a series of modulations, with the basses pumping out the first bar of the main theme for a few bars, until the composer recovers his temper. His hand relaxes and he gently permits the orchestra to fall back into their familiar key of B flat, in a moving cadence, which brings the first part of the movement to its conclusion in delicious lightness and grace:

The second part opens in the dark colour of the beginning, now made darker than ever by the ominous sound of the strings forced up a semitone to C flat, and playing the main theme in unison. Thence the movement becomes full of uneasy tension, accentuated by restless changes of key and heavy pent-up sounds. The slow-moving quavers of the main theme have now lost their quiet thoughtfulness. These are urged forcefully onwards, while the ever-present demisemiquaver figure has taken on a new quality of charm, as the woodwind instruments with agitated cries call to one another. After being made to traverse many keys the orchestra finds itself very near G major. The composer has at last overcome his apprehensiveness. He gives to the woodwind a little cadence ending in G major, the 1st and

2nd violins chirruping the everlasting figure, until the wood-wind joins them again in a passage of most lovely chromatic harmonies.

The orchestra subsides into the key of C minor, the bassoons harking back to the main theme, over which the woodwind plays this phrase four times in all:

Fig. 15
W. Wind

modulating each time to a different key until we are in E flat again, and the mood is now completely restored to that of the beginning. This woodwind phrase, it should be noted, is the cello and bass harmony of the opening bars, and is now to appear frequently in this music of recapitulation, which in perfect serenity rocks quietly over nearly related keys.

The second subject (Fig. 13), when it returns again, now in E flat, needs most careful handling by the violins, which tend to sound harsh in that particular register. The composer, as before, rudely breaks in again, as if too much sweetness were disagreeable to him, but the movement closes with the same exquisite and tender charm we enjoyed at the end of the first part.

This great movement, as I have said, is difficult to perform. If the string tone flags and becomes dull the music loses all its colour and grace. The demisemiquaver figure needs the utmost care, both in ensemble and character. Many are the opportunities for bad habits on the part both of conductor and orchestra—thus discrepancies in the length of short notes, imperfect phrasing, lack of balance between strings and woodwind, lack of rhythm. Within the orchestra we remember too many performances when this slow movement seemed interminable. Whose the responsibility and the blame? The reader will guess.

The third movement is in the usual form of Minuet, Trio, Minuet. It affords a grand opportunity for the orchestra to show its true style—and the strings in particular. The Minuet, in the customary two sections, requires great verve and brilliance of tone, and wonderful is the sound from the strings when the bows, quick in movement and straight as a die, make every nook and cranny of the instruments resound.

With all this intense life and firmness, there must be no coarseness or trace of scratch and scrape. One may often observe an impressive look as of hard work going on, yet with a resultant sound not corresponding to the amount of elbow-grease used, and a tone that is forced into instead of lifted out of the instrument. The tune is picked out in the upper octave by flutes, which add more sparks to the scoring:

The second section of the Minuet is a continuation of the first:

In the continuation there is a brilliant passage in counterpoint which the composer suddenly brings up short. In a miracle of contrast and inspiration he uses the last refrain of the main theme to round off the Minuet. Instead of forte it is now piano, and we hear the delicate sound of the flute accompanied by some startling chromatic harmony on the wind and the strings on tip-toe, having the final say:

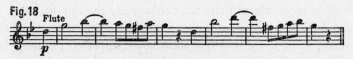

The Trio is in G major and, like the Minuet, in the usual two sections. It is as smooth and flowing as the Minuet was energetic. A lovely spot of viola colour is heard under bar 5:

HAYDN

MOZART

In the second section there is an interesting piece of scoring with the horns reinforcing the violins, when they return to the tune of the first section again to round off the trio.

Fig. 20

It is the first time in the symphony that the horns come into the limelight. Then the Minuet returns.

This Minuet movement is perfect both in its own balance and for the value it provides between the dark slow movement and the dramatic finale that is to come. Haydn's influence shows strongly.

The Finale must have startled Mozart's audience, and his orchestra too, with the intensity of its contrasts and dramatic power. The minor mode was very much the exception in the symphonic writing of Mozart's day. Unprecedented and unique was a characteristic of some of Mozart's later works in the minor: he maintained the mode in the finale, and reinforced its effect of pathos to the end. If this movement is to be played to full purpose the restraining and cultured hand of the conductor must for once be relaxed and the orchestra be allowed in one sense to have its head, though in another it must be well and truly belaboured. Here certainly is an excuse for using all available resources.

The movement is in sonata form and begins and ends in G minor. The first subject is tremendously exciting even in these days, and with its double character of extreme lightness and heavy violence it must have been the cause of trial and tribulation to the orchestras of the 1790s.

Fig. 21 *Allegro assai*

The initial arpeggio figure is extremely light and pointed,

2

while the quavers immediately succeeding it have to be violently scrubbed, yet clear. The second part of the theme is of four bars:

The whole subject is beautifully rounded off with a repetition of the second half of Fig. 21. In all the opening music the glittering quavers make the running, speedily overwhelming the arpeggio figure. The movement is intensely brilliant, until Mozart clears up the bustle with decisive chords. He has meanwhile brought the orchestra with some surprise into a major key. Instead of giving a second subject in the minor, he quickly allots the violins a lovely tune in B flat major as the second subject. This is one of the most beautiful moments in the symphony.

Like other pages in the symphony written for string quartet, this subject is given to the 1st violins, accompanied by 2nd violins and violas, and is then dexterously handed over to the wind, which provides it with a lovely adornment here and there and finishes the episode by four bars of chromatic harmony. This leads us back into the old turmoil again, which with its brilliant speed and dash continues to the end of the first part of the movement in the key of B flat.

The development that ensues remains and ever will remain the father and mother of all developments. Inside the orchestra this is one of the movements that never cease to rejoice the players, even of an inner part. If a 2nd violin or viola player can keep his ears open and can manage his instrument—which here is apt to behave like a witch's broom—then he knows delights in which even hardened old salts of the orchestra can revel. It is music that makes difficult demands on the orchestra's sense of intonation, ensemble and style.

The development, then, opens with the arpeggio figure of the first subject, now at last come into its own, after its eclipse in the exposition. A great unison of strings and wind crashes out in anger, which should strike terror—Koussevitsky sees that it does! —until the unmoved bassoons and clarinets dispel all the savage temper in two incredibly calm bars of Mozart's characteristic chromaticism. An intricate and unique working-out begins in earnest, first in a series of quiet but sparkling modulations on the arpeggio figure. Then the violas with a crunch of their C strings set going some mighty machine in F minor, which beggars description in its intricate mechanism. The gorgeous sound is something Wagner never surpassed, with all his resources.

The effect of the counterpoint and multitudinous sounds perfectly interwoven is prodigious. This is a great technical study, in which every note makes thrilling music. It is as though Mozart had stolen Bach's genius and at the same time H. G. Wells' time machine, to drive into the future.

Suddenly, in the middle of it all, after a succession of chords that appear to be taking us to a definite key (C sharp minor), Mozart slithers into an A major chord, and bassoons and clarinets in yet another key, like small and cheeky boys, whistle the arpeggio figure of Fig. 1 under their breath. This is too much for the orchestra which, having been caught up in its stride and grossly misled, crashes out into renewed efforts of still more brilliant intricacy, until the composer, played out with so much strain, brings it all to an end. After taking two bars of deep breath he returns once more to the material of the beginning of the movement for its recapitulation.

This time the second subject, when it reappears, is in the expected minor key, and the mood is much changed by this. There is now no consolation. The music takes much the same course as in the exposition, but with scoring and details that are more brilliant. The pace is kept exciting and strenuous to the end. This is music that transcends its period and the categories. Never here do we think—as often in the earlier Mozart—of eighteenth-century elegance. It is music as poignantly pathetic as anything of the romantic period. But we must not call the G minor symphony 'romantic.' It is music both classical and romantic, and rises above all that those terms ordinarily denote. In the electric atmosphere of this finale the orchestra needs a conductor of genius who knows how to inspire it both with extreme delicacy and with a glimpse of unholy fire. Beecham is a conductor who knows these secrets, and to think of this music is to remember his expressive face, one moment urbane as an eighteenth-century exquisite and the next flashing demoniacally.

V

BEETHOVEN
(1770–1827)

W E have come to the prince of musicians.

It is one hundred and fifty years since Beethoven first impressed and captivated the music-loving aristocracy of old Vienna, and since then the world has never ceased to be the empire of his genius.

There are characteristics of Beethoven, a scope in his work, which make him seem different not so much in degree as in kind from all the great composers who had gone before him. I would put it summarily thus: The great composers before Beethoven had in one way or another been servants of society or of the Church, and had written the music that had been expected of them, however greatly they had transcended such expectations. More consciously from the first, and altogether as time went on, did Beethoven compose for himself. Such individualism was a new thing. Beethoven exploited, so to say, his inner self. His work is a self-dramatization. In this respect he may be called the first of the romantic musicians of the nineteenth century in whom these were the characteristic principles; but he was far more than that. Wherein lay that superiority which places him head and shoulders above all his successors? It lay, of course, in the depth and richness of the self that was his to exploit, and in a certain responsibility which makes him, romantic though he was, the great classical composer. Vehement—no artist was more so. But this vehemence was balanced by what I call his responsibility.

And along with the intense personality in Beethoven's music we recognize a new tragic sense. Understand me to mean tragic not as moody, melancholy, agitated or romantically suicidal. Beethoven's music is essentially sane and sanguine. But it is the art of a man who faced for himself the problems of life and destiny; who had his own personal struggle with despair; who had felt himself alone in a world somehow larger, more confused, wild and pathless than any artist of the eighteenth century had known; and who had to fight single-handed for faith. Thus it is that we are aware, in Beethoven's most boisterously vital music as in his most divinely serene, of an element that can only be called tragic. If, after saying so much, I choose for detailed description a symphony in which Beethoven's characteristic tragic vehemence is in abeyance my premise holds good. None but a totally inexperienced listener can think of the Pastoral Symphony in isolation. One of the values of this great but sometimes underrated composition lies in its representation of a momentary conquest of serenity and faith in a life that was an heroic tragedy.

Once again, I am not undertaking a biography. Let us glance only at the circumstances of Beethoven's life that had the most immediate bearing on his music. He was the son of a professional musician, like Mozart and nearly all the great composers of that age and the earlier centuries. Not until the nineteenth century do we find such composers as Berlioz and Schumann, who were not brought up to music but who had more or less to fight for a musical career (in Berlioz's case, with a life-long handicap, from not having learnt the language of music at his mother's knee). Like Mozart's father, Beethoven's was a musician employed at the court of an ecclesiastical principality (at Bonn on the Rhine, the capital of the state of the Archbishop-Elector of Cologne).

The elder Beethoven was a different type from Leopold Mozart. He was a ne'er-do-well, and Beethoven had not a happy childhood. But what has often not been taken enough into account by compassionate and romantic biographers is the thoroughness of Beethoven's musical education and the opportunity he had as a child and youth, in that small town, of acquainting himself with the best music of his age and of making the most of his genius. Readers of some of the older and more sentimental accounts of Beethoven's life should ask themselves whether the discomfort of his young years was not a small thing compared with the sufferings which would have been Beethoven's if, later on, he—a man supremely conscious of his genius—had felt himself handicapped or frustrated in his art by lack of an adequate training.

He showed his gift at an early age, though without anything like the little Mozart's brilliancy and winning ways. As a child he was a violinist, pianist and organist, and as a lad he played the viola in the theatre orchestra. A composition of his was published when he was eleven, and a piano concerto was written in his eighteenth year. Haydn encouraged him, and by the time he was twenty he was writing good music. The earliest of his memorable works, however, did not come until some years later —Beethoven was not preternaturally precocious. He went to live at Vienna when he was twenty-two, and soon made his name in the most musical society that has ever existed, principally as a pianist—as a pianist with a wonderful gift for improvisation.

We cannot understand Beethoven's life or his art without some appreciation of the passionate cultivation of music among the Austrian nobility and burgesses of that time. He early won the patronage of aristocratic music-lovers, and their support was his economic mainstay all his life. At the same time, Beethoven very soon showed a temper and independence that mark him as a man of the new age. He was *fin de siècle*. It was another world from that of Mozart's Salzburg in the 1770s. The French Revolution had come. In spirit, if not everywhere in form, all Europe was changed.

Beethoven accepted patronage on his own terms. His behaviour must have seemed uncouth. It would have seemed intolerably uncouth a generation before. But young noblemen like Prince Lichnowsky were also men of their time. There is nothing to show that in that earlier period Beethoven's independence of attitude— one may say, the grossness of his behaviour—did him any harm. It was the age of a new individualism.

We have spoken of Beethoven's consciousness of his genius. This consciousness, with the duty it entailed, the sacred duty, was the ruling factor in his whole life. It stamps him as an artist of a new type. The attitude of his predecessors had been rather that of the craftsman. Often we seem to see the man Beethoven as the victim of a strange and tyrannical guest—a guest in his mind and soul. The rough and almost gross man, the peasant that he was, sacrificed his ordinary instincts, his creature comforts, his whole life, to this wonderful and terrible visitant.

He quickly became famous. There was no obstacle in the way of his getting a hearing or of his finding publishers. At the age of thirty he produced his first symphony. As the years went on he became almost legendary, almost a divinity. It is true that the public could not keep pace with his development. During his second period the works of his first period were the more popular, and when those of the third period came they were generally regarded—naturally enough—as obscure and terribly difficult. And still, when the Ninth Symphony was first performed, together with movements from the Mass in D, there was a scene of immense enthusiasm. Beethoven was then fifty-four and had been deaf for many years.

Volumes have been written about Beethoven's deafness, and the doctors disagree. Some time before he was thirty Beethoven suffered from an obscure illness, and when he was thirty-one he realized he was losing his hearing. The loss was gradual but relentless. It reduced him at one time to something like despair. In his latter years he was, to all intents and purposes, absolutely deaf.

Laymen may overrate the disability. Beethoven had not the need of physical hearing which a layman imagines indispensable to a composer. We may say that the scoring of the Ninth Symphony might, but for this disaster, have been different, but not the music itself. A disaster, however, it was, and one ineffably tragic. Beethoven seems at first to have despaired chiefly because of the wreck of his career as a pianist. But perhaps the worst aspect was the effect upon his character—always eccentric—of the peculiar suspiciousness in social relationships which is commonly entailed by deafness. This was the source of much of Beethoven's misery.

Always a difficult man, he became almost impossibly difficult; and, while worshipped, he could hardly be said to have a friend— I mean in the full sense of the word, something more than a mere admirer or a mere hanger-on. That was Beethoven's tragedy—

he, that warm-hearted, ebullient man, to live lovelessly! He did not marry; and volumes have been written about his shadowy relations with women, to small effect. Some believe that his illness was the principal reason for his celibacy. The balance of evidence seems rather to be that the principal among several reasons was his inner heart's devotion to his genius. He certainly loved at times and at times toyed with the idea of marriage; but there seems always to have been something half-hearted in these moods. The god within him was a jealous god.

I have spoken of the tragic element in Beethoven's work and I have spoken of his deafness. Let not these two things be too closely connected. We misread Beethoven if we regard the darkness of his utterances as reflecting merely a personal misfortune. Beethoven's tragic music is the expression of a profound mind that has considered for itself the lot of man, the mystery of life. It is a tragic music that is also the most triumphant of music.

Something must be said about the sources of Beethoven's musical language. Haydn was his teacher and he was saturated in Mozart. He took over from them what may be called symphonic draughtsmanship. Temperamentally he was more akin to Haydn, a peasant like himself; but without Mozart's piano concertos we should not have had Beethoven's. He also greatly admired Cherubini; and when we hear music composed by Cherubini in the 1790s it often strikes us as having a Beethovenian ring of earnestness and severity, which did not belong to the Viennese tradition. Nothing was farther from Beethoven's mind than musical revolutionism. He had a profound respect for Bach and Handel; but he knew them imperfectly and must have felt them to belong to another world. Formally there is in early Beethoven no departure from Haydn or Mozart. The difference is in the imbuing spirit.

There are three categories of Beethoven's music in which is fully illustrated the working of this spirit upon familiar forms and material—Mozart's symphonic manner and Haydn's harmony—until, as time goes on, we are translated into another world. These three categories are the piano sonatas, the string

2*

quartets and the symphonies. The sonatas are a record more intimate than the others of Beethoven's manifold mind until the close of his life, when he preferred the string quartet. But the nine symphonies also represent his principal phases, though one only belongs to the last period.

Even though one may have played these symphonies year after year, until one's performances reach nearly three figures, they still sound fresh and great. I recall the whole cycle played in 1938 under Toscanini, and there remains an indelible impression of contact with Beethoven's very mind. The conductor's intensity and his relentless power and rhythm carried us through the colossal cycle with no intervention of an alien idiosyncrasy between composer and orchestra; and Beethoven seemed to tower behind the conductor's shoulder like an almost visible genie. The orchestra felt itself straining to the utmost of its power to respond to the demands that Beethoven himself seemed to be making through Toscanini. That strange feeling of being very near a composer's mind! For my part, I had never felt anything like it before in so extended an enterprise. A cycle of a composer's works is generally an abomination from the artistic point of view, for the greatest symphonic masterpieces sound their best as a rule in juxtaposition with other carefully chosen works. But this Beethoven Festival, dreaded at first by the orchestra, as promising a mere endurance test without relief, became a steady crescendo of interest and power. It was an experience without which the orchestra of my time might never have measured the full grandeur of Beethoven so clearly.

The First Symphony, in C, representing Beethoven as a man of thirty years, is written in the tradition and style of Mozart. No difference in the orchestration appears except in the more extended use of clarinets. But hints of things to come are not wanting. Beethoven hurls the aspidistra out of the window in the very first bar, by beginning his C major symphony on a discord in F. But it is the Minuet and Trio which break more fresh ground than the other movements, and foreshadow their great children in the later symphonies. The joke with which the last movement opens is like Haydn's pleasantries.

The Second Symphony, in D, which was completed two years later, is, if we recall Beethoven's physical and spiritual crisis of that time, amazingly free from gloom and despondency. It was the time of his worst despair. To what resiliency does it testify! To what an immense power, and what confidence in that inner voice which was to rescue him! The symphony is full of charm and grace. Though larger than No. 1, it still belongs to the traditional style. The Larghetto is particularly lovely, though often it seems long to the orchestra. Much depends upon the conductor. Toscanini takes the movement faster than usual, to the players' greater enjoyment. A slow tempo brings weariness, but Toscanini captured a rhythmic spirit which made the performance an entrancing experience. Again the Scherzo shows more of the essential Beethoven. It is full of force and varied contrasts.

Only four years separate the Third Symphony, the Eroica, from the First, but here we find ourselves suddenly upon one of the peaks of second-period Beethoven. A saying of his, recorded during the composition of the Second Symphony, is: "I am not satisfied with my work up to the present time. From to-day I mean to take a new road." Whither did this road take him? To the symphony that was no longer a comedy but a mighty poem. Beethoven did not turn his back for good upon the comedy-symphony; but the Eroica was the conquest of an empire of which music had never before dreamed.

Napoleon's name can hardly be omitted here, though the story has innumerable times been told of Beethoven's early idealization of the conqueror, of his proposed dedication of the symphony to him, and then of his anger at Napoleon's assumption of an imperial title and the erasing of the name on the dedicatory page, with the rather naïve ejaculation, "So my hero is only mortal!" The story has been over-simplified by some. Beethoven, immeasurably the superior in mind and character, was not without his Napoleonic moods and ambitions. A recorded expression (1798) is this: "Power is the morality of men who loom above others, and it is mine."

No more than any other man was Beethoven all of a piece. He was inexhaustibly complex, and the interplay of his elements will interest mankind while civilization endures. An unchecked, unclouded career—and might not Beethoven have been a Napoleonically ambitious man rather than the profoundly great man we know? The Eroica is not my subject, but this must be said: that that symphony represents a nothing less than gigantic enlargement of the form, in the richness of its material and development and in its spiritual design and content.

In the hands of a conductor himself great enough and able to charge the music with its due intensity of power and rhythm, the Eroica is more thrilling to play than any other symphony in the world. At the London Festival Toscanini moved oceans away from his restrained and rather formal interpretation of the first two symphonies to a style of terrific intensity and immense range of expression. The Eroica is a great landmark of the great master's life. Not perhaps until the Ninth Symphony did he set out again into such vast, unexplored territory.

In No. 4 in B flat—written after another two years' interval—Beethoven comes down from the peaks into a lovely wooded valley, to warm hearts and to gaiety; and in the Adagio the music becomes so passionate that it is not difficult to trust the suggestion of three love-letters, found in his desk after his death, that in the year of the symphony, at the age of thirty-four, he became engaged to the Countess Theresa, sister of his friend von Brunsvik. No other symphony reflects more happiness. Only the opening Adagio expresses doubt and groping, soon to be swept aside. The slow movement is a passionate and poetical love scene.

The Fourth Symphony was begun after he had written two movements of No. 5, but his blessed period of happiness interrupted that darker work, which he did not take up again until his love-affair had fallen through. The Fifth Symphony, in C minor, which he eventually completed at the same time as No. 6, in 1808 (two years after the fourth), is still the most famous of all symphonies. It is a work much spoilt for the orchestra by excessive familiarity and by the plaguing idiosyncrasies of conductors. How many hundreds of times have

players had to ring the changes on ♪♪♪ | ♩ to suit their different temperaments! Countless are the different tempi, the inserted dramatic commas, the diverse phrasing and breathing, which conductors adopt. Magnificently dramatic the C minor symphony will always be; but so far as the orchestral player's enjoyment goes it is not to be compared with the Third, Seventh, or the Ninth. Here again Toscanini rose superior both to routine and personal whim, and the first movement, so often made the playground of exhibitory conductors, was driven through with such unrelenting rhythm and force that Beethoven's ghost might have been imagined sighing with relief. An almost reckless tempo swept the movement onwards, and we were given the fullest impression of Beethoven in this, his most stormy and violent mood, made all the more agitating by the clearness and taut rhythmic articulation of the softer music. Never perhaps had that quick tempo, held so relentlessly, been heard before in this country. Unique as the Eroica is the C minor symphony. Again it is a poem: a poem, this time, of despair battled with and overcome.

The fact that the Sixth Symphony, in F, the Pastoral, was completed at about the same time should make us beware of connecting too closely Beethoven's compositions with the passing events of his life. The Pastoral* is the work I have chosen for fuller discussion in the next chapter. Four years separated this pair of symphonies from the great No. 7 in A (Op. 92). Deaf though he was, Beethoven conducted the first performance of the Seventh Symphony together with 'Wellington's Victory,' at a charity concert, in 1813, and in the orchestra were musicians so eminent as Romberg, Spohr, Dragonetti, Meyerbeer, Hummel and Moscheles; while probably the sixteen-year-old Schubert, who had already written his first symphony, was in the audience. The symphony was received with enthusiasm, and the slow movement was encored. This great symphony in A is to-day a

---

* A footnote is perhaps the place to mention that Beethoven probably derived the idea of his 'Pastoral' from a programme-symphony by Justin Knecht, 'Le Portrait musical de la nature' (? 1784), which includes a depiction of a beautiful day in the country, a storm and a final hymn of gratitude to the Creator. See art. 'Knecht' in Grove's Dictionary.

rival with the Fifth in popularity. From the players' point of view it is more enjoyable to play, once the difficult and slippery steps of the introduction are safely mounted. The work, besides having the most nerve-taxing introduction of all, has another bugbear, which few conductors worry about. It is the much debated rhythm ♩.♫ which Beethoven alternates extensively with ♫♫ as the central idea of the first movement. The poor strings are sometimes harassed with every type of bowing to mark this subtle difference, seldom to any particular effect. And what is worse, there comes a paralysis that seems to attack the rhythm itself, even of the finest orchestras, and makes the taut 6/8 rhythm degenerate into 2/4. How often have conductors held up the strings to shame before the wind players, who, looking down their noses, are never wrong. (It is far easier to tongue a rhythm such as this than to make it clear with the bow.)

Beethoven regarded this glorious Seventh Symphony as one of his finest works, and it is the most enthralling of all to play. Even at a Promenade Concert one still enjoys its perfection of line and colour, and the lovely contrast between the movements. Its great length never becomes wearisome, and the final stages of the ebullient last movement still provide one of those thrills that are all too few for the hardened player. The work is the embodiment of vitality, beauty and power. The very ruggedness that has always been characteristic of Beethoven is here more rounded, like magnificent rocks pounded by the waves but losing nothing of their grandeur.

Immediately after finishing this symphony Beethoven was hard at work polishing the Eighth Symphony, which he completed in the wonderfully short period of four months. Vastly different from No. 7, though full of exuberant spirits, it is much shorter and less weighty. It is an extraordinarily light-hearted, humorous work. Beethoven gives us a picture of his happiest moods—poking fun at someone or other, revelling in the open air, roaring with fury at an annoyance or making love to the sweetheart of the moment. It was the last time he could capture such moods and spirits.

The so-called 'Battle Symphony,' which dates from the same period, is properly named 'Wellington's Victory, or the Battle of Vitoria,' and is not strictly a symphony at all, but a piece of crude programme music in which 'Rule, Britannia' and 'God Save the King' are introduced. Vastly popular at the time, it has been forgotten.

The years that followed the Eighth Symphony were strangely barren. Beethoven's health deteriorated; he was involved in family disputes and lawsuits. Five years passed before he began the composition of his Ninth Symphony. This is the place in which to make a brief reference to Beethoven's sketch-books, which throw a light upon a method of composition no doubt unique among the masters of music. His mind would work upon three or four different compositions at a time, and in the sketch-books we see the ideas taking shape and a process of experiment and improvement which exhibits Beethoven as the most consciously and laboriously intellectual of artists. We thus find indications of the Ninth Symphony as long as six years before the work was completed. A servant of Beethoven's has left us this account of him at that period:

"He usually got up at about five-thirty, and would then sit down at the table and begin to write, singing, growling and beating time with both hands and feet. Seven-thirty was the family breakfast, after which he would go out into the open air. There he would lounge about in the fields, suddenly breaking out into loud exclamations and throwing his hands wildly about, often scaring cattle and alarming strangers. Twelve-thirty was dinner-time, and then in his room until 3 p.m., when he would take his inseparable sketch-book into the open air again until sunset. After supper he would retire to his room and go to bed about ten."

The Ninth Symphony was finished in the autumn of 1823. Only two rehearsals could be allowed to the first performance of the colossal work. Though Beethoven could now hear nothing of the music, he came into the orchestra, stood by the conductor, and beat time to indicate the various changes of tempo. At the close of the performance, well after the work had finished and amidst the ovation, he still stood with his back to the audience, beating time. He had heard nothing whatever.

The first movement of the Choral Symphony portrays the full force of that indomitable nature. It is the great summing-up of his struggle with life, and there are two ways of interpreting it— that of the great German tradition represented by Weingartner and Bruno Walter, in which the movement grows out of some immense space and builds up into range after range of mighty peaks. Toscanini, on the other hand, sees the movement as Beethoven's final expression of his own irresistible force meeting the immovable mass of nature. His body has to succumb, but his spirit is undying. The relentless power which Toscanini seems to derive from that great spirit behind him drives the orchestra through the mighty movement in one long terrific and pro-tracted effort. No relaxation of tempo, even in the two passages in which Beethoven relieves the pressure himself. Just the slightest drawing up, like the tightening of some equipment, before the next battle, and that is all.

The Scherzo is the finest of all in the symphonies. Technically it is still one of the most difficult movements that exist. The basic rhythm, like that of the first movement of the Seventh Sym-phony, is wickedly difficult for the strings to play to perfection. It is not easy for the wind, but for twenty violins to make it as clear as one player is a frightening task under an exacting chief. The hammering blows of the timpani seem to carry on that sense of titanic strife which inspired the first movement, but here is something regained of the vitality and humour of the happier Beethoven. The delicious horn tune in the Trio is in one of his happy open-air moods.

The third movement might be in the heavens, and here Toscanini made every effort to transfer the playing from brilliant, incisive vitality to the quietest, subdued tenderness. "In Para-diso!" he exclaimed. The strings particularly caressed their music and were never allowed to become passionate—only intensely ethereal. Bruno Walter takes another course, and reads more humanity into the music. A great warmth of feeling is fostered, as against the restraint and other-worldly character of Toscanini's interpretation. Yet the latter's detachment and restrained feeling gave the movement its full beauty of contrast after the terrific performance of the first and second movements, and it ended in exquisite beauty.

The aesthetic question of the choral finale is not within my present scope. I will simply say that it is something of a trial to the orchestra. Is it or is it not an experiment? An experiment not wholly successful? After the clamorous beginning, the wonderful recitative for cellos and basses and the recall of the preceding movements, the announcement of the immortal melody of the hymn never fails to thrill, but no sooner has the choral section been heralded by the bass solo than the orchestra feels it has come to the end of its real task. The orchestral player says that all the rest, with one or two exceptional passages, seems to peter out into noise and trivialities. The test is fearful for the choir, and rarely or never does the solo quartet rise to Beethoven's demands; while the orchestra, already weary from its great exertions, is apt to lose heart. I mention this as the average executant's feeling on a question about which volumes have been and will be written. What, at the same time, must be admitted is that the choral finale is, with all its inequalities—inequalities such as we have never met with before in Beethoven—unique; that, if it is a failure, it is still worth more than a thousand other men's successes; and that there is something unspeakably affecting and impressive in the spectacle of Beethoven failing on this scale. It was like Beethoven to attempt, at the last, the impossible. What he could not, no man will ever achieve.

There was to have been a tenth symphony. Sketches survive. But Beethoven devoted his last years to the string quartet, and in a series of works which have not their equivalent in his orchestral music he expressed his inmost self with a new abundance of ideas, with a new terseness, a new passionate intellectualism.

The symphony reached in Beethoven its apogee. During the century that came after him great musicians composed much beautiful music in the form, but we have only to contemplate Beethoven to realize that the zenith was passed, and all music since is the music of a long-drawn afternoon.

VI

BEETHOVEN'S PASTORAL SYMPHONY

THE Pastoral Symphony is a pure classic, and one of the most difficult to interpret, for all the transparency of the writing. Toscanini was for ever complaining of the difficulty of the first movement. "Ah, it is so difficult—always difficult, this movement, wherever it is played! These long crescendi and the balance—tcts-tcts-tcts-tcts! Violas, now! Firmly the first note—if nobody 'ears, the melody has no beginning! The violins, in time, no ritenuto, no ritenuto to the pause! After the pause we go straight on—yes, no break. Violas, play firmly again after the pause!"

Fig.1 *Allegro ma non troppo*
1st Violins

When he first conducted this symphony in London, he spent half the time at rehearsal on the exposition of the first movement. The interpretation of the work lies in the orchestra's rhythm and the purity of its style. The playing of the opening four bars gives the key to the rest of the movement. This grows like nature itself, all springing from the parent stem. Offshoots and blossoms in any number derive from some figure of this subject; and nature's repetitiveness, repetitions without sameness, is in Beethoven. Only a wooden or flippant mind makes this music monotonous. Unlike the others, it is a symphony that relies completely on the integrity and fineness of sensibility of its interpreter.

Immediately after these opening bars we come upon this

characteristic repetition. Beethoven takes a group of notes formed out of the first subject:

and repeats it ten times. So is a leaf repeated on a branch. Monotonous? No! For Beethoven writes a gradual crescendo to forte and then down again, finishing pianissimo without any accompaniment, and the little figure trips up the scale for the oboe to return innocently to the opening bars again. Another bar is tacked on to take the music onward, instead of pausing as before:

(New bar instead of pause)

Clarinets and bassoons repeat the passage crescendo, and then violins and full woodwind join in, adding yet another two bars to the oboe's suggestion,

while the violins finally round the whole thing off:

So does the music germinate, like nature herself, entirely of such short, tripping figures. Every imaginable change is wrought in a group of four or five notes, and nothing is without significance. Even a little reiterated triplet figure:

without interest at first, grows into an integral, rhythmic part of
the movement, later actually to dominate the whole.

The second subject is different. It does not belong to the
'nature' growth, but by its smooth character serves as a contrast.
It consists of three separate ideas which have the happy knack of
fitting in with one another in any way that may be chosen.
Sometimes one figure is in the treble, sometimes in the bass.
Here are the three separate ideas altogether in one long melody:

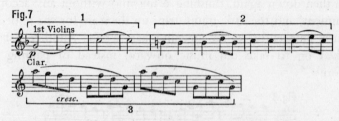

The orchestra will not forget how Toscanini worked at this
passage. Labouring to get a perfect dovetailing of the quavers
(No. 3) between 1st and 2nd violins and cellos, he does not rest
until the music sounds fresh and clear as if its beauty had never
been noticed by man before. The violins are asked to sing with
natural expression, while he keeps the accompaniment down so
that these two bars of undulating quavers are handed over clearly
and smoothly between the departments. It is quite entrancing to
hear the effect for the first time, for this is often made to sound a
dull kind of churning accompaniment, quite obscuring the beauty
of its features.

So this little phrase wends its way from 1st violins to 2nd
violins, down to cellos and basses, and then up again as if over a
lovely, undulating countryside, through clarinets, to the flutes,
whilst the original bass somehow finds itself in the treble. All this
time there is a gradual crescendo working up to a C major chord
and a new subsidiary tune on the strings, still with the same bucolic
character:

is sweetly answered by woodwind, only for the strings to insist rudely on their own tune again, playing it fortissimo. The little triplet figure, which first came on the scene like a shoot in the ground, has now grown to a sizeable tree, first by its rhythm imposing on the woodwind and then in alternate bars serving as bass for a new theme:

Fig.9 Violins

With the rhythm of the last phrase gradually disappearing to pianissimo and rumbling softly in basses and cellos, Beethoven calls an end to the first section of the movement and places the usual sign for repeat.

At rehearsal there was a doubt whether there was to be a repeat. For once, Toscanini is undecided. "I don't know. I have always Da capo until now, but I think I may be wrong. For the balance of the movement perhaps it is best that we make it. Yes, we will go back!" Toscanini seldom makes this first repeat in a long symphony—never in Brahms, for instance, and never in a long first movement. But in Beethoven Nos. 1, 2, 5 and 8 he observed the *Da capo*. And so again here, since this exposition is comparatively short. In the bar before the repeat Beethoven's forte is played too roughly by the orchestra. "Via, via, via! It is the fortissimo! Take care, take care!"

In a few bars after the double bar begins a great passage of accumulated repetitions and steadily increasing sound. "Ah, this passage, it is always difficult! It must be in gradual crescendo and perfect balance! Yes, yes, strings, you must begin pianissimo, otherwise there is no crescendo."

This is a good instance of Toscanini's making an alteration in Beethoven's marking. By reducing the tone to a pianissimo, he ensures that the whole great ensuing crescendo becomes doubly effective. For eight bars Beethoven now repeats this figure:

Fig.10 1st Violins

on a chord of B flat, with the original little triplet figure spread over an arpeggio—lightly dancing on the strings. Then for four bars, still on the same chord, he slightly alters the figure, until at last a change of harmony lightens the colour to D major. Now the tone has become firm, with the orchestra under Toscanini's broad, rhythmic beat strongly swinging over the bar lines, instead of the usual heavy rhythm, bar by bar. The figure is repeated again and again, and added scoring caps the whole crescendo in a grand fortissimo, still in D major, with the basses for ever playing with the obstinate idea that must have obsessed our Beethoven in his country clothes. Still it goes on—thrown about this time between the strings, till at last bassoons and violins are left to themselves in a comic little duet:

having at last thrown off the  part of the figure. This popping little duet, with delicious naïveté, suddenly brings us back to the first subject again in G major, with another delightful little counter-tune on the 2nd violins:

Fig.12

This little theme on the 2nd violins was strongly focused by Toscanini for perfect clarity and ensemble after the tied note.

but only by way of a joke, for Beethoven has been so pleased with his great crescendo that he takes us back for another ride, this time in G major, with the favourite obsession like a dog twitching his nose. E major is the summit we make for this time, brilliant in the sunshine of a sharper key. Violins and bassoons engage in their cross-talk as before, and the first subject now returns in A major. The little counter-theme that Toscanini criticized before now has the 2nd violins wary—not to be caught again!

But Beethoven now lets the first subject have its proper say, and for the first time since the beginning of the movement we hear the second part of the tune again:

Fig.13 Violas & Cellos

So much so, in fact, that he allows it to go on its own way through one or two modulations, until the 1st violins sing a minor version of it with strong accents, giving it a different character:

Fig.14 1st Violins

A climax for this tune marks the next landmark, before Beethoven thinks about the recapitulation. This he approaches after a sudden piano in which a tentative little figure

Fig.15 2nd Violins

first on 2nd violins, then violas, and finally cellos, turns back naïvely to the first bar of the main theme again. Now he reminds us of the pause in the fifth bar of the movement, for instead of going on he gives the 1st violins an unaccompanied trill and a charming little cadenza in place of the original pause. This is another place where Toscanini took particular pains. It is trying for the nerves of twenty violins, for there is no cover by the rest of the orchestra.

He exclaimed, "No stringendo, no allargando! In strict time! But look at me! Via, via, via, it is not clear! Some of you make stringendo! See!"

Near the end of the recapitulation Beethoven transforms the subsidiary tune:

Fig.16 Strings

which had come early in the movement, to:

Fig. 17 Strings

altering the rhythm to triplets, and he uses this material to work up to the biggest climax of the movement, which sounds grand if there is sufficient reserve left for the crowning fortissimo. Here was another of Toscanini's particular points. A diminuendo brings us the coda, which begins pianissimo in the violas

Fig. 18 Violas

and contains a quaint passage for clarinet, rather reminiscent of the farmyard. Beethoven rather enjoyed trying to make the clarinet squeak. A similar passage in the scherzo of the Eighth Symphony always leads the orchestra to wonder what the clarinet is thinking about when he is approaching the last top note. But the expert player of our day makes light of it, though the height looks dizzy.

So Beethoven ends the movement with a charming little ladder shared between 1st violin and flute, and finally full orchestra. It ends, as it began, in the pure happiness and sunshine of spring.

In the slow movement spring has turned to summer. The movement has a title—'By the Brook.' Throughout the music, this gentle, slow-moving stream wanders through quiet valleys, full of sweet air and the sounds of midsummer.

Fig. 19 Andante molto mosso   1st Violins

Strings (The Brook)

In one of the notes which have been found in an old 1st violin part Beethoven said: "All painting in instrumental music, if pushed too too far, is a failure." Until we get to the actual bird-voices this music is not imitative, but Beethoven's rendering

with his own classic means of myriad little noises that enchant us
in the sunshine, when we rest near running water, is all here.
Like nature's own sounds, Beethoven's material here is elusive
and often a theme has almost gone before we have caught it.
Such elusive shreds of sound are suggested in the first bar, where
the first part of the principal subject on the 1st violins is broken
by long rests, as though our ears had picked up some delicious
little sound, only to lose it again. Beethoven completes the first
subject with two inspired bars of continuous melody:

Fig. 20

The whole movement consists of a number of motifs that
come and go over this ceaseless background of water and this
principal theme. After the 1st violins have played it through, the
clarinets repeat it, with the violins murmuring little trills of
approving comment.

Toscanini here took infinite pains to set the movement going.
First of all the brook motif was strongly criticized for 'heaviness.'
"It must be so light, and gently rocking like a berceuse!" The
lovely sound that eventually came forth was made by the shortest
possible bows in the strings and the slightest rhythmical swing at
the beginning of each triplet. He dropped this tone down one
grade, practically to pianissimo. The little turn of the tune on the
violins in the second bar, and later on the clarinets, he had to sing
himself over and over again before we could please him. I can
still hear him singing that "tra-leala."

The clarinets having now concluded the principal theme of the
movement, the 1st violins quietly wander to a new strain of
thought for two bars, in the same mood, as if in exquisite day-
dream:

Fig. 21

The clarinet then once more repeats the 1st violin's remarks, while violins join with the bassoon in a new accompaniment for him.

We are now so used to the sound of the continual murmur of the brook that we almost fail to notice its disappearance for a moment, while a little distant thrumming underneath another disjointed remark of the 1st violins again changes our trend of thought. But the music soon comes back to the main idea again. The stream gently returns to our ears beneath the 1st violins, as at the beginning, only this time Beethoven—instead of keeping their little broken phrases on the same notes—takes them higher, and modulates into F major, while he ornaments the continuous melody with new figures and grace-notes. The colours are enchanting, as if the sun had suddenly picked out new beauties from the shadows. Generally the bassoon seems more at home there, but Beethoven's sunshine persuades even him from his lair, and his tenor voice is heard for the first time by itself, imitating a tender phrase of the flute. So encouraged is he that he expresses himself in one of the loveliest tunes ever given to the bassoon— the second main tune of the movement:

Fig. 22

The choice of the bassoon for this tune is extraordinarily apt. The hearts of cellos and violas are melted and they feel they must join him. Beethoven brings these thoughts to a gentle conclusion with a bar that forecasts the Brahms of fifty years later. He alters the slow, rocking movement in 12/8 to 6/4, and a lovely change is given to the movement of the brook, as if its course had suddenly been altered. Toscanini slightly stressed the phrasing of this bar by shortening each second quaver:

Fig. 23

It is a famous bar of music, beautifully punctuating the ceaseless flow of the movement without breaking it.

In the next bar a trill * on the 1st violin over two chords leads us over much the same ground as we have just passed—the music suggested by the bassoon.

The whole passage is repeated, with much increased figuration and scoring, until, after a fascinating arpeggio passage between flute, bassoon and 1st violin, the violas and cellos lead us back to the main idea again.

Beethoven begins the working-out section by widening the river, which now streams with more sound underneath the violins, who enrich their first little broken phrases. A new tune, in perfect harmony with drowsy contentment, occurs to Beethoven, which he uses extensively in all the ensuing development:

Fig. 24   2nd Violins & Violas

while a lovely little arpeggio, which is only an accompaniment at first to this new tune, presently turns from its chrysalis into a brilliant little butterfly flitting with happy freedom all over the score:

Fig. 25   Flute

All the themes and material which have now come into use are thereupon woven together with wonderful ingenuity and charm. The music wanders through the keys of E flat, G flat, E minor and B flat in much the same way as it had begun, with carefree thought and no sense of labour. Repetition occurs much in the

* This trill has been the subject of some argument as to whether it should finish with the natural little turn, or whether Beethoven really meant it to finish abruptly without one. Toscanini himself seemed doubtful, and said: "Ah, yes, First Violin—I know Beethoven did not write a turn, but I don't think I like it cut off. Try, just try, bitte, for me now! Try it with turn!—Ah, bene, bene! It is more natural. Yes, we will play it so."

same way as in the first movement, but there is often the disguise of a different figuration. Home again in B flat! And the exposition is repeated with enrichments of its original simplicity. In the Coda come the famous bird-songs, over which pundits and aesthetes have written volumes. Tovey must be quoted here:

> "Much nonsense might have been spared about this passage if the superior persons who regard it as a violation of the absoluteness of music had taken the trouble to notice that the three birds make with this motto a perfectly normal four-bar phrase."

It greatly depends upon the conductor how this Coda comes off. Clownish treatment is shockingly out of place, and the ending itself is so beautiful in its simplicity that a trace of bad taste in its performance brings shipwreck. Toscanini takes immense pains here with his three prima-donnas, Nightingale, Quail and Cuckoo. First the flute makes the nightingale gently expressive, with a slight stress on his trill. Toscanini then makes a slight crescendo for the quail, whose little pipping song on the oboe is as short as possible. Quail and cuckoo each enter a shade louder than marked, and finally the three of them fade in diminuendo for the 1st violins, whose phrase then grows naturally out of these little bird-songs, as if they had been listening in the quietude of a wood. The bird-songs are repeated, and this time Beethoven makes a lovely ending to the movement by repeating the phrase on the violins three times more, first on the bassoons, then the clarinets, and finally the flute, with oboes and horns—joining in on the last four notes—to round off the whole movement with a firmly stressed B flat chord.

Toscanini builds up the whole passage imperceptibly from pianissimo on the violins to almost forte on the flutes, each instrument passing his tune over to the other in perfect balance. He rehearsed the dovetailing and handing-over until it sounded like one long phrase with the graded colour of a rainbow.

As in most slow movements marked 'con moto,' he adopted a slightly quicker tempo than usual. "Con moto, con moto, bitte! It is terrible when it is too slow! Movement, always movement—

à la Berceuse—gently rocking—en bateau, and so softly!"
He insisted that the lower strings, which begin the movement of
the brook, should use the shortest possible bows, with the slightest
tremor of the left hand at each beat of the bar, to obtain that
lovely imperceptible current of the stream which must never
become lifeless and mechanical.

Rustic merry-making is idealized in the third movement.
Accustomed as the modern world is to violently realistic music,
this idealization or stylization is something to be borne in mind
by the listener throughout the Pastoral Symphony. In a measure
the symphony is programme music; but with much more music
than programme. Think of an example in which the balance was
different—Strauss's Alpine Symphony, with its shocking banality!
What could be more banal than Beethoven's programme? A
mere day in the country! But no such good music as the Pastoral
Symphony has been written by anyone since. This scherzo is to
be read as no realistic representation of holiday-making hobble-
dehoys, nor yet with an inhuman daintiness.

The principal idea has two contrasted parts—the one short and
sparkling, the other smooth and sunny:

Fig. 26 *Allegro*

This sounds entrancing when played absolutely pianissimo. The
first phrase affords a fine little opportunity for the strings. If
played in one up-bow, with tiny strokes, the effect is fairylike,
though this is a rather nervous undertaking for the players, for it
is not easy. Toscanini does it in this way himself, at a quickish
tempo, and also gives it another lovely, light little touch; he
plays the last three notes in diminuendo, so that an inartistic
bump on the last note—formerly of frequent occurrence—is
avoided. The sunny part of the phrase he plays no louder, but
with great rhythm and life. Soon the orchestra combines in a

crescendo, and the really boisterous element comes in with the heavier-footed maids and men joining in the dance.

The second tune of the Scherzo is again a light, elfish-like little oboe tune, with an unexpected nuance at the end of it.

Fig. 27 Oboe

It is characteristically announced by the 1st and 2nd violins in the true village-band 'chuck, chuck' style:

Fig. 28 1st & 2nd Violins

(With bassoons)

Note another joke of Beethoven's in the coarse remarks that are interpolated by the bassoon, like an old gaffer sitting in the corner of the inn. Yet another delicious little piece of will-o'-the-wisp humour is the inserting of an extra bar, imitating the last bar of the tune, instead of the sustained note. When the first horn takes over the tune it is significant that Beethoven has doubled his string accompaniment (in case of accidents!). It probably sounded somewhat rough in his day, for it is a tricky passage and needs great artistry.

The Trio is the more boisterous part of the movement. Here there is much stamping, and the dust flies. Toscanini slightly alters the bowing of the strings in this tune, and its heavy rhythm thereby makes much more effect. The basses finish the Trio by pounding away for dear life till they are suddenly arrested by a crash of overturned tables. Then a softly held C on trumpets and violins takes us back to the children again and the first tune. But only for a short statement of it, for everyone breaks in again in a furious Presto. It is a stampede.

Now comes the first rumble of the storm in the basses, who move up one semitone to a tremolando D flat; and in a second the rain begins to patter. No storm ever upset a party as this one of Beethoven's. There is no frantic gathering of odds and ends, and rushing for shelter. Beethoven just sweeps all this humanity aside with one god-like gesture, and the earth is primeval again.

The 2nd violins always look as though they were the only people left on earth, with a satanic Toscanini raging at their puny struggles. How many devoted 2nd violins' hearts have been broken on this Bridge of Sorrows! What did Beethoven do with his 2nd violins when he conducted, besides getting into a rage? Toscanini takes the movement in two beats, and there is generally much anguish and dole, until the notes are all short enough, rhythmic and in perfect ensemble. "Santissimo Dio! Via, via, via, via! Play the bow with your brain!"

Never will be forgotten an occasion at the Promenade Concerts when this symphony was not rehearsed by Sir Henry, but by the leader of the orchestra; who that morning had most carefully rehearsed the passage with four beats to a bar. In the evening about 40 per cent of the seconds started as if for two in a bar, and 45 per cent in four, while the rest steered a middle course and turned the raindrops into a waterspout.

With his fine sense of economy, Beethoven has reserved some power for this approach to the last movement of the symphony, and for the first time he brings in two trombones, timpani, and piccolo. This last is, of course, to play a great part with its flashes of lightning. Structurally the storm is an introduction to the Finale. Its opening is so clear with its falling rain and a frightened cry on the first violins

Fig. 29 1st Violins.

that no quotation is needed, and there is no doubt when the full tempest suddenly crashes out in fury on an F minor chord. The storm music is exhausting for all the strings. The basses must get red-hot from sheer friction, and though they have one less note to play in their furious scales than the cellos:

Fig. 30

they have more ground to cover. The main theme of the storm is a Valkyrie-like motif, descending through the orchestra:

and a hacking unison passage:

Short, brittle chords break out here and there like flashes, which Toscanini makes as short and explosive as possible. The fury waxes until a supreme height is reached. Four bars of the same chord, a diminished seventh on F sharp and a series of heavily accented sustained chords with the strings scraping for dear life mark the climax. Now the clamour begins to lessen, as the basses begin their great descending figure underneath the still shivering tremolando of the strings:

Toscanini holds this climax until the last possible moment, and actually maintains the whole bar—where Beethoven writes 'sempre diminuendo'—fortissimo. He directs the strings to continue to tear at their instruments for some bars, to make the gradual diminuendo as long-drawn as possible. His climax is raised to an incredible height by the conservation of forces for as long as possible, both in the crescendo and diminuendo. The summit itself, under Toscanini, somehow produces a rush of extra power beyond anything the orchestra itself knew it was capable of.

BEETHOVEN

SCHUBERT

When at last the sound dies to pianissimo the orchestra breathes a little prayer of thankfulness:

Fig. 34   Oboe & Strings

It is the same figure as the 'rain motif,' only now in slow minims. The rumbling now fades out altogether and, like the first precious ray of sunlight, the flute in a final scale lights up a changed world and, touching the violas and clarinets with a magic wand, takes us into sunlit country again.

Toscanini's treatment of this passage between the two movements is something never to be forgotten. One reason why his interpretations are so satisfying is his art of maintaining a sense of continuity. With him the line of life is never broken. He checks the slightest sign of slowing tempo in the long diminuendo from the storm, and, tenderly though the prayer is sung, it is yet in perfect rhythm, and the scale of the flute, which is frequently slackened at the end, is instead made to run straight into the next movement as Beethoven directed.

The beginning of the Finale ('Shepherd's Song of Thanksgiving') is in the nature of a yodel, first by the clarinets and then the first horn, with a droning bass on the lowest open strings of the violas.

Fig. 35 *Allegretto*
Clarinet
dolce

Essential to the interpretation of these pages is that the join should be perfect. What more lovely than to hear the flute scale imperceptibly merged into the distant yodel! Toscanini particularly asked the violas to accent firmly their first three bars, so that there be no hesitation whatever in the setting of the new 6/8 metre. The yodel was an after-thought. Beethoven thought at first of beginning the movement with the main theme. In the fifth of these bars, preludial when the horn imitates the clarinet, Beethoven used the device of playing in two keys at once (violas

3

continue to sustain in C major, while horn and clarinet play in F)
—a device he had used once before in the Eroica.

The atmosphere has now become clear and sunny again for
the 1st violins to play the lovely song of thankfulness. The theme
is simplicity itself:

Fig. 36 1st Violins

In an unusual piece of scoring Beethoven writes crescendo in the
last bar of the theme (throughout the score), and then hands the
tune over to the 2nd violins an octave lower, with additional
accompaniment. Toscanini cuts the crescendo out of this bar and
inserts diminuendo, so that the 2nds start fair anyway. Otherwise,
"Nobody hears," as he so often exclaims. The 2nds have to play
consistently stronger than at Beethoven's direction. This leads to
a great fortissimo when the theme swings its way onward on the
full orchestra. At the end of this great chorus a new two-bar
phrase enters:

Fig. 37

Note the unusual 'tenuto,' which demands the utmost held power
for each crotchet.

The swing of Toscanini's beat in this new, heavily stressed
phrase seems to become immense, like an enormous pendulum
that suddenly gathers a new momentum. He knocks the two
6/8 bars into one of 12/8, building the phrase up to the top note
and down again. The tune has an extraordinary power in this
way, and gives Beethoven's 'tenuto' the utmost effect.

Beethoven finds the last group of this phrase too good to leave,
and so indulges in some enjoyment with it, first playing about
with the figure itself:

Fig. 38

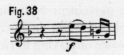

and then turning it into a more fluid form altogether:

Fig. 39

A new short phrase brings us to a return of the music of the opening (the movement is a rondo), with the yodelling now extended.

Toscanini makes no alteration in Beethoven's dynamics before the return of the main theme, but instead of a biggish crescendo in the bar with the scale which reintroduces it he requires this crescendo to be very slight and gradual, so that the yodelling leads easily to the return of the tune. Abruptness is avoided.

On the key changing to B flat clarinets and bassoons remind us of the brook again, and particularly does the flowing accompaniment of the violas:

Fig. 40 Violas

But it is a mountain stream now. Modulations through the key of D flat to C again lead us back to the yodelling, now on the woodwind, with a flowing semiquaver accompaniment. The main tune at the same time is disguised in broken quavers:

Fig. 41 1st Violins

2nd Violins with main theme broken up

This accompaniment becomes a line of continuous movement, linking up the broken form of the tune. Beginning in 1st violins, it runs into the 2nds, when they take over the actual theme from the 1sts. Just as it finishes, Beethoven rushes up to a big fortissimo, followed by the second subject. The music now grows into variations of the themes already quoted, and eventually the full climax of the movement comes after a short fugal passage on the flowing semiquaver theme.

We have come to the Coda. So far the movement has, with

all its beauty, been sedate and homely. Something more is wanted to raise this thanksgiving to a noble level, and to give universality and spiritual grandeur to the whole. The Coda is Beethoven's vehicle for this purpose. The final gathering of his forces is clear as the orchestra joins in a long, sustained organ-like fortissimo on an F major chord. The wind all sustain, strings break into quick bows which become practically tremolando to get the utmost power, and the basses in this figure:

Fig. 42
ff Cellos & Basses   *sf*

stride up to the summit of a mountain top, chord by chord. This climax of the symphony is majestic. The violins descend from their highest notes to their lowest, while the basses range up and down on their seven-league boots. The whole passage is held fortissimo for over twelve bars, and then gradually fades. The strings play a few bars reminiscent of the principal theme, and this, after two heavily accented bars of truly Beethovenian contrast, is wistfully repeated by the oboes. The symphony comes to an end after the first horn, very distantly, plays the original yodel.

Particular to Toscanini's interpretation of this Finale is the wonderful swing of the unchanging 6/8 rhythm. Often this has been known to become heavy and lifeless. With Toscanini it is intensely vital, and the momentum with which the orchestra is imbued gives the music a power that is not less than its charm.

Have I suggested in this chapter—written under the influence of a great performance—a kind of vividness and colour in the Pastoral Symphony which does not belong to the music and which may lead the inexperienced listener to expect something that is not there? The Pastoral is not romantic music. Its landscapes indeed belong to the eighteenth century. The range of the colour, like the range of the emotion, is severely limited. Any cinema organist could produce a more hair-raising storm than Beethoven's. But art consists of proportion and gradation, and not of the employment of any and every means for sensation's sake. The longer one lives with the Pastoral Symphony, the more adequate, the more insurpassably fine, appear the style, the balance, the discretion of the colouring. "Not so much painting as the expression of feeling," was Beethoven's note, quoted a thousand times, on the score of the slow movement. It is music that expresses feelings so deep that nothing but the most rigorous, the most classic restraint was appropriate or effective. More effusiveness, more protestations! We have only to think of anything of the sort to see how they would have lessened the simple grandeur of Beethoven's subject and clouded the purity of his treatment. The Pastoral Symphony is not music for the young. It takes half a lifetime to appreciate what Beethoven has here not done, as well as the faultlessness of what he has done, the shapeliness, the proportions of this symphony, and in the very modesty of its subject-matter and the subdued colouring the supreme control of the artist who was the most ebullient and vehement of men, but who had the power of mind to attain classic simplicity.

VII

SCHUBERT
1797–1828

SCHUBERT'S life was shorter even than Mozart's, and as long as civilization lasts there will be mourning for the world's loss of that lovely genius, dearer to some hearts than any other in the whole realm of music, at an age when none of the great composers had done their best work. If Bach had died at thirty-one he would be forgotten; and so would Haydn. Mozart, dead at thirty-one, would indeed be remembered, but we should have been without 'Don Giovanni,' 'The Magic Flute' and the great symphonies. Beethoven? We should be left with first-period works only. And Wagner, the composer of 'The Flying Dutchman' only—would he be well remembered? A thing to bear in mind about Schubert is that all his works are early works; and another thing is this: down to the very last weeks of his life he was developing prodigiously. The last year or so was the time of his greatest symphony, his greatest Mass, his greatest chamber music, his greatest piano sonatas, and a quantity of marvellous songs. But the chief consideration is not what Schubert did not, but what he did accomplish—that wonderful outpouring of a profoundly poetic as well as profoundly musical nature, which made Ethel Smyth, for instance, exclaim: "All my life his music has perhaps been nearer my heart than any other—that crystal stream welling and welling for ever!"

At the same time, Schubert has sometimes been disparaged as none of his three great predecessors of the Viennese school have been. In this connexion one should bear in mind that practically everything Schubert wrote from his fifteenth year onwards—and he wrote incessantly—has been preserved and published. And there is the fact, which has been allowed to weigh in some estimates down to our own day, that for a variety of reasons Schubert did not succeed in fully imposing himself on his contemporary world. There has been much misunderstanding of Schubert's character because he did not shine in ordinary society (he did not care to). Any Tom, Dick or Harry, scribbling about music, has fancied himself fit to patronize Schubert. Cecil Gray, author of *A History of Music* (1928), is one of several superior persons of these times who have pooh-poohed him. Gray wrote: "There was a lack of intellectual fibre and grit about his whole personality—a flabbiness and superfluity of adipose tissue in his mind as in his body." I prefer Grove's verdict, uttered eighty years ago with more sense and recognition of the eternal verities than is shown by some of the lively sparks of our century. "One of the ten or twelve topmost men in the world!" said Grove. Schnabel went farther, saying: "The last of the great composers!"

The truth is that Schubert, obscure by birth and standing deliberately aloof from the official musical world of his Vienna, was the life and soul of his chosen circle, a group of intellectual young men, artists, poets, civil servants, several of them talented, most of them of superior social position to himself, who one and all acknowledged him as their leading spirit and revelled in his genius. 'Schubertiads' was the name they gave to their meetings and parties. Outside this circle and that of his family Schubert was ill at ease—and above all impatient. He had time for nothing but friends and his art. Once or twice, being hard-pressed economically, he half-heartedly put in for salaried appointments, but one can see that he did not seriously wish for them.

One thing salient about Schubert's life is the determination with which he gave himself to composition. Much of the pity expended over his penniless lot is misplaced. It is true that he was miserably rewarded by the publishers of his compositions. But even this is something we should consider with the justice of remembering that publishers, in those days of an incoherent copyright law, were not in their established position of to-day, and the royalty system did not exist. In their dealings with

Schubert they were hard. He never had the luck of hitting upon a publisher of any generosity. But this was hardly more than an inconvenience, not a misery, to Schubert. His music was published—a hundred works in the seven years before his death. The important thing for Schubert, as for us, was that he should be free to write. He was free to do so: he had worshipping friends; and, hard up though he was, he certainly never starved.

The tragedy of Schubert's life had nothing to do with his circumstances. He was happy in the exercise of his wonderful genius. He had no unlucky love-affairs, so far as is known; there is, in fact, no substantial evidence of any such affair of any seriousness. If penniless, he had no family claims. The disaster was an illness that afflicted him when he was twenty-six. It was not in itself mortal, and in those next few years he worked like a man possessed; but it undermined his health. The nature of the illness of 1823 will be found discussed in various biographies. It was not the immediate cause of his death on that dreadful day, November 19, 1828. The immediate cause was typhoid. But what we can divine in the records is essentially something like Mozart's death —Schubert was killed by the exactions of his inner demon.

He was born not, indeed, into a family of professional musicians, but into one in which music was the prime recreation, the daily delight. We shall not begin to understand the great Viennese classical period if the extraordinary cult of music of the time is not appreciated. The passion for good music that had characterized the aristocracy and upper burgesses of Mozart's time spread a few years later to more modest circles. Schubert's father was an elementary schoolmaster of peasant stock, with a large family and an income that would in our days appear a starvation wage. Schubert's boyhood was a time of national crisis and military disasters. As a boy he saw the French occupation of Vienna, and the years of his adolescence were those of a severe *post-bellum* stringency. But the cost of living remained surprisingly low. Grove, Schubert's passionate champion in mid-nineteenth-century England, was generously indignant at the thought of his hero's economic straits:

"Good God! it makes one's blood boil to think of so fine and rare a genius in want of even the common necessaries of life. To want bread! It is too dreadful to think of."

But this is an exaggeration. Schubert did not starve. That the modest Liechtental family was above the danger-line is proved by the present Schubert's father gave to his seventeen-year-old son of a five-octave piano on the occasion of the production of the lad's first Mass, composed for a festival at their parish church. It is characteristic of Schubert that four years later he should have offered the instrument as a present to his brother Ferdinand, who was then in need of a piano. Schubert's family attachments were deep—to his father, his step-mother, to his brothers and sisters. The story of a breach with his father (told in nearly all the biographies) has the flimsiest of foundations.

What of Schubert's musical education? It was somewhat less thorough than that of Mozart or Beethoven. His father was an amateur, and the child's marvellous gifts excited more wonder than ambition in his circle. But the commonly held belief that Schubert was an uneducated genius is nonsense. His father gave him violin lessons when he was eight, and sent him to be taught singing and the rudiments of music with the local organist. The child already knew his way about the piano, and his elder brother Ferdinand gave him lessons. At the age of eleven he easily won a choral scholarship at the Imperial Seminary ('Konvikt'), the best school in Vienna. He was there for five years, and in the next period of his life, when he was already writing masterpieces, he was a composition pupil of the famous Salieri. In some ways the regimen at the Seminary was harsh, as all boys' schools were thenadays; but the musical opportunities were important. As well as the Court Chapel choir there was a school orchestra which practised every day. The small Schubert was soon promoted to be principal violin. From his twelfth year Schubert composed copiously. Dated 1811 is the enormous vocal piece, 'Hagar's Lament,' which stands first in the collected edition of his 600 songs. At the seminary he made life-long friends. In the autumn in which he quitted the institution he completed his first symphony, in D, and began his opera 'The Devil's Pleasaunce.'

3*

Is his father to be censured for not trusting to a musical career for Schubert and for starting him at school-teaching? In any case Schubert cannot have let his pupils greatly distract him from his music. The volume of music he produced at the time was enormous—in 1815, for instance, 144 songs, six stage works, another Mass, and two more symphonies. In the next year, 1816, when he was nineteen, he left his father's school and took to the bohemian way of life in which he remained until his death.

Our concern is with Schubert the writer of instrumental music, the symphonist. But one phenomenon cannot be passed over. While the boy Schubert was practising his art in symphonies, quartets and sonatas—all pleasing music, but youthful prentice-work—he already achieved in the domain of song what no other musician of his years, and indeed no other artist of any sort in all the centuries, has done, namely the creation of absolute masterpieces, songs of insuperable value and absolutely mature beauty. At sixteen he composed 'Gretchen at the Spinning-Wheel,' at seventeen 'The Erl King.' The miracle that these pages represent will amaze mankind for ever and ever.

Such achievements have had the curious effect of leading many writers into disparaging Schubert's instrumental works, without taking the trouble to consider the date of composition. A rough guide is this: disregard, first of all, the opus-numbers attached to Schubert's works—they are anything but chronological. Then bear in mind that Schubert was twenty-three before he matured as an instrumental composer. His twenty-fourth year (1820) is that of the wonderful string quartet (unfinished) in C minor. Charming as is much of the earlier music—the 'Trout Quintet,' for instance, the first six symphonies and quantities of other things—it is all properly to be regarded as prentice-work. Remember this and you will see it in the right perspective, and you will avoid doing Schubert the injustice of which many clever, superficial writers have been guilty. After all, twenty-three is not so very advanced an age!

But everything that Schubert wrote from then onwards may fairly be judged by the severest standard. Putting aside the multitude of incomparable songs and many beautiful part-songs, and also the unlucky operatic works (one and all stultified by hope-less librettos), what do we find? The following: the two great Masses in A flat and E flat; the two wonderful piano trios in B flat and E flat; four string quartets (the unfinished C minor, A minor, D minor and G); the octet for strings and wind; the marvellous string quintet of Schubert's last year; eight great piano sonatas (including the unfinished C major); the 'Wanderer Fantasia' for piano; a quantity of fine music for piano duet, including the Grand Duo in C, which is really a symphony transcribed; and two symphonies, the unfinished B minor, No. 8, and the great C major, No. 9.

Schubert's symphonies are the following:

No. 1, D (1813); No. 2, B flat (1815); No. 3, D (1815); No. 4, C minor, 'The Tragic' (1816); No. 5, B flat (1816); No. 6, C (1818); No. 7, E, unfinished (1821); No. 8, B minor, unfinished (1822); No. 9, C (1828).

The early works, composed for performance by amateurs of his circle, are all modest in scope, again and again charming in their ideas, rather stiff and prim in their behaviour. The inspiration and imaginative adventures of the great contemporaneous songs are wanting. One sees Schubert humbly sitting at Mozart's feet. Each of these little works deserves the attention of amateur orchestras. No. 4 used to enjoy a vogue that it has of late years lost to No. 5, which Beecham and others have frequently performed. String players and woodwind alike find these unpretentious symphonies delightful to play; and from the very first there are characteristic felicities of harmony.

The unfinished symphony in E, the manuscript of which is at the Royal College of Music in London, is a curiosity. Schubert sketched the whole work, and evidently had it all in his head. Why did he abandon it? The problem of Schubert's unfinished compositions would need a chapter of its own. There are five unfinished piano sonatas. The truth, in brief, may be guessed to be that the pressure of new ideas and the impulse to launch out on different enterprises were too much for him. Another time would do for works he had practically finished—music that only wanted writing down! Two concert arrangements of the symphony in E exist, one made many years ago by Barnett and another in our own time by Weingartner; but the work remains practically unknown. Pleasing though it is, it is completely eclipsed by the unfinished symphony in B minor, the history of which is curious. The first two movements—to-day famous and familiar as anything in the orchestral repertory—were completed and dispatched to Schubert's friend Hüttenbrenner, at Graz. The beginning of the scherzo exists. For no known reason Schubert broke off; and posterity is left guessing what the finale would have been like. One thing certain is that Schubert cannot have intended to let it remain in that state. Tovey suggested that if a finale were wanted it might be found in the Rondo, Op. 70, for violin, which is also mature Schubert and is also in B minor. The other strange thing about the symphony is that Hüttenbrenner, a musician, indolently put it aside and seems no less than Schubert to have forgotten its existence. It was lost to sight until 1865. As extraordinary, for that matter, was the fate of the glorious string quintet in C, which lay in obscurity until Hellmesberger first played it in 1850 (it was published in 1853). And we shall see how, thanks to Schumann, the last of the symphonies was brought to light.

A word must be said about a symphony, the so-called 'Gastein,' which such great Schubertians as Grove and O. E. Deutsch believe to have been lost, while Schumann and Donald Tovey were inclined to think we possess it, though only in the form of a transcript for piano duet (the Grand Duo, Op. 140). The Duo was composed at Zseliz in Hungary in 1824. In the following summer, when Schubert was on holiday at Gmunden, a letter from one of the circle mentioned his being at work on a symphony, and this symphony is referred to by others a little later as the 'Gastein,' Schubert having stayed at Gastein in August. He is known for certain to have composed some famous songs during his three weeks' stay there, but the evidence for a symphony lacks much substance. The next year Schubert dedicated to the Vienna Philharmonic Society an unidentified symphony and the society made the composer a present of 100 florins. After Schubert's death his friend Sonnleithner, in an obituary notice, spoke among other things of "three grand symphonies." Deutsch thinks he referred to the B minor, the lost 'Gastein' and the great C major. Another friend, Spaun, then spoke in a memoir of "a grand symphony for which the composer had a great preference" as dating from 1825, at Gastein. Spaun, however, attributes to Schubert only six symphonies all told, and in other respects his enumeration of Schubert's works is sketchy. No one in the circle ever makes a direct reference to the B minor symphony in the obituary notices.

It will be gathered that the existence of a Gastein symphony is questionable. Tovey did not commit himself absolutely to the opinion that the Grand Duo was a transcription of a symphony but he came very near doing so, pointing to the peculiar ineffectiveness of the writing for piano duet:

> "An arrangement of Beethoven's C minor symphony would hardly make the players feel more as if they were trying to play cricket with ping-pong bats. From beginning to end there is not a trace of pianoforte style in the work."

Joachim in the past and, among others in our own time, Anthony Collins have scored this fine work for orchestra, and the result is an unquestionable symphony. It is an insincerity to lament a lost work and at the same time neglect so splendid an example of Schubert at his prime. A grand piece!—although less poignant than the B minor and less grand than the C major, to which we are coming.

VIII

SCHUBERT'S NINTH SYMPHONY

SCHUBERT lived under Beethoven's shadow, and his reputation, except as a song-writer, has been under the shadow of Beethoven's ever since. He owed much to Beethoven, especially to the works of the second period; but we are guilty of a radical vice of mis-criticism if we look to him for Beethovenian qualities and blame him for not carrying on Beethoven's life. The two were pro-foundly different men. If their art can be characterized in two words, it must be said that that of the one springs from strenuous intellectual labour while that of the other is a torrential out-pouring from a man who was like one possessed. But that is to simplify. It is to misrepresent Schubert to suggest that his was an irreflective art. Someone should give us a full-dress study of Schubert to show how every year his music was affected and enriched by what he absorbed, by what he felt and what he learnt. It is clear that in the last year of his life—while his old fertility was more wonderful than ever—a new force and sub-stance entered into his music. The three last piano sonatas give evidence of a new study of Beethoven; and we are leagues away there from the simply charming Schubert of ten years before. We pore over these compositions of 1828; and imagination fails at the thought of what another few years might have brought from Schubert. Within a few days he wrote that set of Heine songs which have a searching quality and intensity of poetry unpredictable even on the strength of so many earlier lyric masterpieces.

From this year, from the month of March, dates the great C major symphony, which is a classic and yet a symphony like none of the earlier classics. A classic; and at the same time a

romantic symphony, the greatest of the romantic symphonies.*
Were the two immortal movements of the B minor more perfect? It may be; and it may be that something disturbs us in the
wildness of Schubert's last symphonic outpouring. But the
grandeur of it is something beyond anything he had ever before
conceived.

On a famous day, New Year's Day, 1839, Schumann came
upon the symphony among manuscripts which Ferdinand
Schubert had not managed to dispose of to the publishers. The
result was that Mendelssohn gave it the first performance in the
following March—eleven years after its composition. Mendelssohn also tried to persuade the Philharmonic Orchestra in
London to accept it—without success—whereupon the Prince
Consort had it played at Windsor. The Philharmonic Society
would have no titanic music that was not Beethoven's.

That the symphony is to be huge is immediately apparent
from the spaciousness and length of the opening tune, which can
only mean an introduction of majestic proportions. Two horns
in unison announce this:

Fig.1

You will hear those notes in the second bar again and again.
This impressive opening must be perfect in technical performance,
perfectly serene in mood. One blemish will frighten one, seeing
all that is to come. Schubert, who never heard his symphony
played, cannot have hoped for perfection here, as on the old
horns two of the notes (marked by crosses) had to be stopped by
the hand, with the result of altering the quality. Unless he had a
prophetic soul he would be astonished to hear his tune played
as it is at the present day, with the homogeneity of tone and
assurance which the coming of the valve horn has brought.

The woodwind has a smoother version of this theme, accompanied by strings, and violas and cellos continue with a second

* But Edmund Rubbra has called it: "The finest of all classical
symphonies" (in 'The Music Teacher,' Jan. 1948).

part of the tune, fading into a lovely cadence before the main tune bursts out again fortissimo, reinforced by the trombones. The oboe, with an effect of that exquisite lyrical beauty which Schubert is to exploit later on, now brings in a new note, and its enchanting voice insistently continues, despite the interjections of the whole orchestra, which seems to be growing impatient for the Allegro. Schubert, however, has not yet finished, and with the last appealing note of the oboe he unexpectedly slips into the key of A flat and amuses himself with a little octave figure (which has already appeared accompanying the oboe):

Fig. 2

together with, of course, the inevitable ♩. ♪♩ rhythm which is

hardly ever out of the music. The woodwind restores the key to the dominant for the return of the main tune, this time with a lovely running accompaniment in the strings. And now Schubert delays no longer, but allows the orchestra its head to run into the Allegro, with a splendid building up of power.

With the new tempo the significance of that ubiquitous second bar of the introduction is appreciated. It forms the basic rhythm of the principal theme.

Fig. 3 *Allegro ma non troppo*

Schubert, who rarely revised, did so here. Originally the subject stood thus:

Fig. 4

He wrote the whole movement before realizing that it could be improved by altering the last quaver of the bar from G to D.

His penknife had to work overtime—he scratched out the inferior note hundreds of times from the score. The music is exuberant and exciting, with these vital rhythms: ♩. ♪♩. ♪ and ♩♩♩♩♩♩ urging each other on.

Suddenly oboes and bassoons announce the second subject, on an abrupt change of key into E minor:

Fig. 5

It is one of Schubert's great ideas, full of character and life. The first two bars dance into the entrancing lyrical strain that is typical of Schubert's inspiration, while he rounds off the whole subject with two bars accentuated with a touch of character.

The accompaniment of the strings is of the usual Schubertian simplicity:

Apart from an occasional counterpoint, Schubert's accompaniments are mainly secondary affairs which require care rather than skill, and contain little interest of themselves. Yet this simple quaver accompaniment can sound lovely if the conductor allows it shape and life.

Making much use of those first two dancing bars of the second subject (Fig. 5) and vigorous chords, the music builds up to the first climax of the Allegro. Now there is a variant of the dancing bars, effected by a strong accent on the last note of the bar instead of the first:

Fig. 6

After changing the key into E flat Schubert settles down to a rhythmic and pianissimo background, consisting of the running accompaniment between 2nd violins and violas and the dancing crotchet figure between cellos and 1st violins, this time with an accent on the second crotchet while woodwind softly breathe supporting chords. This background is delicious if an imperceptible swing keeps the rhythm alive. Toscanini and Boult are for ever insisting on the imperceptible swing and lilt that must never leave a running accompaniment such as this. Dvořák, later on, used this kind of background a great deal, with richer Bohemian colours in the scoring.

All this background is set for a wonderfully impressive passage for trombones:

This motif, again derived from the second bar of the introduction, enters pianissimo on the trombones—a wonderful invention of Schubert's orchestral imagination—and thence gradually grows into a triumphant climax. At the peak Schubert reveals a particular feature of the whole symphony, and incidentally foreshadows the later Brahms. With three prodigious efforts, each stronger than the last, he crowns the gigantic mountain-top:

Everything here depends on the conductor's sense of climax. Unless he has left something in reserve for Schubert's final effort at the double fortissimo top G, the peaks are only wrapt in mist. Not only must the tone grow in brilliance and strength throughout these titanic efforts, but the rhythm itself must carry the orchestra onwards in a wonderful momentum. Boult manages this superbly. Later on, in the last movement, Schubert builds up his forces even more extensively with similar means. The exposition is now brought to an end in G major.

The working-out begins by the key stepping up a semitone into A flat. A big climax fades into a lovely episode of quiet reflection, and the brass meanwhile, in a passage similar to those already quoted, has slightly changed its original motif to

Fig. 9

The woodwind and lower strings carry on with it, and all the time the triplet figure of the first subject of the Allegro acts as accompaniment. The brass motif becomes darker and darker as the violas, cellos and basses brood over an extended idea of it:

Fig. 10
Cellos & Violas

Schubert, with characteristic delight in a sudden change of mood, then surreptitiously slides by the back door into the whole first subject again in its original key. The recapitulation is for long kept in an exciting *piano*, thus enabling a greater climax to be built up than before. This magnificent gathering of forces is spread over twelve pages of the score, and the energy of the basic rhythm ♩ ♪♩. ♪♩ ♩. never flags. The strings are beginning to feel the strain of that taut rhythm, which is unrelenting to the end of the movement. It induces cramp as much as any other music written.

After the climax Schubert brings back the second subject in the tonic minor. Then once more we climb and the three pinnacles seem higher than ever, if the conductor has had the foresight to reserve some power. The coda, as if toppling over the edge, shoots off at greater speed, as though the enormous energy exerted to reach the summit had suddenly been cut out, and we slide downhill on our own momentum. But Schubert has not done with all the force he has generated. The music again gathers intensity and ever pushes onward, until the great theme of the introduction comes back again, fortissimo, in the woodwind, and in its repetition the strings bring the movement to an end.

The scoring of this ending was revised by Schubert, and his second thoughts here were not lucky. Tovey has said:

> "The scoring, as Schubert finally left it, is notoriously miscalculated; but there is a better remedy for it than the horrible marine-parade custom of giving the tune to the trumpet. All that need be done (beyond the usual precaution with the trombones) is to restore Schubert's first version of the string parts, which happened to be perfectly transparent until he altered them, though not one listener in a hundred could tell the difference in sound or sense, except for the all-important fact that in the first version the theme in the woodwind can be heard, and in the second it cannot."

Fig. 10ª

The slow movement is one of the loveliest inspirations for the delectation of woodwind soloists ever given to man. Like the horns' task in the introduction, the performance demands perfection. A whole volume on the art of phrasing might be based on this one movement. Many a performance has been marred by an unfortunate reed or some colour that just fails to blend. One touch of dull phrasing and we are brought down to earth. As rhythm and unflagging vitality were demanded in the first movement, so now Schubert calls for the utmost delicacy and imaginativeness of phrasing, and perfection of intonation and tone colour. Seven bars of dark, march-like steps in A minor open the scene.

Fig. 11

Then comes the oboe's song. A song of what? A song of the wandering gypsy life?

To this, in the softest repetition, the clarinet adds his darker colours and slight variation. The oboe, still enchanted, continues his song in a smoother cantabile, and, again encouraged by the clarinet, he expresses himself in a further strain of exquisite tenderness:

But the orchestra now crashes in upon the quiet melancholy of the mood. It is strife between opposing elements—on the one side a kind of stern pageantry,

and on the other a musing spirit and the most intimate pensive thought.

The second subject:

is prepared for with a dramatic lowering of the lights. It is the 2nd violins who here are most unusually honoured by Schubert with the first part of the tune. True, the bassoon shares their delight, but a glance at the 2nd violins reveals a look of self-conscious gratification on their faces.

Schubert seems never to need to come to the end of a great

melody. It flows from him with nature's own inexhaustibility. Here for instance the melody unfolds blossom after blossom, with exquisite sprays and tendrils. Presently comes a summons from the horn, an episode that has never been surpassed for its effect of mystery :

Fig. 16

With just the one note, answering the quietest of stroked chords on the strings, Schubert's horn takes us worlds away, to some subterranean cavern where breathlessly we listen to a weird tolling, lost in the depths. The illusion fades, and on his magic carpet Schubert restores us home again in A minor. Back comes the lovely oboe song, now made more solemn by the adornment of this little figure :

Fig. 17

suggested by the trumpet, copied by the horn, and keeping the violins perpetually involved, until the clarinet once more whispers the lovely cantabile of the second subject. Schubert seems himself to be infatuated with the creatures of his imagination, as we assuredly are with him, until a new mood supervenes with impending excitement. The rhythmic figure in the march:

becomes increasingly important. A climax approaches, and all the lyrical beauties are driven away by hard, unyielding rhythms and chords which surround the orchestra in an atmosphere of extraordinary tension. The climax crashes out on a thunderous chord of the diminished seventh, sustained fortissimo by the whole orchestra and reiterated twice by the tearing bows of the strings. Stunned, the orchestra is silent for a bar and a half. The effect of catastrophe is appalling. To this, what has our Schubert to say? Upon softly breathed chords the cellos have an immortal melody, deriving from the original oboe

tune. It breathes sympathy and consolation, but the calamity has
been so dreadful that the effect is of ineffable pathos.

This is the very poetry of music. Listen for the modulation in the
fifth bar. It is one of never-failing wonder. The beautiful episode
is easy to distort and maul. It should simply float upon the air,
until it gently loses itself in the returning second subject. Schubert
adds new beauties to his accompaniments as the themes return,
and there is now a particularly lovely counterpoint on 2nd
violins and violas which flows on for over thirty bars:

until the boisterous chords intrude again. Most of the recapitulation is newly embellished, and though the material is the same in
essence, it is slightly different in treatment—even the tolling of
the horn. Schubert, realizing that the great moment of the
symphony is far too momentous to appear again in anti-climax,
abbreviates the whole of that section. Instead of massing his
forces once more, he suddenly lets all slip away, and quiet woodwind chords take us back to A minor. A naïve little phrase on
the oboe

gives a delicious touch of finality, and with true Schubertian
grace suggests that the movement really must be brought to an
end. The closing bars echo the horn passage in its alternating
fortissimo and piano chords, besides reminding us of the clashing
of the two chief characteristics of the movement. With wonderful
simplicity Schubert ends the music with a great sigh, as after an
intensely moving experience.

The opening of the Scherzo, in C major, roughly wakes us out of our dreams:

Fig. 21

With no time even to rub our eyes we are hurtled into violent movement and bustle. After a mediocre performance of the slow movement, in the hands of a dull and tedious conductor, the strings are wont to release their pent-up annoyance in these first four bars. Many are the instruments that have suffered and bow-hairs broken on this account.

This, the greatest of Schubert's innumerable scherzos, with their endless fund of invention, is a sublimation of Viennese youth and dancing spirits. The second tune is this enchantingly graceful thing:

Fig. 22

The first violins reveal it, and the cellos sing most of the tune two bars behind them, while the quiet woodwind chatters of the first tune in the background. Schubert adds another lovely touch by keeping the orchestra down to piano and then suddenly reducing even that to pianissimo. The strings continue to play with the first three bars of the second tune upside down, under the increasing chatter of the woodwind. The music builds up with a great crescendo in a series of modulations through F sharp minor, D major, B minor, and finally to fortissimo on G major. This brings us to the double bar. Next the music breaks out in A flat. There is a wealth of invention and originality in this second section. The woodwind have the first news:

Fig. 23

The next idea is an afterthought of Schubert's, and a marvellously happy one. The flute has a lovely melody in the key of C flat, which in the most entrancing manner is copied note for note by the violin and oboe, but a semitone higher in pitch. A return of boisterousness and a long series of modulations take us to a lively and unexpected little fugato, in the quietest pianissimo on the strings. It is derived from the opening of the Scherzo.

Note that each instrument as it makes its entry must bite on the first note. This is not so easy as it looks. As usual, though this Scherzo is such an immense piece of music, both sections are marked for repeats. The orchestra is not often called upon to make the second repetition. When it is, a feeling of physical distress pervades the desks.

The Trio, in A major, affords contrast to the Scherzo's vigour and grace with a melodious languor and voluptuousness. It is the innings of the woodwind, the strings only accompanying through-out. This accompaniment is of the usual Schubertian simplicity. Uninspiring though it is from the players' point of view, yet it must be full of rhythm and vitality. Here are two of the melodies —a poet's dream of a waltz:

We have had three grand movements; but, after all, the supreme test of a symphonic composer's imaginative power lies

—at any rate, if the gist of the work has been tragic—in the finale. Here is a respect in which the symphony differs from the concerto. In the latter the weight of the argument, the serious task, may well be confined to the first movement; and example after example shows that it is thoroughly satisfactory then for the slow movement to represent relaxation and lyrical repose, and the finale a merry-making, with the consciousness of the day's work done. We have seen that Haydn's symphonies were comedies, however far from being trivial comedies; and the Haydn finale is regularly gay. We are aware that the finale presented to Mozart and Beethoven a problem—and also an opportunity—outside Haydn's range of thought. It has been mentioned how Mozart rose to the challenge of the finale in his last symphonies with an unprecedented effort of the imagination—in the G minor with a wonderful intensification and exacerbation of the pathetic spirit, and in the C major with a miraculous play of dancing counterpoint. A word or two has been said about Beethoven's finales, the subject for an entire book. How exacting the demands were on the poetic imagination is seen from the fact that both these princes of music did on occasion fall short in their finales—Mozart, for instance, in his great G minor quintet and Beethoven in the second of the Rasoumovski quartets.

Only towards the end of his life did Schubert squarely face the problem of the finale. A comedy ending was fully adequate for all his early instrumental works. We have to admit that the finale of the beautiful little A minor quartet fails to live up to the first movement. A little later, and he becomes aware of the problem in quartets, trios and piano sonatas. Sometimes, while still having recourse to the rondo, he expands the form with a wild torrent of music, as if to submerge the listener. It is principally these movements which have given rise to the legend of Schubert's uncontrolled diffuseness. A glorious success is the passionate dance of the finale of the very late quintet in C, though it is on a less than symphonic scale.

Nothing exemplifies Schubert's mighty poetic genius so magnificently as the Finale of his ninth symphony. It more than matches the gigantic proportions of the previous movements.

Far from being exhausted, he brings up such astounding reserves of demoniac energy that the last movement, for irresistible force and impetuosity, leaves the others behind. We feel that he wrote it down at the dictation of a superhuman power, and never is there a halt or hesitation in the amazing inspiration. This is the movement at which our Philharmonic Orchestra jibbed in Mendelssohn's day, and indeed, from the players' point of view, the demands it makes are really unfair on an orchestra that is by now no longer fresh to face its fearful attacks and strains. The strings, for instance, have to use brute force to keep up that demoniacal rhythm and speed; yet a fearful pace is the essence of the idea.

One of the greatest exponents of the symphony, Bruno Walter, takes it at a reckless tempo, and a performance is remembered when he came from the platform white as a sheet under the strain he had undergone to keep the orchestra in control. Only a barely perceptible slackening was felt at the second subject and in the development, which enabled him to work up still more furious excitement in the coda. If the movement is allowed to flag the whole symphony begins to be felt oppressively long; but that is not Schubert's fault—it is a criticism of the treatment. Like Beethoven's Ninth, this symphony should have a concert practically to itself and should certainly never be played at a Promenade concert, or in any circumstances precluding adequate rehearsal. Even if a flawless second movement is achieved by the woodwind the last movement will inevitably fail through the sheer exhaustion of the orchestra, if the rest of the programme has made serious demands.

The opening is a flash of lightning. What picture or legend had Schubert in his mind? Phaeton and the horses of the sun? Is it Faust's ride to the abyss? The listener may indulge his fancy privately. It is a derogation of such music to pin it down in public to a material programme. Here is the lightning-flash:

Fig.27

This is a difficult opening. The whole orchestra must leap to life with perfect articulation, and this it often fails to do. One often hears just 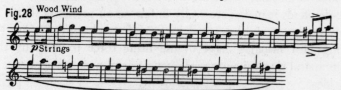 . Yet the semiquaver is all-important. It acts as a kind of devil's goad throughout the movement. Immediately a galloping motif breaks out in the strings and carries us over rough, jagged ground to the first subject of the movement:

Fig.28

It swirls and eddies on the woodwind and strings, while the pricking of the goad is felt at regular intervals. Another riding motif formed out of the  sweeps up and down the orchestra, after a strenuous climax, on the strings alone:

Fig.29

It is the forerunner of future developments, and one of the heavy tasks of the strings in this movement is to make it sound clear at the right speed. The second outstanding feature shows up on the horns—four bars of tremendous minims:

Fig.30

Schubert makes immense use of these later on, when continually they ram home their hard-hitting blows. The second subject is thirty-two bars long:

Fig.31

Whenever the second subject appears, always there are these galloping triplets in attendance:

A new urge to prevent the motion from settling down to a trot is begun by the cellos and basses, who stride up and down on arpeggios of the accompanying harmonies, and with untiring energy drive the orchestra forward. A delicious change to B major, alternating with E minor, and a hush to pianissimo allow the orchestra a short breathing space. A sharp return to G major, fortissimo, however, reveals the strings coping with more severe tugs and strains:

From this point Schubert makes for his first climax, which is built on a series of harmonies which seem to be leading us to F, only to slip back finally into G major again at the last moment, on a terrific crash from the whole orchestra. From this great peak, Schubert takes us on a long descent, step by step and softer and softer. The basses climb down a range of two octaves until the bottom is reached in a murmur on a low G major chord.

We are at the double bar. Unfortunate the orchestra that is required to make the repeat! In true Schubertian style, the development begins by the cellos moving down a tone to F, and then further to E flat, for the clarinets to lead off in that key with a re-casting of the second subject which this time, in its tranquillity, shows up a striking resemblance to the choral melody in Beethoven's Ninth symphony. The trombones—with an

audacity extraordinary in Schubert's day—join in this motif, and are again entrusted with solo parts as in the first movement: another instance of the composer's extraordinarily imaginative use of these instruments.

There comes an expansive working-out of all this second-subject matter, with the four bars of warning minims now hurled forth on the brass, and passed about amongst the orchestra, while the smooth character of the second part of the subject is altered by a heavy staccato. After a great mass of sound has been accumulated, Schubert relaxes the tension, and over a long G pedal the music subsides to an ominous and unnatural calm. The horns' warning notes are heard in the distance, and the goad, pricking intermittently, adds further uneasiness. This passage, leading to the recapitulation, is amazingly exciting in its sense of impending disaster. The pricking becomes more frequent and brutal, the warning notes, though still pianissimo, begin to come from all quarters, until, with a flash of lightning again we are back to the swirling winds of the first subject. So we rush by the same landmarks again, until there comes the great coda, with Phaeton's last appalling rush to destruction.

Schubert, seemingly fresh as when he began the symphony, sets the final scene with wonderful skill. After the long diminuendo for the second time, when the basses again climb down out of the key—this time from C major to B flat, and finally resting on A—the strings are off again on their galloping motif whilst the continually tortured bass urges the rhythm ever onwards. A series of violent, ungovernable tugs from the steeds—the luckless strings again—show that no longer can they be controlled. An enormously prolonged crescendo, in which the bass moves up step by step from A to C, leads to a last warning, which bursts out on a great unison C. Time after time Phaeton tries to drag us back to another harmony, but inexorably he is pulled onward until the bass falls on G, when with three colossal efforts:

Fig.35 Full Orchestra

—the third the greatest of all—Schubert gathers together all in one gigantic mass. The strings, now wildly galloping, pressed on by the rest of the orchestra, make mad rushes from piano to fortissimo, to their final ruin on a dominant chord (triple forte). All is now over save for the final C major chords.

More than the more strictly classical symphonies does Schubert's C major depend upon the conductor. Bruno Walter, with his deep lyricism, and Boult, with his long views and constructive sense in the building of climaxes, have given the work its finest interpretations in our time. The C major is not music for every day. Its wild life languishes in perfunctory hands. None but a first-rate orchestra should dream of tackling it. Let us remember that in 1828 it was considered too difficult for the Vienna Philharmonic even to try over. Schubert no doubt was disappointed, but the refusal should be remembered by some who have stepped in where better men than they have feared to tread.

PART II

IX

SCHUMANN

1810–1856

ONE of the best-loved of nineteenth-century musicians—composer of a multitude of songs and pianoforte pieces that will never grow old—Schumann, we may at once admit, was only secondarily a symphonist. Yet there was a wonderful period in that short life when its every moment brought forth delightful musical thoughts, some of which went into chamber and orchestral works which we neglect to our loss.

In the earlier centuries the typical musician had been born to his craft. Over and over again we find whole families of musicians or a kind of dynastic line which may or not produce, sooner or later, a man of genius; Schumann is a different case, rather typical of the nineteenth century. Like Berlioz and Wagner, he had all the potentiality of a man of letters. We feel, for all his musical genius, that another turn of the wheel of fate and he might as well have become a poet or painter. Beethoven's example and immense prestige, reflected in romantic literature, put it into ambitious young men's minds that the composer of music could wield a sway incomparably beyond that of musicians of olden days—comparable rather with that of vatic bards, Homer or Pindar. We may guess that in another civilization, lacking Beethoven's example, men of such overbearing willpower as Berlioz and Wagner would have chosen a career other than music to impose themselves upon mankind, while Schumann might have chosen to become no more than an amateur musician. A thorough professional he made himself by his passionate persistence, but he was especially masterly in the smaller forms, and his large compositions are our delight less by reason of any great power of draughtsmanship or dialectic than for the lovely lyrical ideas scattered therein.

Schumann was the son of a bookseller and publisher at Zwickau in Saxony. His father died at the age of 53, under the shock of the suicide of his young daughter Emilie, who was mentally afflicted. Robert was then sixteen. Thirty years later his end was not unlike Emilie's. There remains a good deal to be done in the way of pathological examination of Schumann's case. From his first nervous breakdown at the age of thirty-three he recovered; but, generally speaking, his music composed thereafter has more sombre hues, and by the time he was hardly middle-aged the fire was almost out and he was writing an old man's music. At thirty-seven he was again threatened; then recovered, and indulged again in furious over-work. At forty-one he could only be considered as mentally unstable. At forty-four he attempted suicide. He died in an asylum a little more than two years later.

One of the famous musical romances is that of Schumann and Clara Wieck, a pre-eminent pianist, to whom he dedicated his sonata in F sharp minor when she was sixteen. They fell in love, became engaged—against the will of Clara's father—and at last married when he was thirty and she twenty-one. Their relationship was wonderfully happy, but of their many children more than one disastrously inherited their father's taint. But let us look at the young Schumann, before his affliction had turned him into a moody, unsociable, haunted man. A school friend in later years described him thus:

"Robert was an ordinary enough schoolboy, though dreamy and absent-minded. One thing soon struck me—he was dominated by his certainty of soon becoming a celebrated man, though in what direction he was not clear. He threw himself for a time into philology, then heraldry. Later on we both fell into the arms of German poetry and remained there. His talent shown in both verse and prose was altogether remarkable, as well as his attempts at music. I must add, to his honour, that he was not only the most ambitious man I have ever known but also the most assiduous and tireless, and I am inclined to share Roller's opinion that he became a great musician less perhaps by force of genius than by his iron will."

And the same writer, Flechsig, goes on:

"What brought him to his lamentable end? I recall how, when he was a small boy, he was wildly attracted by tales of men of genius who destroyed themselves by their own creation. Byron was his ideal, and the fantastic life and suicide of the poet Sonnenberg impressed him enormously. At the age of ten he knew about Hölderlin's madness and spoke of it with timid veneration. He would almost have liked to resemble Beethoven, with tangled hair and grim features."

Schumann himself has left us some memoirs. At eighteen he looked back on himself at thirteen and jotted down:

"Free improvisation several hours a day. Circumstances propitious to my extra-musical formation. Love of liberty and nature. . . . At my highest in free improvisation. Fiery talk . . . morbid desire for music and the piano when I had not been playing for a time. Enthusiasm for Jean Paul (Richter). Conception of music especially as Jean Paul understood it, a blessed consolation in hours of solitude."

And another jotting about himself reads:

"Strong musical inclination from my earliest years. A good master who was fond of me but who himself played only moderately well, I had no instruction in composition until I was nineteen. I early began to compose. Outside Mozart and Haydn my favourite composers in youth were Pixis, Moscheles and Prince Louis (Louis Ferdinand of Prussia). I knew Beethoven only by his piano works. I had heard no great executant. From that period until my twentieth year date several attempts at poetry. The chief poets of nearly all lands were familiar to me. At eighteen, enthusiasm for Jean Paul. I heard Franz Schubert's music, then, too, for the first time. Goethe and Bach had until then been closed books for me. I heard good music. Then Schubert and Beethoven rose in my esteem, and Bach began to dawn upon me."

Schumann was later on to regret his addiction to extemporization. He warned Clara against the habit. "Too much flows to waste that way. Make up your mind to write everything down at once." But all teachers of composition will agree that nothing is more promising in a pupil than an improvising talent.

Everyone has heard of Schumann's attempt at a short cut to virtuosity as a pianist, and of his injuring one of his fingers by his contrivance. This was soon after he had abandoned the law (Leipzig and Heidelberg, 1828–9). The next decade was one of a marvellous outpouring of music; and Schumann was at the same time writing musical criticism which is still full of interest. It is exuberant, picturesque—a young man's writing. Not only great composers—Chopin, Berlioz—were hailed, but also a good many insignificant composers whose attitude or sentiment chimed in with Schumann's. He wrote a symphony and had it performed at Leipzig when he was twenty-three, but the work—a prentice hand's—remains unpublished. His early music, as we have it, is all for piano, and includes such ever-familiar and ever-attractive pieces as 'Papillons,' Op. 2 (composed when he was 19–20), the Toccata in C, 'Carnival,' Op. 9, and the 'Symphonic Studies' (variations in C sharp minor), Op. 12. The year of his marriage, 1840, saw a great production of songs. In the next year, when he was thirty-one, he finished his first symphony, the B flat, Op. 38; he composed another work that is virtually a symphony, the 'Overture, Scherzo and Finale,' Op. 52; the first movement of his famous piano concerto; and the first version of the D minor symphony, which we know as No. 4, Op. 120. The symphony in C which we know as No. 2, Op. 61, was composed in 1845–6, and the "Rhenish," No. 3, in E flat, Op. 97, in 1850–1. The D minor was revised in 1851, after ten years.* Schumann was at this time engaged as a conductor at Düsseldorf. There is no doubt that he was less than an indifferent conductor. He had no aptitude at all in that direction. In the masses of music of his last phase some of the old charm breaks through now and again, as in certain pages of the violoncello concerto. Other works, such as the violin concerto, were kept from the light of day on the advice of Joachim and Brahms.

---

* Schumann's original version was published in 1891. The revision consists largely in a thickening of the orchestral texture.

X

SCHUMANN'S SYMPHONY IN
D MINOR

ALL the symphonic works of 1840–1 reflect the composer's new-
found happiness, all are like a lover's rhapsodies—the outpourings
of a lover who has gained his heart's desire and sees life as a sky
without a cloud. The B flat was originally called a 'Spring
Symphony.' The 'Overture, Scherzo and Finale' is an unjustly
neglected work; and we might suppose this was because of its
cumbrous title if it were not that the symphony in C, too, is for
years on end absent from our programmes.

A question that cannot be avoided is Schumann's orchestration.
It is one that every conductor has to face, for Schumann—
although not so inept at instrumentation as is sometimes
suggested (there are delightful and original effects in his scoring)
—was not at home with the orchestra, and in the interests of the
music conductors are bound to do something to lighten the
thickness of the texture. Whether or no Mahler went too far in
rewriting or virtually rewriting Schumann is matter for discussion. Mahler was a man of genius who could afford to forget
more about orchestration than Schumann ever knew. A man of
genius and a supreme master of the orchestra—but also most high-
handed when dealing with music outside his own century! If the
tales one hears are true he went leagues farther than Wagner in
daubing preposterous colours on Gluck. But Schumann belonged
to Mahler's century, to his range of sympathy and sentiment. I
suggest that any conductor who is in doubt had better use
Mahler's scoring. There is no pretending that Schumann's
symphonies are as well-known as they might be. Mahler's
clarity and the sureness of his touch might give them a new
lease. How far he went will be seen from the fact that he restored

the opening bars of the first symphony to the form in which
they originally stood. Schumann had, at the eleventh hour, to
modify the 'Summons to Spring' because of an oversight. He
had forgotten what the limitations were of the horns of 1840.
First he wrote:

But that was before the day of valve-horns; and on natural
horns the sixth and seventh of those notes had to be "stopped"
—in other words, they were of a totally different quality from
the B flats, and indeed as though produced by a different instrument. Schumann had to rewrite the theme a third higher. But
then came the valve-horn to supersede the old instrument. There
was now no difficulty; and Mahler started the symphony on
B flat and not D. But the D minor and not the B flat is the
symphony we here propose to look at.

It is a symphony that will always be associated in the minds of
certain London orchestral players with a particular occasion.
Hamilton Harty had had a long illness, and most of us had
resigned ourselves to the belief that he would never return to the
scene. But return he did; and with this symphony—the very
music, with its warm and joyous spirit, for so happy an occasion.
Like Mahler, Weingartner, Bruno Walter and many others,
Harty modified Schumann's scoring. But there is something else,
too, a performance of Schumann needs—and this was something
Harty could bring—poetry and a spontaneous interpretation. It
was his spontaneity of expression and the inspiration of a mind
refreshed and thankful that charmed us in the orchestra and gave
us a contact with the heart of Schumann.

It must be admitted that a Schumann symphony does not
always mean a stimulating experience for the players. The work
of reading between the lines to bring out the essence and meaning
of the music is laborious as it is not in, for instance, a Brahms
symphony, which quickly repays intelligent application. What
is wanted in Brahms is a slightly exaggerated care, and everything

is clear. But Schumann's scores are confused, and if one is playing from the original or from an inferior revision one is aware that obedience to the letter, no matter how scrupulous, is not helping much. There is also the need of great flexibility and unremitting attention to accents. As in Schumann's quartets, freedom of style and imaginative phrasing play a vital part. Schumann's own expression marks are quite inadequate, and no other composer of his quality sounds so dull and uninspired in a humdrum performance. Beethoven and Schubert can get their message through in conditions which would be the death of Schumann. Harty's modifications of the score were more discreet than those of some of the Germans, but he obtained perfect clarity. Did the audience miss any detail? I cannot say; but the player's feeling was of taking part in a lovely work of chamber music, one that sparkled with happiness and beauty in every line.

The first of the four movements has an introduction ("somewhat slow") leading to an Allegro in 2/4 time. The second is a Romance in A minor, whose last chord is in the major. The Scherzo is linked by an impressive Adagio to the D major Finale—a movement full of light and joy. The lovely introduction, in 3/4 time, is quiet and contemplative in character, with this as its main theme:

Fig.2 *Ziemlich langsam (Somewhat slow)*

This expressive and flowing tune broadens to a climax, when the 1st violins make a tentative suggestion for the principal tune of the coming Allegro.

Fig.3 Violins

Struck with the idea, they become more insistent and push the tempo onwards, to such effect that the orchestra finds itself running straight into the Allegro, with the 1st violins' tune now unanimously approved, but altered in character to a strong

4*

rhythmical subject taken hold of vigorously by flutes, oboes, 1st violins and violas.

A feature of this subject is the strongly marked accents on both first and second beats in the bar. The danger of the second accent is that it is apt to make the rhythm sound laboured, but in spite of this Harty asked for it to be played particularly heavily and, surprisingly, seemed to obtain added life; while Boult more logically seeks a rather weaker accent than the first. As for the Introduction, there are differences of opinion about its interpretation. Some conductors take it very slowly and give it a deeply emotional character, as though Schumann were setting out to write an immensely serious work. Others lighten it with a much quicker tempo, nearer to the mood of the whole symphony.

"Schumann marked this 'somewhat slow,'" said Harty. "Gentlemen, I like this introduction to flow smoothly and freely. I do not like it held back and too measured."

Still in the same energetic mood and with very similar material comes the second subject.

It does not settle down until about eight bars later, in F major; but from later developments it is clearer to make this quotation. How the violas wish they were not always doubled by bassoons when anything important turns up! But that kind of thing is characteristic of Schumann's scoring. It is a feature of his treatment of the second subject material, that he continues the first four semiquavers right up the score—thus:

A feature of the development is the composer's way of frequently breaking the flow of the music by stopping the orchestra dead in its stride. This has already happened at the end of the exposition, which he rounds off with two conventional chords in F. He sets out on the development by sustaining a strong E flat unison. The second tune, as before on violas, cellos and bassoons, leads off, and has just time to climb up the score when Schumann calls a halt, as if he had made a false start. Once more the same instruments start again as before, and the composer thereupon allows the music to flow evenly with a new and most impressive entrance of trombones and an exciting arpeggio passage breaking out on the cellos beneath them.

Fig.7 Cello

This always sounds like mice venturing out of a hole, and bolting home again at the sight of a cat. (Possibly the strong accent at the top which every player strives to get in causes this sense of fright in its performance.)

The music increases in power, and the first climax approaches, with woodwind playing short explosive chords of D flat, backed up by the brass. Two keys are passed through, A flat and G flat, and Schumann again calls a halt on F major. A similar course of events takes place, taking us to another landmark—C major—and then, with a delicious feeling for contrast, the key comes back to F major again and the violins sing out a new joyous tune of four bars, repeated by the wind.

Fig.8 1st Violins

The peculiarity of the whole movement is that there is no recapitulation. What happens, through a great range of keys, is an exciting bubbling-up of life leading to a climax, in A major, when the whole orchestra crashes out the gay tune (Fig. 8) in a hardened and more military style. A sudden piano comes, for the orchestra to take breath, and then—a headlong ending.

If any movement needs conducting with inspiration it is this. Not to be forgotten is Harty driving along the last lap of this movement, like a coachman with a devil in his eyes. The orchestra needs to see the sparks fly.

The Romance follows on without a break. This movement opens with an appealing tune in A minor, full of tenderness, allotted to oboe and a solo cello, between which it is a bone of contention. Each wishes he had it to himself.

Fig.9 ROMANZE *Ziemlich langsam (Somewhat slow)*
(Oboe & Solo Cello in octaves)

It is extraordinarily difficult for a solo stringed instrument to play either in unison or in octaves with a wind instrument. They often do not sit near each other, and intonation thus becomes a matter of anxiety, while the concentration necessary to match the other instrument's every note militates against spontaneity.

At the conclusion of this tune we find ourselves listening again to the flowing theme of the introduction to the first movement. Its return here makes a most lovely effect. Then Schumann signs to the oboe and solo cello to play the last few bars of their own tune again, and this is so entrancing that violas—and bassoons!— add a final remark which ends with a resolution on the major chord instead of minor.

The second part of the movement has a famous violin solo which in nine cases out of ten falls short of perfection because of the scoring. This solo is simply a delicate pattern woven into the main texture of the subject in the strings, but Schumann's marking is precisely the same for everyone, and consequently his glowing 'piano, dolce' for all the strings in full harmonies overwhelms the soloist unless precautionary measures be taken. Often the soloist has to play out forte, to the ruin of the mood. Fig. 10 is the main theme.

Fig. 11 is the solo violin's arabesque:

Harty used to overcome the difficulty by reducing the players to one desk only of each section. When the first tune returns it is as a trio for oboe, solo cello and bassoon, and now, curiously enough, it is less difficult with the added instrument—the sound is not so transparent. It is always easier for three instruments to play in perfect ensemble and intonation than two.

The Scherzo, back in D minor again, is full of exuberance and light-hearted dancing. A five-finger exercise provides the first tune:

and some boisterous leaps on the strings give a rollicking and very masculine character to the dance:

which is soon offset by an obviously feminine reply, in much quieter accents:

The Trio is in B flat, and has a more wistful character. It is as though a couple had withdrawn from the noisy gathering, and were dancing quietly to their own time. With lovely inspiration, Schumann uses again the solo violin's music in the Romance (Fig. 11), giving it to the 1st violins, who delicately embroider the most longing phrases sung by the woodwind, violas and 2nd violins. Each phrase begins with a tender little sigh,

Fine feeling on the conductor's part makes this little episode, which was one of Harty's particular joys, quite delicious, but the poise is easily lost. The 1st violins' part is not easy, and any raggedness will bring it tumbling to earth.

The boisterous Scherzo crashes in again, but instead of ending the movement with a coda, the composer repeats the trio, nearly intact, though it eventually seems to break into pieces when the violas, cellos and lower woodwind, in the rhythm of the trio, finally reiterate two chords, very softly.

The sky has suddenly lost its brightness, as though light-hearted gaiety was to be at an end, and preparations made for a serious—perhaps even tragic—character.

The strings begin a quick tremolo under the 1st violins, who begin playing over their original tentative figure of the introduction to the first movement. After a warning rumble on the timpani, the trombones make a solemn entrance and declaim in patriarchal tone that we must prepare for the sterner realities of life. As if to give portentous effect to their warning sentences, they finally drop an inexorable fifth—a veritable 'We have spoken!' But the violins still persist in their arpeggio figure, which impertinently refuses to be silenced, and over a long pedal on A, with the help of the woodwind, they quicken the tempo and bring the Adagio to an end on a dominant chord. After a breath all the momentous words of the old gentlemen are scorned, and the

Allegro breaks out, impetuously, in D major—with precisely the same theme as the first Allegro, only in the major mode, and preceded by two sharp chords. The accent on the second beat of the bar is now removed, and the time being altered to 4/4 instead of 2/4, a much lighter and grander swing flows into the music, which is punctuated by a rhythmic figure in the woodwind, also taken from the first movement.

Fig.17

In the highest of spirits the movement swings along, with this subsidiary figure adding to the material.

Fig 18.

After much discussion on this subsidiary tune around the orchestra, a diminuendo reveals the second subject—as light-hearted as you please and with any amount of character. First violins, flutes and oboes, very quietly at first, introduce it, to the simplest of accompaniments.

Fig.19 Violins, Flutes & Oboes

This is one of Schumann's most happy inspirations, and if played with tremendous life and colour, yet subdued in tone, it provides just the foil for the heavier parts of the movement. Harty got the utmost from its possibilities—free as air and with a tempo slightly rubato, perhaps even hurried a little, the accompaniment itself came infectious in its life. It was even whipped up, and the slightest sluggishness anywhere was immediately pricked.

Harty's trick, with his left hand particularly, of imperceptibly bringing the orchestra on with him, without unduly affecting the actual tempo, showed up typically here, and it cheered the orchestra with the assurance that he had lost none of his vitality.

Played vapidly, this movement can be terrible. The music calls for freedom and an onward drive, and almost every bar must be handled with skill and imagination. In Harty's hands it sparkled. Colours appeared and disappeared, and every atom of interest, every nuance, was brought out, yet without apparent care.

Schumann concludes the second subject matter with two groups of four bars in crescendo, on this rhythm, derived from the wood-wind punctuation at the beginning of the movement:

Fig. 20 Strings & Wind

A new figure comes on the scene now—a fast and brilliant scale always followed by a held note:

Fig. 21 Cello & Bass

Instruments and sections all over the orchestra take up this exciting, rushing scale, and hang on grimly to their held notes whilst the others in their turn climb as quickly as they can.

Schumann begins the development much as he did at first by dropping a whole tone and sustaining a strong unison—G this time. The violins and violas, as though not knowing what to do next, shiver in a violent tremolo, but this is only another false start. Cellos and bassoons begin a little Mendelssohnian rhythmic theme (from the third bar of Fig. 17) which is the subject of a fugato.

Fig. 22 Cellos & Bassoons

The importance of this rhythmic figure has been steadily growing and now it dominates the scene completely until the horns and violas firmly announce the following idea, which eventually calls an end to the fugal discussion:

Fig. 23 Violas & Horns

and brings us back, not to the first subject of the movement, which Schumann ignores for evermore, but the subsidiary theme:

Fig. 24

which works up an exciting crescendo for a few bars, only to dissolve again into a recapitulation of the second subject. This is more heavily scored this time, and is more passionate in mood. It leads to the scale motif which works to a big climax. This section he rounds off with the same bars of his false start—the shivering tremolo—now still more violent and dramatic, after the long-sustained unison.

His next move is delicious and Schubertian. An entirely new tune turns up—and inspired by the same light-hearted mood as that of the violin tune of the first movement.

Fig. 25

From this point the music gets reckless. The tempo changes to "Quicker" and then Presto. This is the most thrilling part of the symphony for the orchestra. We feel like horses about to bolt! A wild rush ends in two fortissimo and panting chords and complete silence, while everyone prepares for the last effort. This silence recalls a remark once made by Maurice Sons, a famous leader of the Queen's Hall Orchestra. The 1st violins are the first to break it by one solitary, almost unobserved note, just as though the composer had so often heard some wretched violinist, losing his nerve, crash in too soon that he actually made it official in the score.

"This miserable note," Sons was once heard to remark bitterly, "is the one of the whole work in which the strings are allowed to play without the wind!"

Never did Schumann, or anyone else for that matter, write a passage for such violent attack as the final frenzied charge to the end. It is one of the great moments in the symphony when, in breathless silence, with every eye fixed to the conductor, the cellos wait to swoop on their victim.

This is clutched from them by violas and violins and passed up the orchestra. With everyone going full out, the end comes in thrilling, joyous excitement.

XI

BRAHMS

1833–1897

BRAHMS was a Hamburger of lowly birth and sound stock. His life was humdrum. Not the most unscrupulous of film-mongers or concocters of musical comedies has been able to find in it the least excuse for a romance. If there was a dramatic aspect of his career it was external to his nature and not of his seeking. By a quaint freak of fortune his name and art were seized upon by Wagner's enemies as a rallying-point. For reasons more personal than artistic he was set up as an anti-Wagner, and consequently came in for extravagant adulation and extravagant disparagement. Hans von Bülow—whose wife, Cosima Liszt, had left his rooftree for Wagner's—bracketed Brahms's name with those of Bach and Beethoven. The Wagnerians, on their side, went for Brahms with tooth and claw. Here in England, for instance, Bernard Shaw, a Wagnerian standard-bearer, called Brahms's Requiem a "colossal musical imposture" and said that by comparison with Goetz—composer of a symphony in F and an opera, 'The Taming of the Shrew'—Brahms was a dolt. Here is Shaw on the symphonies:

> "Strip off the euphuism from these symphonies, and you will find a string of incomplete dance and ballad tunes, following one another with no more organic coherence than the succession of passing images reflected in a shop-window in Piccadilly during any twenty minutes in the day."

So far did musical politics go in the nineteenth century! Here is Vincent d'Indy:

> "Brahms left four symphonies of classical shape which, in spite of good qualities, deplorably confirm what I have had to

say about Schumann and his disregard of Beethoven's principles with respect to tonal order. Brahms's developments, crowded with details charming in themselves, are almost always wearisome as a whole by reason of a disorder in the modulations analogous to the faults of perspective which spoil otherwise excellent pictures. Brahms's orchestration has the same shortcomings, often aggravated, as Schumann's. He proceeds by entire doublings of different tone-qualities, with a doughy, heavy result."

The Brahmsian need not feel self-distrustful at all this. To speak only of opinion in England, he has Parry, Stanford and Tovey with him and also the mass of the musical public, which has quite forgotten Goetz and cannot be said to care much for d'Indy, but which, year in and year out, never tires of Brahms's symphonies and concertos. At the same time, appreciation of Brahms must be allowed to be in some measure a matter of temperament. Germany, England—in spite of Brahms's fanatical antipathy towards us—and America are the countries where he is most beloved; while he has always left the Latin countries indifferent.

Brahms's music is an idealization of the German middle classes of the nineteenth century. He was both a learned and a sentimental composer. (Understand 'sentimental' in not an unduly disparaging sense.) He was, like Mendelssohn and Schumann, a romantic composer of the domestic sort, but there is in him more solidity and a deeper pensiveness than in his elders. He was a great student of the classics, and from his firmness of character there developed a fine taste and beautiful certainty of style. At the centre, beneath the man of learning and the rather narrow, unattractive and almost uncouth person represented in any number of memoirs, was a naïve and tender heart. As for Brahms the artist, he was not one of those who squandered his gifts. We have the feeling that every inch of fertile soil was cultivated.

Brahms's father was a humble theatre musician. His mother, seventeen years older than his father, was a woman of superior mind whose lot, in conditions of almost squalid poverty, must have been hard. There was no question about the boy's vocation, and he was lucky in his first teacher, O. F. W. Cossel, a name always to be reverenced by Brahmsians. The pianoforte was his instrument. He became a fine executant, and would no doubt have been a great virtuoso if he had not devoted himself to composition. The tremendous 'Paganini Variations' could only have been written by a highly accomplished pianist. Brahms's boyhood was not easy. From the age of thirteen he had to help balance the family budget by playing at taverns and dancing saloons and by giving ill-paid lessons. But it would be a mistake to exaggerate. Brahms was, at least, not distracted from his vocation as many a gifted boy of a superior social stratum has been. And his troubles were over when he was twenty. Joachim met him and opened all doors, and Schumann wrote an enthusiastic article on his early compositions. When he was thirty he settled at Vienna, his home for the rest of his life. He did not marry.

Brahms's earlier compositions sometimes show ambitions in the heroic vein which he did not pursue in later life. Such are the D minor piano concerto (first intended to be a symphony), and the piano sonata in F minor. Brahms was forty-two when he composed his first symphony, which, however, he had designed years before. This is the famous C minor, which represents his last essay in the grand heroic manner. All the later works are more or less in the intimate vein which we think of as essentially Brahmsian. There are but nine orchestral works, all told, by Brahms, outside the four concertos and the choral works with orchestra. This enumeration may suggest that the symphonies lie outside his true periphery, but it is not so. In these works we are as much at the heart of Brahms as in the best of his chamber music. All four were composed within nine years. Two points are thereby illustrated—the first being that the young Brahms, like the young Schumann, hardly thought of himself primarily as an orchestral composer, and the second, the solemnity which, after Beethoven, filled a conscientious composer's mind at the thought of attempting a symphony. It is characteristic of Brahms, who was above all things respectful of the art he practised, that he should have put off so long the day of his approach to the highest form. As we have it, then, his entire symphonic output is absolutely mature, and no trial and error is to be found therein. From the great tide of sound that opens the first symphony to the last variation of the noble Passacaglia of No. 4, the quality is all of his finest period of composition. There is no movement of any of the four symphonies we would be without.

The four symphonies are the following:

C minor, No. 1 (1875–6); D major, No. 2 (1877); F major, No. 3 (1882–3); E minor, No. 4 (1884–5).

The first performance of the C minor was given at Karlsruhe under Dessoff; of the D major at Vienna under Richter, and of the F major likewise; and of the E minor at Meiningen under Bülow. We shall see in the next chapter how large the scheme is and dramatic the unfolding of the first symphony. The second, which was for many years the favourite of all, is more lyrical and charming.

If this is music of late summer the no less beautiful symphony in F is autumnal in feeling, with its sweeping winds and falling leaves. There are two strong preludial chords and then comes— if the orchestra can play—one of the greatest moments in romantic music, when the violins swoop down from the heights with the main theme, which so quickly takes on an elegiac tone with the minor third of the scale. To hear thirty or so first-rate violins play this is to think of Shelley. The performance of all this first movement is a supreme test of the orchestra. Warmth of phrase —therein is to be found the effect. Anything wooden in the playing of Brahms kills the music. The slow movement is deeply serious, with characteristic clarinet colour. The third is a bewitching love-song, with a famous tune for the cellos. The finale is all autumnal wildness and exhilaration. Then, at the end, comes a regretful reminiscence of the first theme of the first movement, to give the poignancy of "the days that are no more" to the close.

The fourth symphony, again, is autumnal music, of yet more tragic cast. The beautiful and masterly first movement is profoundly elegiac, the slow movement is solemnly processional. The third is extraordinarily boisterous. Here, for once, Brahms recalls Beethoven. The fourth is the tragic and passionate

Passacaglia—romantic music in a pre-classical form. All Brahms's music is a wonderful pleasure to play, and this in spite of the fact that his string-writing is clumsy. There are places of atrocious difficulty which do not sound out of the way. The public listens placidly, while the player curses. And yet no symphonies give the orchestra more general cause for enjoyment. It is like playing chamber music, in which everything matters, everything has its sense and point. Brahms's chamber music yields a more glowing satisfaction to the player than any other, and the symphonies are but an extension of those works—the trios, the quartets, quintets and sonatas.

XII

BRAHMS'S FIRST SYMPHONY

AT the opening of the symphony it is as though we are borne on a great and sombre tide. It is no ordinary beginning; the first great slow-moving phrases of woodwind and strings break upon our ears as though they had long been resounding. This portentous introduction sets a mood of tragedy, and in cloudy form in these first thirty bars of heavy presentiment appear most of the themes and ideas of the first movement.

Great features confront us as we are swept into the symphony. The ominous hammering of the timpani on a pedal C supports a huge structure of slow-moving harmonies, created by the 1st and 2nd violins climbing in octaves by slow steps to a peak, while the woodwind descends in heavily sustained chords. The characteristically Brahmsian phrase of the strings in the first few bars is to play a great part throughout the first movement:

The stream of sound accumulates in a bar of 9/8 to be abruptly checked on a short G major chord, as if the torrent had been suddenly dammed. In great stillness the woodwind plays this tentative theme, which is lightly emphasized by strings pizzicato.

A long and intensely emotional phrase, shared by 1st violins, flute and bassoon, concludes this quiet mood, fading to pianissimo on an arpeggio-like figure on the strings.

Fig.3

There is a feeling of waiting and expectancy about these two bars, and even now they suddenly fill up with such force that the dam is wrecked and we are swept into the great stream of the opening bars again, this time in the dominant key of G minor.

Brahms checks the power of the music as before, and gives the oboe a new and wonderful melody, which is a test of the player's power of expression and skill in legato, to say nothing of breath control:

Fig.4

The cellos then have their chance to improve on the oboe, and at the same time bring the introduction to an end.

The Allegro opens with the main subject (derived from Fig. 1) divided between woodwind and strings, and it is one of violent anger and strife. The smoothness of the opening of the symphony, the smoothness of a great river, is now broken up by the jagged rocks and swift eddies of the semiquaver figure tacked on:

Fig.5

The significance of Fig. 3 is now apparent, for it is the central idea of the first subject, which continues:

Fig.6

All this principal subject-matter is thick with tempestuous life and vigour. In a few bars the 1st and 2nd violins catch hold of the tentative phrase of the woodwind (Fig. 2) with stormy gestures.

Fig.7   1st & 2nd Violins

The superb style required of an orchestra for playing Brahms will have been apparent from the beginning of this symphony. We have said how important it is for players to adapt themselves to the different composers they interpret. In Brahms there are essentials which may all be observed in the introduction and the opening of the Allegro. In the opening bars, observe the power of the strings in sustaining each note to its utmost value. There must be no gaps in the sound, and the great difficulty of legato-playing in perfect ensemble is that it must sound natural and without effort. Notice, above all, the orchestra's approach to the real peak of climax. There is one peak in this introduction, and one only—at the repetition of the opening bars in G minor. The wind have to sing their phrases with a far greater warmth and freedom than for the earlier masters, and great breadth and spaciousness of phrase must be apparent in the music from beginning to end. Take the upward leap of an octave by the oboe in Fig. 4. The lower note must grow into the top one as if it were possible to play both at once. No singer can suggest this, but an oboe can—and string players perhaps better still. There must be no shade of difference of colour between the notes.

Then take Fig. 6. Does one hear each separate note of these arpeggios on the strings—do they make the first bar sound clearly? Or are they uncertain or fluffy? Does the phrase mount up to a brilliant, perfectly confident high A flat? How do the strings play the contrasted separate and staccato notes in that last bar?

Brahms's glory is his art of building up a phrase. There is scarcely a theme that does not grow to a definite point. Yet how often does perfunctory playing blur that very point! It is the stuff between the notes that tells so much in Brahms. The vibrato of the string player—his power of getting sound from beneath his bow throughout its whole length—his control in short, sharp, jabbing strokes in contrast—in all this the strings must think alike. Rich sonority and the glowing colour of a Rembrandt should be the background. Such colour must be matched in sound if one is to hear a Brahms symphony in all its glory. The directions in his scores are barely adequate. He did not generally mark his accompanying instruments below the soloists, though his scoring demands it. The understanding of orchestral balance by the players themselves is wanted. A great orchestra will show that Brahms is its business and not only the conductor's. The latter must look after the interpretation as a whole; the orchestra will seize on the music and play a phrase like Fig. 6 as only Brahms must be played.

The themes quoted follow and alternate with one another—sometimes changing over from bass and treble—modulating through different keys, all as it were struggling with one another angrily, while the timpani can be heard hammering out this

rhythm intermittently:

All this fighting rather suddenly lessens after coming to the key of B flat, which is to take us as the dominant key to the second subject in E flat. This is in complete contrast of mood, as foreshadowed in the introduction, but with a new and poignantly tender theme, in which Fig. 6 supplies the bass:

Notice the way in which this typically Brahmsian phrase grows in the bass, and how beautifully it is rounded off. The theme itself, so bald and unpromising on paper, is yet, when played with all its harmonies, entrancing in its climb and its appealing fall.

The oboe carries on in the same mood, the clarinet imitating one of his figures with touching sympathy:

The smooth, warm tone of the clarinet, after the long, plaintive song of the oboe, is wonderfully friendly, and Brahms takes this phrase for a few moments, as if extemporizing amongst the various instruments. But this movement is too surely destined for tragedy and strife, and the precious period of quiet tendencies is now to be utterly banished by the violas, whose angry, broken phrases

sinister in colour and feeling, arouse the orchestra to the old passions again. Fig. 6 once more supplies the bass—now upside down:

The whole orchestra gives vent to its fury, the themes are hurled about in every position until there comes a sharp check to the rhythm by some vicious chords in E flat minor.

A few bars of hacking notes from the strings force the key back to C minor, for the traditional first repeat, unless we go straight on to the development. This opens in the strange key of B major with a struggle between lower and upper strings for Fig. 6 and a sudden frightening drop to pianissimo. The violins recede to a

trembling background while Fig. 6 is played by bassoon and later
basses and cellos in long-drawn notes:

The tune in its new character is heard all over the orchestra, from
flutes to basses. Keys change in the mysterious atmosphere until
F minor is reached. This is the signal for the violas to burst in
rudely as before—with their same instant success of infecting the
orchestra with violence. This time, however, a new tune, broad
and hymn-like, is introduced over the timpani's insistent rhythm.
It modulates in a series of sequences until the dominant key of the
movement returns and G major chords suddenly appear in ironic
contrast to the dark, angry surroundings. In wonderfully moving
harmonies the upper strings and woodwind gradually subside to
a pianissimo pedal note.

   This extraordinary impressive subsidence—lasting a considerable time and with imperceptible gradations of tone—takes us
to the heart of the whole tragedy. As the sounds diminish the
feeling of sorrow increases, with a laboured breath between the
broken phrases. The drum, softened indeed, still keeps up the
fateful rhythm until finally the double bassoon with most telling
effect sinks the pedal note a semitone down to F sharp, and the
moment of all comes when, in this gloom and despair, Brahms
begins his preparation for the supreme climax.

   In extreme pianissimo, the composer takes the first bars of the
second subject (Fig. 8) minus the bass, and two other features, the
drum rhythm and the figure allied to it, expanded from the
violas (Fig. 11, treble).

   The pressure becomes almost intolerable when, at the height
of the climax, at last the strings, in superb Brahmsian style,
dominate the orchestra with this figure from Fig. 5:

It depends entirely upon their style and skill whether they succeed in getting through the mass of wind placed against them with the top line of Fig. 11 and the basses thundering out the basic rhythm.

They rush down a violent scale, as if to the home key again, but instead the orchestra makes a sharp swerve into the unexpected key of B minor for the return of the Allegro again. This only lasts a bar or two, because the lower strings, backed up by bassoons and double-bassoon in a magnificent effort, force the key first into D major and then G major, until finally Brahms launches upon the recapitulation of the movement in its original key of C minor. This section takes its previous course. Much that may have been too complicated to grasp in the exposition will now, when heard for the second time, become clear. The coda grows naturally out of the turbulent picture, and Brahms closes the movement with a favourite tempo indication, 'poco sostenuto.' Woodwind and upper strings wail their grief over the drum's inexorable rhythm, and the end is despair.

If the lovely Andante is a consolation, it is at the same time deeply pathetic. The key is the distant one of E major. The keys of the movements of this symphony go up by major thirds— C, E, A flat (G sharp), C.

The principal theme is in two great parts. The first opens in deep tranquillity (notice the tender hush in the third bar).

Fig.14 *Andante sostenuto*
p Strings & Bassoon   *pp*

This goes on to expand unexpectedly in impassioned love-strains,

Fig.15 1st Violins
pp   *f*

and still further, until with perfect sense of line and symmetry it subsides to the pensive tranquillity of the opening bars again, when the violas on their C strings (much beloved of Brahms!) colour the harmony and echo the violins. The second part is taken up by the oboe.

Inside the orchestra, when one has been driven to the limit of emotional and, indeed, physical endurance in the first movement, but is now enjoying a delicious calm, how magical is the sound of the oboe on these first three expressive notes!

The tune is so different in feeling from the first part—as simple and touching as the other becomes impassioned. It is one of those precious melodies that every artist wishes he had to himself.

The next section, still in the same key, clearly opens on the 1st violins, which, entirely alone, climb up on a major chord:

The violins eventually rise to ecstatic heights with glorious free-dom, over a soft syncopated accompaniment in second violins and violas, who are unable to restrain themselves and are irresistibly drawn into the tune themselves for a brief moment, before relaxing again into still more delicate accompanying. The next theme is for the oboe again in the key of C sharp minor:

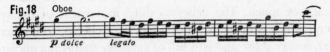

It is imitated by the clarinet in an exquisite change of key into D flat, and grows to a considerable climax for the whole orchestra.

When this is spent a quiet dialogue of broken phrases between woodwind and strings:

leads us back to the original key and the whole principal theme of the movement returns with the scoring grandly enriched and elaborated, trumpets and drums entering for the first time. On the return of Fig. 16 we hear that matchless sound of the solo violin playing in octaves with oboe and horn. The horn after a bar or two carries on with the tune and the solo violin, in inspired improvisations, lifts the music to the very skies until its ethereal voice is lost in the flutes.

Beginning with the flutes, Brahms, with infinite tenderness, leads us back to earth with repetition and variants of the most expressive bar of Fig. 16:

Fig. 17 returns again, now shared by all the upper strings, but instead of the previous romantic development the composer gives us a warm phrase with a clear sense of finality in it, keeping the mood completely tranquil. The movement ends with the solo violin once more lifting us to celestial heights, on a chord of E major.

When Brahms heads a movement with the word 'grazioso'— a favourite with him—it means that grace and charm must abound in the performance, with lightness of rhythm and delicacy of touch. The delicious third movement of the symphony, which is in the form of a scherzo (scherzo, trio, scherzo, coda), is very short, and is as full of exquisite things as a miniature painting. So perfect is Brahms's sense of proportion that a considerable climax is managed within the small picture. The scoring

SCHUMANN

BRAHMS

is without trombones and drum, and the trumpets appear for a
few bars only.

The theme with which the clarinet opens the movement, in
A flat, is a lovely piece of symmetrical line drawing, the second
phrase being an exact inversion of the first:

It is the extension of each phrase to a fifth bar that adds so much
charm.

The clarinet's liquid sound gives the whole essence of the
melody, which flows with the utmost smoothness. The strings
quietly emphasize the phrase, while the clarinet sustains; and this
becomes an important feature. As background to the theme, the
first horns move in an opposite curve in smooth crotchets, while
the bass is taken by the cellos moving in regular quavers, pizzicato.
This cello accompaniment makes or mars the music. If it is
plucked without a delicate sense of rhythm and sensitiveness the
clarinet solo will lose its magic.

The second theme follows immediately after the clarinet's, and
is given to woodwind:

The strings accompany them with arpeggios of the same rhythm:
the theme expanding freely in lovely undulations. Next, the first
theme returns on the first violins whilst the clarinet weaves a
liquid little arpeggio around it. All this takes place in a few
moments—so much in so little time! Thus the easy flow of the
movement continues, colour and sparkles of light everywhere,
always touched with a most delicate miniature-painter's brush,
until Brahms changes the key to F minor.

5

The clarinet is again favoured with the new theme, an agitated
one,

which flute and oboe immediately carry on.

The agitated accompaniment is difficult, though it is merely a
matter of perfect fitting of a simple rhythm, broken up amongst
the strings:

It depends where the cellos and basses are placed in the orchestra. If they are together this passage of accompaniment will
be smooth, but if on opposite sides of the orchestra, there will be
trouble. Toscanini became extremely upset on one occasion, when
the pieces could not be fitted together. It was anything but a
smooth passage! It is impossible for the five string departments all
to be close together, so here the one wretched department that is
out in the cold will inevitably become the scapegoat.

All this section is in agitated mood until violas and 1st violins
bring the clarinet back to the main theme in A flat. This is
eventually drawn out beautifully into a cadence of three notes in
E flat. These three notes now become part of the opening theme
of the Trio. Typical of Brahms's use of his material and means to
an end!

The Trio in B major and 6/8 time, in complete contrast to the
Scherzo, is vigorous and purposeful. It is in the usual two parts

with repeats, and rises to a considerable climax when the trumpets
add brilliance to the scoring.

There is an interesting effect here available to the interpreter,
and Boult, true to Brahms's style, always insists upon it. The
climax to fortissimo is built up in the second repeated section and
Boult always keeps something in reserve for the second time, so
that the climax becomes cumulative throughout and not merely a
repetition. This also tends to show up clearly the highest peak of
the movement, which should shine out in brilliant outline, for the
Trio ends in B major at the height of climax. In the next bar there
is a change to a darker key, the D sharp becoming E flat.

A few more bars take us back into A flat again, for the return of
the Scherzo. The scoring is fuller, and instead of the original
second strain of the clarinet, the 1st violins make a delicious
change, turning the old inversion into a new strain of great
beauty:

The second theme (Fig. 22) is then changed in key (the D
naturals becoming D flat). It expands richly in a big crescendo to
forte, subsiding into E flat minor until the tempo slows to "poco
più tranquillo" for the Coda. The Coda is a lovely summary of
the Trio, and with charming grace ends with the first three notes
of the Trio theme.

The Finale begins with an introduction that carries us back to the tragic mood of the first movement. Longer than the great opening introduction by twenty-four bars, it is still darker, more fraught with foreboding and even terror. Like the immense introduction to the last movement of Beethoven's Ninth Symphony, it is one of the outstanding things in all music. Momentous events must happen after this, and meanwhile we are shaken by the power of these concentrated sixty-one bars.

It is magnificent to play and at the same time difficult, for the orchestra is faced with peculiar problems in the great range of expression and in maintaining the ensemble proper to a Brahmsian style.

In very slow tempo three descending crotchets open the introduction on the strings, and massive harmonies rise in the second bar. The 1st and 2nd violins and horns should be heard dominating with their significant, shadowy form of the theme of the coming allegro:

Fig. 29   Violins & Horns

The woodwind harmonies descend in slow-moving steps, as in the opening of the symphony. Next the strings are heard in a great pizzicato episode—dead slow and soft at first, but gathering speed and power through seven bars:

Fig. 30   Strings pizzicato

to a savage slash across the strings on a chord of D flat. This huge plucked chord sounds grand if it really reverberates through the hall; and every player does his utmost to make it sound. It needs care with all its savagery.

Brahms then repeats the opening bars in another key, ending

with another vicious slash, but this time on the last quaver of the
bar, the whole pizzicato episode having been cut down to only
four bars. This gives the effect of greater anger and impatience,
which is a hundred times intensified in the next bar. Here, the
strings sustain a long note and then make a furtive rush at a scale
as if scared. (These passages are troublesome and if they are to
sound terrifying, ensemble must be perfect.)

Ominously grim in the background, the woodwind plays the
gloomy first bar of the introduction. Immediately this boils up to
a thick and suffused crescendo from the whole orchestra, less
heavy brass and drums. This theme is predominant in the woodwind:

A sharp climax is quickly built up, first and second violins rushing
downhill in two brilliant passages, curiously scored by being
broken up between them. The second passage is a semitone lower,
leading us to an uneasy piano. In two terror-stricken bars the
whole orchestra bursts into a shriek with a thunderclap from
the timpani. Only cellos, basses and bassoon remain on a
held A natural, falling to A flat and finally to a dominant pedal
note G.

As they touch this pedal note, pianissimo, the tempo quickens
to "più andante" and a great triumphant song peals out on the
horn over an exciting shimmer on a C major chord from the
strings. This great bridge-passage, linking the introduction to the
allegro, is a wonderful inspiration. One is always reminded of a
glorious deep-tinted sunrise. In the foreground, dark angry
clouds lour; far in the east the low sun begins to light the whole
sky with gorgeous colours. This is tremendously apparent when a

sudden darkening of the harmony sets off the horn's top note in the fifth bar as if with the most brilliant shaft of light:

Fig.33 *Più andante*

The pedal note on the dominant has meanwhile dropped to C and the flute takes up the triumphant song. The gorgeousness of the sunrise fades, and a solemn hymn is announced by bassoons and brass. This is not to be heard again until near the end of the symphony. Once more the horn peals out, joined by the second horn in an exhilarating paean expanding the first bar of the song, and gradually the music fades and entirely disappears on the dominant of C major on a quiet chord in the woodwind. So far the introduction. What does it lead to?

In C major, the 1st violins on their lowest strings, helped by the 2nds, sing out the broad melody of the finale. This is the famous theme which Brahms's critics have often accused him of imitating from that of the last movement of Beethoven's Ninth Symphony. There is no doubt a family likeness but the two are distinct as any individual men. Both are great melodies. Here is Brahms's:

Fig.34 *Allegro non troppo ma con brio*

This resounds all over the orchestra and is brought to fortissimo for a change in its character. The tempo is slightly quickened, and a new figure, vigorous and jerky, adds animation:

Fig.35 *Animato*

whilst another brilliant scale motif derived from Fig. 31 brings excitement into the music broadly sung:

Fig.36 Strings

The furtive little rushes at Fig. 31 have now become confident, and they lead the orchestra up to a climax for the first strain of the horn theme to peal out again. The key is now the dominant of G major in preparation for the second subject. This is one of those smoothly swift tunes in which Brahms's invention was inimitable. It has a joyous feeling, and the tempo has yet again slightly quickened:

Fig.37 Animato Violins
p dolce

This tune, as usual, expands naturally. Notice the bass, which never changes.

This tune quickly and unexpectedly works to a rough out-burst. This alters the jubilant mood to one of agitation for another subsidiary tune to the second subject, falling into the minor mode on the oboe:

Fig.38 Oboe
p dolce   p

which Brahms soon turns into a bustling scamper on the violas (the same notes as the above but twice as fast):

Fig.39 Violas
marcato

infecting the other strings and boiling up to a high-spirited tune on the violins, springing from Fig. 32 of the introduction in the key of E minor:

Another important triplet figure takes a big part in this greatly developed second-subject matter:

With great vigour this complex episode is brought to a jagged close in E minor. Brahms holds a sustained chord, changes the key to the dominant again, and once more launches out into the main theme (Fig. 34). After its complete restatement we are led into E flat, and the pizzicato passage of the introduction (Fig. 30) reappears, shorn of its dramatic and violent hurry. It is dramatic enough here with its heavy crescendo and alternating attempts of the woodwind to keep the main tune going through various keys; but there is no fury about it. The animato (Fig. 35) returns again in its original key of C major; then a grand development section ensues in which a giant figure arising from Fig 36 strides about the orchestra:

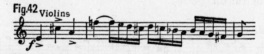

It magically transforms itself into a quiet accompaniment for another important ingredient in this melting-pot of precious metals:

This comes, of course, from Fig. 35, and as the great cauldron grows fiercer and fiercer in its heat, this figure takes complete precedence, even over Fig. 42. At last the molten mass bursts over the top, with a shower of sparks. Flute and violins scream this broken figure:

then cascade for six bars to a breathless, unbelievable silence.

This is another moment in great music where everything is caught up and concentrated in one solitary crotchet rest for a supremely dramatic effect. A huge sustained chord crashes out from the whole orchestra, the 1st violins with thrilling tone play out the first notes of the song of triumph:

We realize now the significance of that broken figure (Fig. 44) in the last few bars of the climax—it was the identical figure striving for completion. Words can never convey the power of this climax. It is sufficient to say that it is the peak of the whole symphony. If the conductor has driven the players too hard and has kept nothing in reserve for the supreme effort, then he has failed in the interpretation of the symphony, however fine certain portions may have been. The climax of the first movement was terrific, it is true, but this must somehow grip with a fiercer clutch.

The triumphant song on the two horns does not fade in a shimmering background as before, but over warm and excitingly rich string tone, with a reminiscence of the main theme of the movement, the horn phrases expand and widen, softening to piano in gradual slowing of tempo.

Brahms has yet another delight for us, and by the exercise of his sleights of hand we find ourselves suddenly in the smooth and almost slippery jubilation of the second subject again (Fig. 37), though we are scarcely aware how the subtle change of tempo and amazing brightening of mood have come about.

5*

We are now given a complete recapitulation of all the second-subject material until we reach the point where the violas sustain a long note for the harmony to prepare for the return of the main theme. This time they play a minor chord, and in quiet repeated notes; it is the beginning of the coda. The bass is heard growling with the initial theme of the movement (Fig. 29) in canon with the woodwind high in the treble. The strings in swift passages urge on the speed, the rhythm of the theme is broken up and becomes fiercer. The great crescendo rises until a mighty concentration of the orchestra on five repeated dominant chords brings us to the triumphant peroration in C major.

The tempo is quickened to 'più allegro' and a new idea of the main theme of the movement breaks out:

We are taken swiftly to the great hymn, which has only appeared once before. This peals out fortissimo in solemn grandeur on brass and strings. Tradition allows a considerably slower tempo here, and the only conductor who drives on relentlessly at Brahms's apparent direction is Toscanini.

On the last chord of the hymn the strings, followed by horns and trumpets, burst into wild jubilation on one more version of the initial theme:

and thence, with all the fire and vigour it can muster, the orchestra dashes to the end only checked by three exciting gaps, in which the timpanist is heard violently hammering, as if to remind us of his earlier and more fateful task in the first movement.

The C minor symphony is unique in Brahms's works. Nowhere else has he celebrated spiritual victory as in this superb finale. The underlying poetic vision is that of Beethoven's symphony in the same key—the progress from darkness to light, from despairing doubts to triumphant confidence. We may allow that without that other C minor symphony there might never have been this one. To say as much is no derogation of Brahms, but rather a tribute, seeing how entirely his own are the new contents within the old framework. That Æschylus should have treated a subject did not mean that Euripides was forbidden it. The despair of his first movement is wholly Brahms's, so the relief of the middle movements, and so, not least, the gorgeous triumph of the finale. If this is music of the silver age it is still an enduring masterpiece.

XIII

DVOŘÁK

1841–1904

THE Czechs think more of Smetana, the founder of their national school of music; but from the year 1880 onwards that school has been represented in English minds and English affections by Antonín Dvořák. It is true that none of Dvořák's operas has won such a place as Smetana's 'Bartered Bride'; but in the fields of choral, chamber and symphonic music Dvořák stands for Bohemia. No later-comer from that land, whose people so long ago as in Burney's time had the reputation of being the most musical in Europe,* approached his fame.

When Dvořák arrived on the scene the idea of a national music, a music coloured by folk-song and folk-dance and by peculiarities of scales and rhythms, was familiar but still fresh. There had been hints of it in Haydn and Mozart—in the former's 'gypsy rondo' for instance, in the Turkish music of a few of Mozart's works (e.g. the violin concerto in A, K. 219)—and still more in Weber and Schubert. But Chopin was the first composer to idealize the folk-music of his own fatherland in a passionately patriotic spirit. What may be called the poetry of nationalism was a creation of the nineteenth century, and it made a noteworthy contribution to the music of the age. At that time there was something romantic and appealing about the small nations that were agitating for freedom from imperial bonds. The Balkanization of Europe had not been foreseen, nor the ferocity with which various Ruritanias, as soon as liberated, were to set about tyrannizing their own minorities.

---

* "I had frequently been told that the Bohemians were the most musical people of Germany or, perhaps, of all Europe." (*The Present State of Music in Germany*, etc., 1773.)

The Austrian oppression of the Hungarians and the Czechs, which stirred generous hearts to indignation in those innocent times, looks like paternal benevolence by comparison with what Europe has experienced in our century; but the passionate objections to which a relatively mild imperialism gave rise were genuine enough. Not that all the national schools represented a bid for independence by a downtrodden people. Often it was simply a case of self-assertion. The remarkable Russian national school rebelled against Western culture. Huge Russia and small Norway (represented by Grieg) alike felt that their music should be less a contribution to the European pool than an expression of differences.

A national badge of some sort became indispensable to the musician's costume, and such a cosmopolitan as Liszt had to call to mind where he had been born. It had been in Hungary; and although he did not know Hungarian and did not know the difference between Hungarian and gypsy music, he wrote Hungarian rhapsodies—and with immense success. Some nations, like Spain, were slow in joining the movement, and Frenchmen, Germans and Russians obligingly filled the gaps by composing pieces in a more or less Spanish idiom. The French composer Lalo wrote a Spanish violin concerto and a Norwegian orchestral rhapsody. The motive was like any other; that is to say, its outcome was good or bad according to the quality of the artist.

Such Russians as Balakirev and Mussorgsky attempted to create a music radically independent of the West. There was no such ambition among the Bohemians. These had had far too much to do with Western music, which was in a considerable measure of their making. Vienna, after all, was their imperial capital, and Czech names abound among the minor masters of the classical age. Smetana naturally made Mendelssohn his springboard, as Dvořák did Brahms. We must beware of ascribing too much to the influence of folklore in the work of these two delightful musicians. The number of the tunes that either borrowed is insignificant in the mass of those that they invented for themselves. National dance-rhythms certainly contribute something, especially to their operas and lighter instrumental forms; but it is not necessary to be a Bohemian to write a polka. Important, no doubt, but difficult to assess is the extent to which the 'national character' enters into the individual, and the extent to which an artist's work represents a racial or national character. No one could possibly have divined from his music that Schubert was a German or Mendelssohn a Jew. Anyone guessing must have said that Mendelssohn was French, a superior Saint-Saëns; and that Schubert was a Bohemian, a superior Dvořák.

National and racial character is altogether very boggy ground. With the influence of environment we are on a much safer footing. Dvořák came of sturdy peasant stock, and to the end a peasant he remained. Even in the miserable, war-blighted Bohemia of Burney's time music was a great diversion in the villages. Burney found music in the churches, the schools and the inns. The country picked up after the Napoleonic wars, and from the accounts of Dvořák's childhood we get the idea of a prosperous countryside and of a cheerful people, hard-working in the week and given on Sundays to religious observances and to merry-making wherein music entered largely. Dvořák's father was an innkeeper and butcher. The boy joined the church choir when he was eight, and before that had begun to play the violin.

When he was sixteen he was sent to Prague for serious study. He was poor, and for years earned his living as a theatre musician (violin and viola). Although composition had from early days been his one ambition, he was not precocious. A good many of his youthful works he destroyed, and others have come to light only since his death. He was thirty before he became even locally known as a composer. When he was thirty-four Brahms took a lively interest in him, and his path thenceforward was without difficulties. The 'Slavonic Dances,' composed more or less on the example of Brahms's popular Hungarian Dances, made his name in Germany and England and earned his publisher, Simrock, a fortune; but Dvořák's ambitions lay in the direction of opera, chamber music and the symphony. Not one of his ten operas won the ear of Europe, but in other fields he was triumphant.

He paid his first visit to England in 1884, and was lionized. He came back here in the autumn of that year to conduct his 'Stabat

Mater' and sixth symphony, in D, Op. 60 (then called 'No. 1'), at the Worcester Festival. His cantata 'The Spectre's Bride' was composed for the Birmingham Festival of 1885, and his oratorio 'St. Ludmilla' for the Leeds Festival of the next year. He conducted it himself, this being his fifth visit to England. On his seventh visit, in 1891, he received the honorary degree of Mus. Doc. at Cambridge. In 1892–5 Dvořák was in America, as director of the new 'National Conservatory' at New York. From those years date the ninth symphony, in E minor, 'From the New World,' the splendid violoncello concerto in B minor, and much chamber music. Dvořák spent his latter years at home, composing symphonic poems and operas.

The word 'naïve' is never to be avoided in discussing Dvořák, and it is true that he was not a learned or intellectual composer. But we must see that this word 'naïve' is not used patronizingly. Many a learned and intellectual composer would have given years of his life for a few of the enchanting ideas which sprang up in Dvořák's mind like flowers in spring. Nor was he the composer only of melodious thoughts. He could write not only tuneful lines but also what Tovey used to call 'paragraphs.' He may not have been as brainy an artist as Brahms, but capable in the head he certainly was, and dogged and honourably ambitious. Or why, when the easy path was opened to him by his Slavonic Dances, should he so steadily have devoted himself to the exacting forms of quartet and symphony? If we call Dvořák naïve it is to indicate the range of his sentiment. Happiness and sorrow, delight in nature, the healthy man's satisfaction with the good things of life, tenderness of heart, home-sickness at times and the gaiety of simple pleasures—something like that is his range, which does not embrace the sublime or the intense, or any extreme of emotion or intellectual problem. An average man, an average butcher's son! But no—for to him belonged the power of expressing the poetry of a simple soul in a way all his own, in a way that makes out of simplicity richness.

For the executant Dvořák is an adorable composer. His music is enchanting to play. Always friendly and human, it seems to spring out of the countryside itself. Perhaps we like him best of all in his chamber music—so satisfying in the richness of the part-writing and in the full use that is made of each instrument's range of colour. And always the tunes are fresh and virile, and dressed in attractive and remarkably individual clothes; tunes that are full of emotion without sentimentality. Viola-players, in particular, venerate him as a faithful friend of their instrument, at that time generally unloved. True, he did not write for the stringed instruments with quite the ease and natural feeling we might have expected from one of his practical experience. His viola parts, especially in his chamber music, are apt to be awkward, and one realizes that he can have been no very wonderful executant. But for this he makes up by the interest of his part-writing. As long as chamber music is practised, so long will Dvořák's name be held dear. No doubt one is aware of less of an intellectual control than in Brahms. Dvořák resembles Schubert in an inclination to discursiveness before the right moment—that is to say, before the exposition has been fully stated. Sometimes he does not know what to do in his finales. The conclusive idea escapes him, and he rambles. But to set against that—"here is God's plenty," as one of our poets said about another.* And one can find not only many whole movements that are perfectly controlled and shapely, but also (if more rarely) entire compositions. Who can detect a shortcoming in the design of the piano quintet in A?

Before I come to the symphony chosen for particular discussion mention should be made of two orchestral works of Dvořák's which must never be dropped from the repertory. These are the Symphonic Variations, Op. 78, and the delightful Scherzo Capriccioso, Op. 66, which would be one of his most popular pieces if it fitted better into our orchestral programmes. There is much confusion in the numbering of Dvořák's symphonies; and a word of warning is needed to guard against anyone's taking his opus-numbers as a chronological indication. I give (with acknowledgment to Alec Robertson †) a list in the right order:

No. 1, C minor ('The Bells of Zlonice'). Originally Op. 3. Composed 1865. Unpublished.

* Dryden on Chaucer.
† *Dvořák*. Dent's 'Master Musicians' series, London, 1945.

No. 2, B flat. Originally Op. 4. Composed 1865. Unpublished.

No. 3, E flat. Originally Op. 10. Composed 1873. Published 1912.

No. 4, D minor. Originally Op. 13. Composed 1874. Published 1912.

No. 5, F. So-called 'No. 3.' Originally Op. 24. Composed 1875; revised 1887, as Op. 76. Published 1888.

No. 6, D. So-called 'No. 1,' Op. 60. Composed and published 1880.

No. 7, D minor. So-called 'No. 2,' Op. 70. Composed and published 1885.

No. 8, G. So-called 'No. 4,' Op. 88. Composed 1889. Published 1892.

No. 9, E minor ('From the New World'). So-called 'No. 5,' Op. 95. Composed 1893. Published 1894.

XIV

DVOŘÁK'S SYMPHONY IN G

IT is a misfortune that the popularity of Dvořák's ninth ('New World') symphony should have been allowed more or less to eclipse its predecessors, two of which, at least, are superior compositions. There is no doubt that the seventh in D minor is the finest of the series. It shows Dvořák at the nearest point he approached to Brahms, and yet is profoundly characteristic. The moods are serious, and even the scoring is dark for Dvořák. Four years later came the lovely symphony in G, the prevailing moods of which are happy, tender or jubilant. To anyone who knows these two symphonies well the 'New World,' a work in which simplicity becomes mere obviousness, is a disappointment. Moreover it has been pitilessly hackneyed, as the others have not.

The symphony in G, although composed for an English publisher, is rarely played by comparison. Whenever it is brought out it seems as fresh as youth itself, given the right sort of performance. The first need of this music is an effect of buoyancy and spontaneous inspiration. It must be played as though all were a discovery. There must be a sense of delightful surprise and enthusiasm in our meeting with the tunes; and the rhythms must be rendered with flexibility and a vigorous swing. A stodgy performance drains such music of its life. It must be coloured by the warmth of the playing as a charming landscape is by spring sunshine.

Cellos and clarinets open the symphony immediately with the first subject in G minor—a lovely tune intensely characteristic of Dvořák in its confiding appeal. Like some of Schubert's, it is

more in the nature of a second than a first subject, and this gives
the movement a character more idyllic than dramatic:

Notice the last phrase. So artless-seeming, it yet rounds off the
tune to perfection with its unexpected rise to the D. It suspends
the tune in mid-air, so to speak, for the lovely G major chord
from which springs a second theme, in that key. If the first theme
is a country song, then the second (introduced by the flute) is
evidently a contribution by the wayside birds:

The piccolo sustains the flute's last note, and now some subdued
bustling begins on the strings and woodwind, with this idea

 hurrying the movement along to an outburst on a D

major chord. The cellos and violas immediately, in rich thirds,
take hold of part of the opening tune:

Fig.3 Cellos & Violas

which develops with new rhythmic figures in the wind and
brings us to the first landmark in G major, for the whole orchestra
to take hold of the flute tune. Immediately then the bass drops a
semitone; the last three notes are echoed down the orchestra and
in most expressive way finished up by the violas, playing in sixths.
A very quiet section on the strings, in four-part harmony,
modulating through A minor, brings us to B minor. Here
Dvořák settles down to one of his moods of cheerful song and

easy, swinging movement for the second subject, which is given
to woodwind over flowing triplets in the strings:

The swing of the rhythm is delicious, and always there is
bustling movement. The 1st and 2nd violins then take over from
the wind, and the triplets become more boisterous, with the
basses pounding away. After a climax a new tune comes on flute
and clarinet:

repeated fortissimo by the whole orchestra and rounded off by
the brass returning to the significant bars of the first tune (Fig. 3).
A long diminuendo brings the exposition to an end.

The development opens with the original cello tune. The key
is G minor again, and it is as though Dvořák was thinking of
repeating the exposition, and then changed his mind. The flute
follows on as before, and discusses his last phrase:

with the oboe. As before, the violas—forsaken by cellos but
befriended by clarinets—launch out with part of the main theme
(Fig. 3), and now develop it at greater length and with some
embellishment. It is repeated by oboes amid new, lovely surroundings, and Dvořák therewith prepares for the central climax

of the movement. This begins with a fugato on a quickened form
of Fig. 3:

The whole orchestra eventually lays hold of the bar with the
four quavers and hammers them out on a chord of the diminished
seventh, the horns and brass blaring through the gaps between
the chords with the first three notes of the fugato subject. The
full climax crashes on an unexpected E minor chord, and the
power of the orchestra is exultantly displayed for about thirty-
five bars of intense vigour, while all the main themes of the
movement are brought in, the initial cello tune coming last on
trumpets. The recapitulation follows, with much beauty of new
orchestration.

The slow movement is an adagio in C minor and major;
and the moods are alternately pensive and joyous. For a time the
composer is impressed by the seriousness of life; then comes an
outburst of high spirits. The serious portions are largely built on
a dirge with this phrase as its motif:

The figure is repeated twice in a descending sequence, and the
sentence is finished by three bars of funeral-march-like steps:

The clarinets, in their darkest clothes, then wail a variation of
the dirge:

At the end of this section the violins repeat the little sobbing figures of the flutes (Fig. 10) in a wonderfully poignant harmony. As the music seems to be fading away the woodwind and horns burst in fortissimo with the original motif of the dirge, punctuated with a violent form of the flute figure on the strings. Twice they exclaim and then, as if with the sudden fall of a curtain after a dark scene, flute and oboe bring comfort by means of a subtle alteration of the dirge motif itself, extending it with a phrase of entrancing tenderness:

At this point the composer escapes from the funereal mood, and the little triplet figure of the dirge associated with slow, measured tread is used by the basses to lead us into an entirely different scene. With the use merely of queer little short chords on the horns and this little triplet on the basses, Dvořák with magical skill makes a transition to a mood of sparkling joy.

This middle section of the movement, which is in C major, contains some fascinating music, and the scoring deserves to be analysed in detail. A tune of joyous, lyrical inspiration, for flute and oboe:

springs from a scintillating background, made out of pizzicato arpeggios on the lower strings, rapid descending scales on the 1st and 2nd violins, and quaint little 'ponk-ponk' chords on the horns and lower woodwind.

Then a violin solo gracefully takes the wand from the flute and oboe, while the woodwind breaks into the flashing colours of the strings, and the violas, in quick pizzicato chords, give the effect of a mellow guitar in the bass. Such wonderful lightness and joyous singing affect the whole orchestra, and after the solo violin has finished with an unusual little cadenza, everyone joins in a fine song of gladness.

But now the sun is overclouded, and pensiveness returns, with the dirge (Fig. 8) fully in evidence. The horns enter dramatically over a mysterious tremolando background for the strings, and the next section is a far more powerful picture than we had at the beginning. Passionate crescendos and explosive chords modulating through various keys culminate in B minor, for the woodwind to make a clamour with the timpani. They hammer out the triplet figure of the dirge in an extended form, which is finally carried down the orchestra from piccolo to double basses and turned into three slow quavers. Now again the sun breaks out, but before the end of the movement there is a powerful return of the funeral march in F minor. The music closes in great simplicity, with the original little tearful motif of the flutes (in Fig. 10), now in C major, fading away on the violins and echoed by the brass.

The Scherzo begins in G minor and ends in G major. Its tempo-direction is one that was a favourite with Brahms, 'Allegretto grazioso.' The movement is delicious in its grace and enchanting in appeal. The composer gives us here the same intimate feeling of delight as in his chamber music, with the enhancement of the myriad colours of the orchestra. The scoring is exquisite.

The charming principal theme is given to the 1st violins:

It is repeated with simple embellishment, and then a greatly contrasted idea, almost harsh, breaks in on the woodwind:

Dvořák skilfully softens this new mood, and in leading us back to the principal theme interposes a delicious little feathery link of four bars in the strings, in this style:

Then back again to the theme, but with considerably more colour and movement in its scoring. Fig. 14 returns, in G major this time. Dvořák softens the mood again, and uses another little link, in the style of Fig. 15, but now in a single arpeggio line throughout the score:

The key is now decidedly G major; and the Trio, of a charm that only Dvořák could conjure up, opens with this quasi-folksong, played in unison by flute and oboe (the accompaniment is on the strings, with a magical rhythmic tap on the timpani every alternate bar):

The second idea is a brightly glowing version of this tune. It expands to a rich climax. When the first theme returns it is with added scoring. The violas have this counter-subject:

—one of those tunes (eventually going right up to top D) which gladden the heart of the most melancholy player.

The music gradually becomes attenuated until the key settles into G minor and the 1st violins run into their original scherzo tune again. After the usual repetition Dvořák proceeds to a coda—a joyous dance with this new variation of the Trio theme in G major:

The Finale is announced by a fanfare on the trumpet, like a summons to a pageant. The cellos are given the principal tune, this time a graceful dance:

All this last movement may be said to resemble a set of Slavonic dances, linked up by various episodes and contrasted themes. The flute, for instance, has a lovely episode:

and this is followed by an orchestral riot typical of Dvořák's manner in his dance-rhapsodies. Many themes appear in the course of the movement. This one, in C minor, of heavy solidity, is one of the most important, in particular the rhythm of its first two bars:

The composer develops this at some length; a climax is built up, and the trumpets blow their opening fanfare again with more elaborate treatment. The music dies away for the cellos to return to their own particular dance. This, however, takes a new turning, and now the flute can be heard as if practising for 'William Tell' over a rather dull tune on violas and bassoons:

Fig.23 Violas & Bassoons
espress.

The mood is now one of quiet reflection, and an expressive cadence on the violins and bassoons in octaves provides the dominant chord for Dvořák's favourite flute and oboe mixture, to close the movement proper in a lovely whispering dialogue with the violins. On the last bar of this, the composer restrains himself from lifting the flute and oboe to the expected note, and simply sustains the D, with charming effect. The end is the general rough-and-tumble, brilliantly coloured, of a Slavonic dance. There is no denying that this is a light-weight movement. But the symphony as a whole is one for which the world will bless Dvořák for generations to come.

PART III

XV

BERLIOZ
1803–1869

SINGULAR is the case of Hector Berlioz. No more to-day than a hundred years ago is the world of music at one in its appreciation of his genius. That Berlioz was a man of genius is as much as the various schools of opinion have in common. How far are the shortcomings of his style and imperfections of his achievement made up for by his qualities, the grandeur of his conceptions, the captivating effect of certain unquestionable successes, and the radiant sound of his orchestra? It is a question on which musicians are capable of quarrelling to-day as they can about no other historical figure. Berlioz would not be altogether displeased if he could overhear some of the twentieth-century disputes that have raged around his name. It would disappoint him, no doubt, to find that his position was not unanimously allowed among the great masters; but still to be so much talked about!—that would gratify him. He was a strange character, to whom loftiness cannot be denied. His aims, if at times more sensational than sublime, were far from being ignoble. But he had a craving for notoriety which to unsympathetic eyes presented him in the light almost of an adventurer. His triumph, however incomplete, has been to keep himself in the public view.

Asked to say who was the greatest French poet, a celebrated critic gave the answer: "Victor Hugo—alas!" French musicians give a similar answer to the question, Who is the greatest French composer?—"Berlioz, alas!" His scope, his impulse, his originality make him look a giant alongside all the others, though those others include so many with gifts of technique and taste such as he never had. The French are keenly disappointed that their great man should have lacked so many of the national qualities. His three operas remarkably lack any theatrical sense. Of a great French artist the first things to be expected are that his workmanship should be accomplished, his matter plastic and his taste fine. Berlioz was awkward, he was a stiff composer; he was not master of a plastic harmony, and his forms are inferior to his ideas and impulse. In this respect Berlioz is the opposite of Liszt, whose ideas were inferior to his forms. There is no mystery about Berlioz, as is sometimes thought. The problem is not obscure. Our appreciation depends on a personal factor—it depends on how much one can forgive or overlook for the sake of the positive qualities of this music, its superb spirit, its largeness, and the clear brilliancy of its colouring.

Generally speaking, Berlioz is not a composer beloved of other composers, but rather of conductors. Debussy, who could be very mordant, said of him: "He fastens romantic curls to old wigs." He cruelly called him "the favourite musician of those unversed in music." He likened Berlioz's music to petals dried between the pages of a book. He said: "His genius found bitter pleasure in airing its longings in an artificial-flower shop." 'Les Troyens' he condemned as faulty in proportions and wearisome in effect. "A monster—not a musician at all," he went so outrageously far as to say of his great compatriot, "he creates the illusion of music by means borrowed from literature and painting."

Nor was Ravel a Berliozian. He once said: "Berlioz is the worst musician of all the great musical geniuses. He had astounding genius—and could not harmonize a simple waltz correctly." ★ Mendelssohn called Berlioz "a caricature without a shadow of talent." Chopin compared the 'Benvenuto Cellini' overture to an enema, and said that such music as the Fantastic Symphony was good enough reason for breaking off friendship with the composer.†

Berlioz has, on the other hand, been all along the conductor's composer. Hallé, Mottl and Weingartner, Hamilton Harty and Beecham—such are the names of some who have stood up for

★ In a conversation recorded by R. Capell.

† Berlioz for his part dismissed Chopin with the remark, "He was dying all his life."

him against his detractors. And he has won the sympathy of considerable critics—in England, in our own times, Ernest Newman,
Cecil Gray and Walter Turner. Newman has combined devotion
to both Wagner and Berlioz, while Turner set Berlioz on a
pedestal rather as a sort of anti-Wagner. "The greatest creative
force in music since the death of Beethoven," so Turner called
him; and said of 'Les Troyens,' "the greatest opera that has ever
been written." Those who give truncated performances of
'Roméo et Juliette' he called "just blackguards"; and when
there was talk of a production of 'Les Troyens' in London he
wrote:

> "I hope, if there is any attempt to present us with a mutilated
> version of Berlioz's work at Covent Garden, that there will be
> young artists in the auditorium who will tear the house to
> pieces in their spontaneous and righteous rage."

Why have there been tides, ebbing and flowing, of Berliozian-
ism? The tide came in, so far as England was concerned, in the
1880s and again about twenty years ago. Berlioz's insufficiency
causes an ebb, and then the necessity for Berlioz brings about its
flood. The necessity is, in a word, the necessity for an anti-Wagner.
Berlioz and Wagner can stand as representatives of the two influences that make us, in England, what we are. Our sentimental
allegiance is Germanic, our intellectual allegiance Latin.

Only post-Beethovenian music is here in question. Music until
Beethoven was, practically speaking, European. But after
Beethoven music by Germans became peculiarly German,
brimming with sentiment. This, up to a point, suits us well. We
all love Schubert, Schumann, Brahms and Wolf; we wallow in
Wagner. Yes—but we wallow in our own way. The English like
Wagner's sound and sentiment, but care nothing for his librettos
as such and cannot bear his theoretical writings. Also, after a
surfeit, they can do with a change. That, the Germans would say,
is not serious Wagnerianism. Germans, who swallow it all—
naturally, for it is their heritage—have been known to express
resentment, in a Bayreuth coffee-house, at an English suggestion
on these lines: "Why make such efforts to be over-serious about

Wagner? The sound is lovely, as lovely as the sound of 'The Faery Queene.' But we do not try to make out the subject of 'The Faery Queene' to be important, so why do so with 'The Ring' and 'Parsifal'?"

At Bayreuth that was put down as English flippancy. Yet who, apart from the Germans themselves, used to get as much pleasure out of Bayreuth as the English? We wallowed there—and after a fortnight of it, bought a volume of Stendhal to read in the train on the way home. A fortnight in the warm Wagnerian waters, and then we escape into a clearer, drier air! That simple holiday experience illustrates the double influence and resource of which history and geography have made us heirs, us Europeans detached from Europe.

Berlioz is the musical equivalent of that volume of Stendhal which brought refreshment after the orgy of Wagnerian sentiment—Berlioz who was, in Walter Turner's words, "a free, grown-up man," and whose music ". . . is never erotic, dubious or pathological, but always fresh, direct and impassioned." Nothing else in the whole history of music is so lamentable as the fact that Berlioz's genius was only partially realized in his work, for no music is more badly needed than that of the Berlioz that might have been if the circumstances of his early life had been more favourable to his development.

The tale of his young years has often been told—most brilliantly by himself, though with the facts often altered by his lively taste for autobiographical fiction. Berlioz's bent for music was an anomaly in his family. His father, a country physician, intended that he should follow his own profession. Berlioz needed all his strength of will to break away. When he took to music seriously he was twenty. What meets the eye is that Berlioz did not learn the language of music as a child, and secondly that, even when he escaped from his medical studies, his musical education was unfortunately conducted. Music in the 1820s was in a poor way in Paris, as in London. The teaching at the Conservatoire was not very intelligent, and there was in Berlioz an arrogance that made him fail to get the most out of it. The age was that of the new French romanticism; and, although Berlioz as a musician was

DVOŘÁK

BERLIOZ

anything but a revolutionary—he disdainfully held aloof from the technique of musical romanticism—he was a romantic in his faith in his genius and in his assumption that sheer Byronian ambition would see him successfully through enormous undertakings for which he was technically ill-equipped. There was, in fact, a good deal of Byron about Berlioz.

His life was unhappy. It is easy to say that this was his own fault; but not so easy to be sure that that is true. His marriage with poor Harriet Smithson, the charming Ophelia of an English theatrical company that visited Paris at the dawn of the romantic revival, was above all a disaster for her. Typical of Berlioz was the recklessness of his passion and the extravagant importance he gave to the creature of his imagination—for that, and not the real Harriet, was the object of his love. When Harriet turned out to be not the figment of his fancy but an ordinary woman he no longer had any use for her. If she wanted revenge fate granted it to her in delivering Berlioz into the clutches of a harpy—Marie Récio, who became his second wife. There is a passage in one of Saint-Saëns's essays which will be new to most English readers:

"Berlioz was unhappy by force of his ingenuity in creating sufferings for himself, in aiming at the impossible and willing it in spite of everything. He harboured the wrong idea—one which, thanks to him, has been disseminated over the world—namely, that the composer's will should not reckon with material obstacles. He refused to recognize that the musician is not in the same position as the painter, who at his own sweet will disposes of inert matter on his canvas, while the musician has to take into account the fatigue of his executants and their varying degrees of skill. In his youth Berlioz required of orchestras that were far inferior to those of to-day truly superhuman efforts. If, in any new and original music, there are bound to be difficulties impossible to avoid, others there are which may be spared the performers without detriment to the work. But Berlioz took no such consideration into account. I have seen him rehearsing a single work twenty or thirty times, tearing his hair and smashing batons and desks, without getting the desired result. The poor players were doing what they could, but the task was beyond them. It took time for our

6

orchestras to become more competent and for Berlioz's music to reach the public ear." *

Saint-Saëns also tells an anecdote illustrating Berlioz's strange ignorance of the music of the past:

"I remember vividly his astonishment and delight at hearing a choral piece by J. S. Bach, to which I once introduced him. That the great Sebastian had written such things was something he could not get over, and he confessed to me that he had always taken him to have been a kind of gigantic schoolmaster, a manufacturer of fugues full of learning but void of charm and poetry. The truth is, he knew nothing about him."

It is a pity that Berlioz did not get on with Cherubini, director of the Paris Conservatoire in his student days. Cherubini was a fine musician, and Berlioz's career might have been rather different if there had been an understanding between the two. But the old man was rigid and the young one arrogant and impatient. That Berlioz acquired so much technique as he did is wonderful enough. His teachers were the academic Reicha, whom he scoffed at as "a mathematician," and the sympathetic, eccentric Lesueur, himself a self-taught musician, rather like Berlioz in many ways, who had little to give the younger man save encouragement.

In truth Berlioz's real teachers were the composers who took his fancy, namely, Gluck, Spontini and Weber. Only later did he become aware of Beethoven, in 1828, when he was twenty-five —and it was a very imperfect awareness. Gluck was the master who determined him, a medical student of eighteen, to become a musician; the work was 'Iphigenia in Tauris.' Before his twentieth birthday he had composed an oratorio, an imitation of Lesueur, 'The Crossing of the Red Sea,' which was actually rehearsed, though not performed, at St. Roch's, Paris. In the next year he began a Mass, some of the music of which was to be used in the famous Requiem of 1837.

Crazy in the eyes of academic musicians must have seemed the enterprises of the young amateurish student those years—an

* *Portraits et Souvenirs.*

opera, 'Les Francs-Juges' when he was twenty-two, 'Eight Scenes from Faust' when he was twenty-four. He had by then failed twice to obtain the Prix de Rome, but he published the 'Faust.' There was something sublime from the first in his self-confidence. As a lad of fifteen, ignorant of the ABC of music, he had thought his compositions deserving of publication. At twenty-six, he composed the Fantastic Symphony. In Germany Schumann recognized the young Berlioz with clairvoyance, but academic Germany, as represented by Zelter, was as unsympathetic as any pedant in Paris. Goethe, to whom Berlioz sent his 'Eight Scenes from Faust' (the nucleus of the famous 'Damnation'), referred the work to Zelter for an opinion, and the latter was not agreeably impressed, reporting that the young Frenchman's score consisted of

"noisy expectorations, croakings, vomitings, the excrescence and residue of miscarriages, the result of hideous incest."

An adverse report, in fact; and Goethe did not even acknowledge the receipt of the score. It is easier now than then to take, with Romain Rolland, a sympathetic view of Berlioz's frustrated efforts and disappointments, yet an effort should be made to put oneself in the place of an ordinary professional musician of the time and fancy what impression would have been made upon one by this ebullient, red-headed Berlioz, who disdained all the lessons of the schools and behaved as though inspiration were the beginning and end of art. But on balance our sympathies must be with Berlioz, when we read of some of the duffers who represented academic eminence in his time. There was Narcisse Girard, for instance. Conductor at the Paris Opera and at the Conservatoire concerts, Girard objected to the use of trombones in symphonic music, and when he was reminded that Beethoven had introduced them into his Fifth and Ninth Symphonies, expressed the opinion that the music would have been better without them.

One of Berlioz's singularities has yet to be mentioned: he played no instrument except the guitar and flute. He became a remarkable conductor, but no other composer has been so little

of an instrumentalist. The fact accounts for some of the peculiarities of his music, which put it apart from all the compositions
of an age when most music derived from the practice of the
piano. It was the age of enharmony, yet no one was less enhar-
monic than Berlioz. When we read his disparaging critique of
the prelude of 'Tristan and Isolde' it is hard to say whether the
prompting spirit is incomprehension or distaste. The verdict,
anyhow, might almost have been that of a musician of the
eighteenth century.

The fluid enharmony of nineteenth-century music from
Schubert and Chopin to Wagner (and thence to its disintegration
in Schoenberg) derives from the all-conquering influence which
piano-playing wielded in the minds of musicians. The octave has
only twelve notes! The sharps and flats of diminished sevenths
and augmented sixths are interchangeably sharps or flats! The
overwhelming flood of enharmony could not have come about
without equally tempered keyboard instruments. In Schubert it
is still fresh and limpid. Becoming more prevalent, it accounts for
the slumberous and dreamy effect of Wagner's music, in which
(in his mature style) anything may merge into anything else without notice. The end of an epoch we see in the total liquefying of
all forms in the music of the Schoenbergians. It is regrettable that
we cannot know what Berlioz would have said about Schoenberg's Op. 11, for he wielded a telling pen. His remarks would
assuredly have made those which Zelter passed upon his 'Faust'
seem bland. What may be summarily called 'harmony in the
melting-pot' was detestable to him; and one reason for the
individuality of his music is the almost archaic reserve of his
modulatory style, so stiff and clear. If personal temperament had
something to do with this, so had the chance of circumstances.
Had there been a piano at Dr. Berlioz's house at La Côte-Saint-
André in 1816 all might have been different. One of the most
appreciative of Berlioz's English critics, T. S. Wotton, has
plausibly argued that his curiously primitive or anachronistic
harmonic practice derived from his playing the guitar as a lad.

A word has been said about Berlioz's pen. He earned a good
part of his living, during most of his life, as a music critic. He

grumbled pretty freely about this, and the more sentimental biographers take him literally (always a mistake with Berlioz), expending themselves in commiseration with his servitude. There is a good deal of nonsense in all this. Berlioz began his long series of articles with an extravagant style and much false eloquence, but every year he improved and there is no better reading in all the prose of the great musicians (it is incomparably better than Wagner's or Liszt's) than his later journalism. The task could not have been so well done if Berlioz had not, on the whole, enjoyed it. He was paid £4 an article by the *Journal des Débats*, and this was handsome by the standard of the time. It is curious that a complete collection has never been made. And typical, too, of the treatment by the French of their great musician is the fact that there has been no adequate publication of his letters, though several more or less scrappy volumes have appeared. Like any other composer who criticizes his contemporaries, Berlioz felt himself hampered by personal considerations and often fell short of candour, but there is always something of interest in his fluent, vivacious *feuilletons*. A moral censor cannot always applaud. Berlioz was nothing more than a blackmailer when one or other of his wives, Harriet at one time and Marie at another, wanted an engagement at a theatre. The shameless pressure he, as a journalist, exerted upon managers is not calculated to win him respect, and the flaw in his character that this betrays may be not unrelated to the inequalities of his work as an artist.

Those brilliant journalists of one hundred years or so ago were no doubt abler writers than the twentieth century knows, but were hardly scrupulous. Heine blackmailed Meyerbeer and tried to blackmail Liszt. Meyerbeer had most of the Paris press in his pay, but Heine's extortions were too much for him. Did Berlioz blackmail Paganini or was the famous present of 20,000 francs extorted from him by Berlioz's newspaper friends, such as the all-powerful Jules Janin? It is a pity that Berlioz's memoirs should not be the truth; but readers of concert programme-notes must be warned that the story—a hundred times repeated by writers who have accepted the memoirs at their face-value—the story of the composition of 'Harold in Italy,' Berlioz's second symphony (so called), is largely a romance, as he tells it.

Paganini's avarice was almost as celebrated as his virtuosity, and the newspapers attacked him for it with a virulence inconceivable in our days of anodyne journalism. The truth of the shady business cannot be exactly known, but the curious should read what Adolphe Boschot had to say in his searching *Life* of Berlioz. In 1834 Paganini was at the height of his fame, earning fabulous money, and Berlioz was in desperate straits. Boschot suggests that the commission from Paganini to write a viola concerto was Berlioz's own bright idea, imposed on the virtuoso, and that the gift later, in 1838, of £800 was an extortion. Early in 1834 the *Gazette Musicale*, for which Berlioz was writing, announced his composition of a 'dramatic fantasy,' 'Mary Stuart's Last Moments,' for orchestra, chorus and solo viola, and added that the solo would be played by Paganini, "who had asked Berlioz for the composition." The truth seems to be that this was Berlioz's way of forcing Paganini's hand. He had determined to associate 'the infernal fiddler' with his music, and announced his wish as a fact.

Having announced the work, he had to do something about composing it. Berlioz was more ready with conceptions than musical ideas. For 'Mary Stuart' he had recourse to his 'Rob Roy' overture, from which he adapted two long extracts for the new work, scrapping the rest. There were to have been two movements. In the spring of 1834 Berlioz desired to add two more and to change the protagonist from Mary Queen of Scots to Byron's Childe Harold. Why Harold? None of the scenes depicted in Berlioz's symphony belongs to Byron's poem. But Berlioz has given us the clue—he saw himself in Harold, "who," he wrote,

"recognized himself as the man the least fitted to live in the human herd. He was too different, too incapable of accommodating his thoughts to those of others, too much cut off in his independence, and able to breathe only outside mankind."

The pensiveness of the doomed queen easily became the lordly misanthrope's moodiness, and—an inspiration!—Byron-Berlioz-Harold was represented by a viola solo. 'Harold in Italy' is not a concerto in the ordinary sense, any more than it is a symphony. The resources of the viola are not exploited, but the work is a classic in which every note is heard. There is a truly Berliozian experiment in orchestration in the slow movement ('Pilgrims' March'), where the viola plays an endless-seeming series of scratchy arpeggios, *sul ponticello*, producing a queer, whistling sound. The idea comes off and is most arresting.

'Harold' was finished and signed at Montmartre on June 22, 1834, but was to be much worked over, as was Berlioz's way, later on. Paganini, back in Paris in the autumn, found himself the victim of a ferocious newspaper agitation. Berlioz himself railed at him for the modesty of his Paris lodging—the wealthy Paganini who owned a palace at Genoa! There is no evidence that Paganini was even shown the score of 'Harold in Italy,' which he, of course, did not play. The first soloist in 'Harold' (November 23, 1834) was Chrétien Urhan, whom Berlioz had probably had in mind from the first. Urhan, an old friend, was the violist of the Baillot Quartet, and to him Berlioz had dedicated his 'Ballet des Ombres' of 1829. Urhan was a mystic and a puritan. He obtained a special dispensation from the Archbishop of Paris to play in the Opera orchestra, where he was careful to turn his back towards the girls of the ballet.

And Paganini's present? At the end of 1838 Berlioz's fortunes were at low water. 'Benvenuto Cellini' had failed at the Opera, in spite of all the composer's friends could do for it in the newspapers. It is a mistake to imagine that Berlioz had no supporters. His partisans were passionate and voluble; but the public could not be won. On a famous day, December 16, 1838, Berlioz conducted at the Conservatoire his 'Harold' and the Fantastic Symphony. Paganini was there, and at the end went to the platform and dramatically kneeled before the composer. Two days later came the violinist's letter, acclaiming him as Beethoven's successor and offering him a present of £800. Sensation in Paris! The money saved Berlioz from cruel embarrassments. Magical was the effect in the press. The word of order went round that the attacks on Paganini were to cease. Janin declared: "Paganini henceforth shall be inviolable!" Liszt, long afterwards, used to say that Paganini had received a hint from Janin to the effect that such a present would soften the tone of the newspapers. The truth of the affair is obscure, but is certainly not so simple as the legend.

There are four symphonies by Berlioz, not one of which is at all a classic symphony. The third of these, however unequal, contains the best music; it is that singular collection of seven movements, with soloists and chorus, 'Romeo and Juliet.' Herein is some of the finest music he ever wrote. Poor Berlioz! Only the delicious scherzo, 'Queen Mab,' has retained a place in ordinary repertories. Entrancing in its dazzling lightness and breathless movement, it is a test of an orchestra's virtuosity. 'Romeo,' as a whole, is an unwieldy work, and the style of some of the pompous movements belongs to the opera house rather than the concert hall. Yet who knows? There may yet be a future for the work. As much is hardly to be expected for the 'Funereal and Triumphal Symphony' of 1840, a pompous and rather empty occasional composition for military band and chorus, which was commissioned by the French government for the tenth anniversary of the 1830 Revolution. Berlioz added string parts for the second version, performed in the same year.

XVI

BERLIOZ'S FANTASTIC
SYMPHONY

THE Fantastic Symphony is a memorial of Berlioz's first infatuation for poor Harriet Smithson. We have said that he first saw her on the stage when he was a student of twenty-three. He had already composed the 'Eight Scenes from Faust' when, in January 1830, just after he had turned twenty-six, he applied his mind to "a huge instrumental composition," which was to figure at a concert where he should make his name. Let us remember that he had not yet met Harriet, nor was he to do so for nearly three more years (December 1832), that is to say, more than five years after he had first succumbed to the charm of her performances as Ophelia and Juliet. In the meantime had come his Roman period and his betrothal to the fickle 'Ariel' (Camille Moke).

There were, in fact, two distinct infatuations with Harriet—the first, the more fanciful, which inspired the symphony, and the second, after his return from Italy, which ended in marriage. There are fashions in emotion as in the shape of hats. Berlioz's infatuation was in keeping with the fashion of the day. How fanciful it was, not to say affected, is seen from the fact that the chance word of a gossip uttered while Berlioz was at work on his symphony—a reflection on Harriet's chastity, which seems to have been entirely without substance—turned his adoration into furious contempt in an instant. The unknown woman whom at one moment he regarded as an unattainable angel he was, at the next, calling a harlot. The absurdity had its bearing on the symphony. Or perhaps did Berlioz not really believe the slander? What really mattered was that it gave him an idea for the finale of his symphony: an atrocious vision of the beloved prostituting herself in the orgy of a Walpurgis night.

6*

The Fantastic is a programme-symphony. Nothing that Berlioz did of any account was without a literary programme. He belonged to a culture in which the music of the theatre was virtually the only music, and he knew at the time practically nothing about the Viennese symphonies. In July 1828 Berlioz attempted to win the award of the Prix de Rome. 'Herminie' was the title of a cantata-text to be set to music by the competitors. (The subject came from Tasso.) The principal theme he then found for this heroine he adopted for his symphony. It is the famous *idée fixe* which, representing the beloved and recurring in each movement of the symphony, is the principal factor of unity in the work. We have said that Berlioz was not fertile in musical ideas, and the fourth and fifth movements of the symphony were taken over from earlier compositions. The concert was to be given on May 23, and the time was not long. In later years the Fantastic Symphony was to be much touched up, but essentially the work we know belongs to January–April 1830. It was the time of Hugo's 'Hernani,' the trumpet-call of French romanticism (February 25, 1830). The notoriety that that sounding tragedy obtained had a good deal to do with the hasty composition of the Fantastic. What Victor achieved in one art, could not Hector rival in another? As Boschot has said, Berlioz, in search of a subject, hatched the idea of a musical autobiography. But so little had happened to him! He had only fallen for the romantic appearance of an actress whom he had never met. His imagination, however, was lively.

"Reveries and passions"—that was subject enough for one movement. A ball, where a glimpse is caught of the beloved in the whirl of the waltz—there was the scherzo. A pastoral adagio, with thoughts of the beloved occurring to the lover as he wanders at the falling of day across quiet fields—a third movement! Yes; and what then? Time is running short. We do not know for certain that the slander on Harriet's fame was ever in reality uttered. What we do know is that, afflicted with toothache that winter, Berlioz was using laudanum to stay the pain. At the same time, Harriet's star was declining in the theatrical world; she, the acclaimed Ophelia, was compelled to accept humiliatingly inferior roles. Well, what then? Berlioz is writing a musical novel, and something striking is due to happen. What if the heroine should fall from purity and the outraged hero slay her? Good! And then the hero must pay the penalty of murder. A march to the guillotine! But more romantic will it be if this is not a crime in vulgar reality but a morphinomaniac's nightmare. Better and better! The novel then need not stop with an execution, but can be continued with further picturesque hallucinations, the more so since Berlioz has in his drawer the music of a Faustian Walpurgis night.

We have seen that time was running short, and after the composition of the third movement it was necessary to see what there was in the drawers of his desk. A march was wanted; and lo! there a march was—one composed for his opera 'Les Francs-Juges.' The *idée fixe* had only to be attached or interpolated, and it was the morphinomaniacal murderer's death-march. Two years before this Berlioz had read Nerval's translation of Goethe's 'Faust' (Part I) with wild excitement. The famous 'Eight Scenes' was the result, and also a projected ballet. There is no Walpurgis night in the 'Eight Scenes,' but here it is in the Fantastic Symphony, with its dance of witches, parody of the 'Dies Irae' and the appearance of the beloved amidst a riot of harlotry. The piece in the drawer lacked only the last of these features. The final note of the Fantastic was written on April 16, 1830. A month later rehearsals began.

Berlioz, never careful to distinguish between fact and fancy, seems by then to have come to the point of believing his symphonic romance of Harriet's degradation. At any rate, he showed no sign of compassion for his victim—for victim she was. Berlioz had flaunted his passion for Harriet and then his contempt. Athirst for notoriety, he had done all he could to make it known that here was a symphony *à clef*, and it was everybody's secret that the finale of the symphony was an exposure of the actress. The first performance was postponed until December 5. An extraordinary day! The concert—which was a success—was in the afternoon, and the orchestral musicians hurried away after the long programme to be in time for the benefit performance which was being given at the Opera for the unfortunate Harriet whose alleged vices they had just been exposing in music. A few days later Berlioz and Camille Moke were betrothed. But Camille was to marry another, and Harriet, the harlot of the symphony, was to become Madame Berlioz.

Berlioz was back in Paris in the autumn of 1832, having—thanks to his Prix de Rome—wasted the best part of two years. Another extraordinary day was December 9, 1832, when the Fantastic Symphony was given again at the Conservatoire, and Harriet came to hear it. Boschot says:

"Miss Smithson came into a box near the platform, and there were eyes for none but her—the heroine of the symphony, tall, decorative, in the splendour of her full-blown beauty, the Irish tragedy-queen! Since her triumphs of 1827 she had passed into the thirties; and reverses of fortune, looming cares and the fatigue of the theatrical life lent her the charms of lassitude and melancholy.

"The cynosure of all eyes, the topic of conversations in which her private life and morals were crudely discussed; represented as a light-of-love in these very programmes that the audience had in their pockets, which described the fallen heroine as 'surrounded at the witches' sabbath by infamous beings, soiled by their caresses, smiling at her own debasement, dancing shamelessly, and shrieking like a Bacchante above the din of the orgy'; she, utterly compromised by this extravagant man, how could she be charmed and how not disgusted and nauseated? And people had the effrontery to tell her he was in love with her!"

A few days later they were introduced. Poor Ophelia! Poor Berlioz too—who was to pay for his confusion between the realm of fancy and of fact!

One generalization must be formulated before we come to the music in detail. Whatever were Berlioz's bizarre or diabolic intentions, the idiom of his music comes from no unearthly world but belongs to the opera-house of his time. This is a word of warning to the naïve listener who, having expected music as detached and original as Berlioz's own social behaviour, may be disappointed at finding the Fantastic Symphony to be composed of early-nineteenth-century ingredients. Berlioz's musical language, so far from being revolutionary, contained no innovation. He sometimes had an admirable idea and at other times fell back on conventional figures. On the other hand, the listener will be unfair who says that the Fantastic Symphony is hardly more than a suite arranged from some old-fashioned opera.

The different movements of the symphony are provided by Berlioz with tiresomely wordy and pretentious explanations, which he asks us to read as opera-goers read a libretto. Let us ignore these—or, at least, not read them too closely. They do the music an injustice. The preface to the first movement, for instance, with its eighteen-thirtyish account of the lovesick opium-eater's hallucinated state of mind has spoilt the symphony for many a listener, who has been led thereby to expect a different and altogether stranger music. Berlioz, for all his crazy behaviour, had a perfectly lucid mind.

The slow introduction (C minor) is long and includes some material that does not reappear in the body of the first movement. This introduction, so quick in establishing a mood, proclaims Berlioz as a born musician of the theatre. The woodwind triplets of the very first bar : *

and the long sigh of the second bar comes as near as may be to illustrating the first glimmer of consciousness after a deep sleep. On this sigh the 1st violins begin a soliloquy devoid of feeling at first, but, as thought begins to take shape, becoming more personal and coherent. Two little double-bass figures, pizzicato, suggest the reviving will. Then with the inconsequence of dreams, the tempo is quickened and the violins dash off into a helter-skelter. This is only another of the fleeting memories that for a moment light up a dark mind. Flutes and clarinets lapse into

* Berlioz did not mind doubled leading-notes.

melancholy again, and the dark and cloudy mood of the beginning returns in a long soliloquy. The first horn brings a new idea, still darkly coloured, but of more determined character:

Fig.2 Horn

The scoring is as telling as it is bare. At the entrance of this horn subject, which stands boldly in the foreground, the 1st violins, with little pinpoints of light, pick out measured arpeggios high in the treble. Basses and cellos hold a long pedal note, while clarinets and flutes intermittently sustain the barest chords, which a little figure in the 2nd violins indicates for each change of harmony:

Fig.3 2nd Violins

The introduction comes to an end after a big accumulation of sound, with the orchestra sustaining a long dominant chord. Characteristic of Berlioz are the dynamic directions of these two bars:

Fig.4 Strings

This is always an exciting moment in the orchestra, and it requires nerve to go pelting on to the end of that fortissimo and then suddenly to jam on the brakes.

The effect of this introduction depends entirely upon the conductor's imagination. One of the finest exponents of Berlioz's music, and of this symphony in particular, was Sir Hamilton Harty, who had the temperament that Berlioz himself would have wished for it. He had both daring and a good head. The

tempo of the opening Largo he took extremely slowly, and he
made the utmost of those early, hesitant thoughts in the violins.
"No expression or feeling, 1st violins! No vibrato! These are
only random thoughts that come into the mind. Use expression
later!" But when the 'più mosso' breaks in, he urged on the
violins to play with brilliance, at a tempo that seemed more than
usually fast. Ensemble is difficult between the 1st violin arpeggios
and the horn tune. These arpeggios Harty took very slowly.
"My dears, don't hurry! Hold these arpeggios back! You spoil
them if the tempo is not held."

Weingartner, who gave a monumental reading of the symphony, kept rigidly to Berlioz's marks and tempos. The work as
a whole sounded wonderful in his reading, but a lack of fever and
phantasy was felt in this introduction. The Fantastic Symphony
is music that gains from having a strongly imaginative mind in
control of the orchestra.

The Allegro opens, 'agitato ed appassionato assai,' with
explosive chords, complete with Berliozian echoes, but it is a
mere flash in the pan, for within three bars this force subsides.
An extreme pianissimo leaves the stage empty for a dramatic
entrance. Quite unaccompanied at first there comes in the *idée fixe*
—a long melody for violins and flute. Only at the seventh bar do
the lower strings begin a panting accompaniment. Naïve listeners
have often been surprised that the *idée fixe* is not sensuously passionate. It is something quite other. This fine melody of nearly
forty bars is superior to the pinchbeck programme. We are
reminded that Berlioz was not only a hothead with sensational
ambitions, but also a Virgilian. The slowly soaring *idée fixe*
belongs to the idyllic Berlioz of the finest scenes of his Virgilian
'Trojans.' The melody begins thus:

Fig.5 *Allegro agitato e appassionato e assai*
1st Violins & Flute

The second phrase of the melody climbs a tone higher. The
third phrase, yet another tone higher, we may recognize as the

source of the violins' soliloquy at the beginning of the introduction:

Fig. 6 1st Violins & Flute

The melody is concluded thus:

Fig. 7 Flute & Violin

The span of this melody, its nobility and expressive value, stamp Berlioz as a distinguished composer. The source of it is the spirit of Gluck's classic operas. As we have seen, it belonged originally to an operatic scena (for that is what 'Herminie,' the so-called cantata, was in fact). Like Gluck's best inspirations, it is a dramatic representation—a melody that depicts a heroine.

Nothing like a classical symphonic exposition must be expected. The woodwind has a subsidiary theme, nobly idyllic:

Fig. 8 Flute

This comes between two orchestral outbursts. There is no second subject, properly speaking, but if one must be found at all costs it may be the three-bar derivative of the *idée* in E minor, which, however, is continued by this codetta-phrase:

Fig. 9 Strings

Three statements of this—each louder than the last—and the remarkably short exposition is at an end. The repeat is usually observed.

The development, likewise, is unconventional, not to say

incoherent. It starts with a derivative of the *idée fixe*, which breaks into even notes as it works up the scale, becoming thus:

Fig.10
Lower Strings

There are two short references to the second subject, and the orchestra finds itself suddenly caught up in a melodramatic storm. The strings play chromatic scales with short, hacking bows, beginning softly and ending fortissimo, and at the top of each scale the woodwind utters a wail. How many times has this unfortunate passage been removed from its home to accompany a film of the Wild West or a blizzard in the Arctic!

There is a crash and a pause, and then, out of the silence, comes the 3rd horn, as if he were the sole survivor, to sustain a long D. The strings begin to whisper an accompaniment figure:

Fig.11
Violins
ppp

for the return of the whole of the *idée fixe*, in the key of G. A big crescendo and much excitement in the strings culminates in a climax of violently attacked and sustained chords, with the usual profusion of expression marks:

Fig.12
ff ———— *p   ff* ———— *p*

The cellos then begin to weave a more complicated texture, on the codetta-theme, taken up in imitations first by the violas, then by 2nd violins. The contrapuntal idea, however, is soon given up in favour of a splendid crescendo which shows Berlioz as Beethoven's pupil—if not in respect of technique, at any rate in the expression of a mounting tide of nobly impassioned feeling. A feature of this extended rhapsody is a new theme for solo oboe:

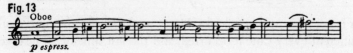

Fig.13
Oboe
p espress.

above a fine development of the *idée* by cellos and violas in imitative style. This leads to what we may call the recapitulation, since it is in C major—a brilliant restatement of the *idée fixe* with all the orchestra's flags out. With this the movement originally ended. But Berlioz's second thoughts were always to the good, and in his revision of the symphony he added a short coda, marked 'Religiosamente.' Instead of the original blatant finish, the music subsides into a series of slow-moving, organ-like chords. The simplicity of these two pages is primitive, but the effect, after the swelling rhetoric that has gone before, quite beautifully effective.

"At a ball he comes again upon the beloved, in the tumult of a brilliant festival" : thus the programme. In the music the bewitching waltz is more in evidence than the troubled soul, and Berlioz does not disguise the fact that his hero was enjoying himself at the party.

In this movement harps ("at least four harps," says Berlioz) add their soft glitter to the pretty scene. The orchestra is otherwise cut down to woodwind, four horns and strings. Berlioz's art is seen in his fine economy. He was never lavish for lavishness' sake. Sometimes he scored for gigantic forces. If so, it was because such was the sound he wanted; but he never gave his extras something to do just because they were there. His harp-writing says much for the technique of his executants. It is still considered to be difficult.

A prelude, full of elegant flourishes, establishes the rhythm and sets the dancers' feet itching. The occasion is one of some stateliness and yet not of stiffness. The violins begin the waltz;

Fig.14

It is not so simple as it looks. Harty used to make the tune sound different every time it occurred, and the last time of all he dwelt

effectively on the top note, played the next two separated notes
very short, and then slid into the 'a tempo.' The continuation
of the waltz is as follows :

Fig. 15

After a recurrence of the first strain there comes an extreme
pianissimo, and on a background of shimmering strings the *idée
fixe* appears again, in new guise but unmistakable. Flute and oboe
are given the theme, which they play across the waltz rhythm, and
it is as though our hero saw the beloved afar in the crowd without
being able to approach her. The rhythmic transformation of the
theme here was the starting-point of three-quarters of a century
of symphonic poems.

A crashing chord recalls wandering thoughts, and the waltz
resumes. The scoring becomes more brilliant and elaborate.
Before the coda comes another appearance of the *idée*. The ending
is Rossinian. Say what Berlioz would against Rossini, he could
not resist his influence here.

On a summer evening in the country our hero hears, in the
deeply peaceful air, two herdsmen who are calling together their
cattle, the one represented by the English horn, the other by the
oboe. The world is calm ; leaves rustle in the light breeze.
Thoughts of the beloved return, and with them forebodings. Is
she true or false? One of the herdsmen plays again his rustic
strain, but there is this time no answer from the other. The sun
sets, and far away sounds the roll of thunder. Solitude . . .
silence . . .

For his pastoral Adagio Berlioz brings in two sets of kettledrums and English horn. This last has a great part to play. There
is no cover for the least of his notes, and his life seems to hang on a
trustworthy reed. If this should fail him it is a calamity. The ordeal
is more severe for him than for his brother-herdsman the oboe,
who plays his answering part *lontano*, behind the platform. The

famous opening of the movement requires good stage-management. The distant oboe has to play a little sharp, and it requires alertness to obey the conductor's stick when seen through an inadequate peep-hole. A little later he has to mind his steps in returning to his place in the orchestra, or he will trip over a music-stand, to the destruction of the mood of the music. The beautifully poetic scene begins thus, with characteristic Berliozian pauses:

Berlioz's fondness for silences is proverbial—whenever there is an opportunity he places a rest instead of a note. The first breath of a zephyr comes from the violas, after the English horn's second phrase. It is a fast tremolando in pianissimo, with a rather dangerous expression mark—rinforzando—in the fourth bar. Harty used to permit only the slightest breeze to mark the harmony. Weingartner played it exactly as Berlioz directed—a gentle though sudden increase of the tone, which only gradually subsides. A gale warning, such as we have sometimes known, is out of the picture here.

The oboe gives a last faint response, and we arrive at the main theme of the movement. Flute and 1st violins play this simple but most expressive tune with only the barest suggestion of accompaniment every fourth bar or so:

The tune expands rhapsodically, bar after bar, until the sound is richly warm. It wanes again in a slowing tempo to a new subsidiary theme on the woodwind:

This works up to an emotional climax, but quickly subsides, leaving the strings quietly descending to two quiet bars which remind one of Beethoven's bird songs in the Pastoral Symphony.

Violas and cellos now set out on the main theme, richly colouring it with their sonorous tenor unison. The violins weave embroidery around the tune, to the chirping of the birds in the woodwind. When cellos and violas are at the height of their enjoyment there comes a dramatic change in the mood. A sudden pianissimo of anxiety and a succeeding passage of gathering intensity and power take us from the quiet pastoral air into the psychological drama again. Bassoons, cellos and basses, with tremendous power and superb style, declaim this foreboding passage:

As the sudden darkening of mood and ominous signs suggested, this is answered by a long-drawn-out vision of the *idée fixe* on the woodwind. All peace has vanished, and the old obsession returns to drive the hero to despair. The strings, after a series of stabs at the cello theme, rush up in a crescendo and accelerando to the climax of the movement—a long, sustained chord of the diminished seventh, held by the whole orchestra fortissimo. It is reiterated with fury, and these bars must be played with such tearing power that the decrescendo that follows must suggest an orchestra panting with exhaustion.

Woodwind, in a lovely, consoling phrase, restore tranquillity, and over the quietest possible pizzicato background on violas and 2nd violins the clarinet plays an intensely expressive and tender tune of much the same character as the main theme of the movement. It is a wonderful piece of lyrical writing, with simple but masterly scoring. The clarinet's song rises ecstatically as he climbs up to one of the top notes of his register and thence gradually subsides in a downward scale to the return of the main theme. This clarinet episode reveals Berlioz's mastery in writing for this (as for every) instrument, with intimate knowledge of its colours and its technique. When the *idée fixe* returns it is in a very calm mood.

We are near the end of the movement, and a wonderful end it is. Here is the Virgilian Berlioz, master of a peculiar sort of poetic music. To hear it again, after no matter how many times, is again to be seized with wonder. So simple the means, so deep the effect! All that happens is that the English horn utters his plaintive call once more, and in the pauses are heard the rumblings of the distant thunder. It is a marvellous example of the workings of Berlioz's musical imagination. The sound of the two sets of kettle-drums never ceases to be fearsome, while the poor English horn waits, and we wait with him—in vain—for the expected answer of the oboe. Lost and bereft, the solo raises its voice a little, then subsides, and the sinister drums sink to pianissimo on their obscure minor chord. This whole movement demands imaginative playing. The conductor must allow English horn and clarinet a large freedom, and the background cannot be too delicate. In humdrum hands the music is lost.

The programme of the March says: "He dreams that he has slain his beloved and, condemned to death, is on the way to execution. The procession moves on. . . . The *idée fixe* reappears a moment—a last thought of love, cut short by the executioner's blow." We have seen where the music originated. But it is no less effective for that, and this march has been known to drive audiences to frenzy. The additions to the score are two cornets, two tubas, two sets of timpani and extra percussion. The two timpani open the scene, ominously tapping the basic rhythm:

Fig. 20 *Allegretto non troppo*
Timpani

and increasing in power until there is the burst of an explosion. The flash of it reveals:

Fig. 21 Cellos & Basses

Berlioz plays with this theme, stirring it violently with an explosion or two. We come to the unique episode for bassoons. This is always entertaining to listen to inside the orchestra. Not only is it grimly humorous with its rattling, hollow sound, but when four bassoons are playing one also hears the quaint noise of the keys working, like a crowd of drilled typists. The first three bars only are quoted:

Fig. 22 4 Bassoons

Harty used to cut even the principal theme down to piano, so that the bassoons might have it their own way.

This leads straight into the second theme of the movement, the March itself, which breaks out on the full military band, with minor upheavals in the strings.

Fig. 23 Wind

In the original Schlesinger edition Berlioz placed a repeat sign for the whole of this first part to be played through again; but in later scores, and one which Weingartner himself edited, it is erased, and the March theme goes straight on to the second part. This begins with a linking-up passage only a few bars long, containing a distorted version of the first theme, and immediately the March returns. The military band is now reinforced by a vigorous arrangement of scoring in the strings. Precisely the same order of events occurs as before, but then a grand Berliozian firework display goes up. Strings in furious clamour accompany the first theme on trombones and tubas, with the woodwind shrieking over their heads the sinister drum figure. A crescendo builds up; the full orchestra blazes away at the same theme and then, with satanic humour, suddenly disappears to pianissimo. The movement abounds in these vicious outbursts and ghostly whispers. After what we may take as a yell from the crowd, the clarinet is suddenly left alone for the condemned man to have a last glimpse of his sweetheart's form, and then comes the catastrophe. The thud of the head as it falls under the guillotine is represented by the pizzicato of the strings. The movement ends with the utmost power that even Berlioz could wring from his huge orchestra—and no one before or since has surpassed him in that line.

In the fifth movement the hero dreams he is at a Witches' Sabbath, and there amid warlocks and monsters the beloved appears—demoralized in a grotesque version of the *idée fixe*. Bells toll; a parody of the ' Dies Irae ' is heard amid the orgy.

The scoring is for the same instruments as the March, with the addition of a peal of two bells. Shivering tremolando and ghostly whisperings chill the air. The tempo is larghetto, and the slower this is taken the more effective are the wind sounds. A grotesque tip-toe passage on the woodwind, descending to the lowest notes of the bassoons, must surely have influenced Elgar at that moment in 'Falstaff' when the poor old wretch tries to catch the King's eye and fails. The flutes play a distant rallying-call, with their last notes dropping an octave in glissando. The revels, of which one never tires in the orchestra, begin with the timpani tapping out a riding motif that is the rhythmic framework of the movement:

Fig.24 *Allegro*
Timpani

The 1st clarinet, very distant at first, plays the theme of the allegro, which is another version of the *idée fixe*:

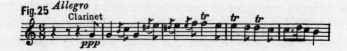

Fig.25 *Allegro*
Clarinet

So is the heroine transformed to a cackling witch with a bawdy
sense of humour. The trills and shakes add to the extravagant
caricature. This strident tune is greeted with a yell of delight
from the crowd of monsters. They welcome their novice and
urge her to further efforts, and she is only too pleased to respond
with all the comic skill that ever came out of an E flat clarinet.
This irrepressible instrument might have been made for the
playing of pranks, with its piercing tone. Bassoon joins in with
flapping skirts, and soon the whole crowd is whirling. Suddenly
the racket ceases, and fear drives them off until scarcely a sound
is audible. This frightened silence is shattered by the clang of a
C bell, which is hit as hard as possible with metal hammer, and is
answered by the other one, a fourth lower. An important theme
then appears on the obviously scared violas:

Fig. 26

It is only a portion of the theme that is coming later. Here it is
suddenly broken off short by a general clatter in the orchestra.
(Harty, by the way, did not use the G bell, but replaced it with
a heavy gong.) To the intermittent crash of the bells the two
tubas roar out a parody of the traditional tune for the 'Dies
Irae.' The burlesque idea needs brilliant playing for its realiza-
tion. The orchestra is not idle during this blasphemous duet, but
spends its time either guying the tubas' phrases in double time or
turning the 'Dies Irae' into a wanton dance, with the riding
rhythm. This episode ends with a shriek from most of the
orchestra, and the violas' motif enters again, quickly taken up by
other instruments until a tumult bursts into the witches' round
dance. Here Berlioz pulls a long nose at his counterpoint professor at the Conservatoire. The dance is fugal, with the following
as its principal subject (the violas' motif now completed):

Fig. 27

Three other features stand out in this fugue—the shout of laughter which generally greets the subject:

a counter-subject:

and a little figure that crackles all over the score:

It is a short-lived fugue. Instead of a development the general tone lessens considerably, the subject and counter-subject disappearing altogether. When they return again to join hands for another violent series of twirls, the round dance suddenly takes on another aspect, as if the hags, becoming exhausted, were resorting to their broomsticks. A quaint motif, which has already appeared once or twice, flaps into the music:

together with another version of the main subject of the dance:

Gradually the air clears; the creatures seem to disperse, and, with but a suggestion of the dance in the lower registers of the bassoon, cellos and horns are heard in the distance, still intoning the 'Dies Irae.' The night, however, is not over. Berlioz has only

cleared the air to start over again, and now he begins a fugato on
yet another variant of the round dance:

Fig. 33

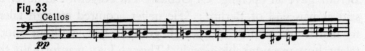

The air thickens again, and a great crescendo is piled up. At the
climax of this fugato Berlioz heads the score: "Dies Irae and
Round Dance together." The strings scratch at the dance theme,
whilst the full wind blare out the 'Dies Irae.' Scale figures rush
all over the orchestra, urging on the music. One particular passage
is too good to miss—it is so typical of Berlioz. The upper strings
are directed to play with the sticks of their bows one of the
rhythms of the round dance:

Fig. 34

obviously to depict clattering broomsticks, while the woodwind
play a final variation of the dance theme, putting a shake on
every accented note:

Fig. 35

The effect is uncanny in its bony rattle and fantastic antics. A
burst of brilliant virtuosity follows in the woodwind. From this
point grinding fortissimo chords gather all the ends together and
the music becomes furious. A last short reference to the 'Dies
Irae' on the tubas brings the orchestra to the coda, *più animato*, a
gorgeous boiling-up of the whole infernal region.

This finale is completely worthy of the symphony. It was a
feat, after the power and drive of the 4th movement, to avoid
anti-climax; but the finale is big enough to surpass it in
conception and brilliance of orchestration. And after it all
we come back to where we were at the beginning: the musical
world will never be at one in its estimate of Berlioz. On the one

hand there will always be disparagement like Debussy's—
extravagantly unfair, no doubt, but disparagement to which
Berlioz gave an opening. Of Debussy and Ravel it can never be
said as was said of Berlioz: "He never acquired enough talent
to match his genius" (Ernest Legouvé). But, without much
talent, how unmistakable a genius! Though Liszt was formally the
author of the symphonic poem Berlioz was the true inspiration of
all that line of music. His influence, great though it was in the
West, was greater still in Russia. We have omitted above to
mention that the Fantastic Symphony was dedicated to the
Emperor Nicholas I. The debt the Russian composers of the mid-
nineteenth-century owed him is hardly mentioned in the history
books, but it is flagrant. Berlioz was twice in Russia, in 1847 and
in 1867, and from the performances of his works he gave them
the young Russian school learnt its orchestration and its
vividness.

Berlioz's experiences in early-Victorian England were chequer-
ed but not altogether ineffective. A disgraceful Italian intrigue
wrecked "Benvenuto Cellini" at Covent Garden in 1853, but it
is pleasant to recall that a number of his London admirers collected 200 guineas for him as a solatium, a sum that was spent on
the engraving of the full score of "The Damnation of Faust."

XVII

FRANCK
1822–1890

THE Paris of the Second Empire was rich, gay and amusing, and
the period was one of brilliant achievements in French literature;
but the musical life was frivolous. Berlioz, scorned and neglected,
died, a tragically disappointed man. Such a composer as Adolphe
Adam was reckoned a person of importance. In those decades an
organist of Belgian extraction, named César Franck, had a name
among ecclesiastical musicians for his gift of improvisation, but
he was anything but a celebrity and earned a meagre living by
working hard as a music teacher.

Then came the Franco-Prussian war of 1870-71, with its
defeats—a blow to French pride, but, as it turned out, not
crippling and exhausting in the way of the wars of our more
disastrous century. Actually the shock seems to have been
salutary to the youth of the next decade, and a remarkable period
set in for French music. Not that the frivolity of Napoleon III's
Paris at once evaporated; but among a few ardent spirits—and,
after all, it is always a few ardent spirits who rule the course of
events—a new musical seriousness appeared, and a determination
to learn from the victorious nation on the other side of the Rhine.

Léon Vallas, in his Life of Vincent d'Indy,* says that Franck
was not quite so obscure a musician in the middle of the century
as d'Indy, who was to be his most enthusiastic and famous pupil,
made out in the widely read book† he wrote about his old master.
The fact remains that for the modest Franck it was one of the
surprises of his life when, in 1872, he was appointed organ professor at the Paris Conservatory. And more remarkable still is the

---

* Paris, 1946.
† Paris, 1906; London (translation by Rosa Newmarch), 1909.

fact that practically all the compositions by which Franck is remembered were written in the last two decades of his life, that is to say, in the period when he was surrounded by the encouraging admiration of a group of pupils, young musicians of the new generation, who saw in his earnestness and religious devotion to music a way of liberation from the tawdriness of the discredited Second Empire. D'Indy was to become the best-known member of this group, which also included Duparc, Chausson and Alexis de Castillon. It is a fact little known that when Franck was a young man he had given lessons to d'Indy's uncle, Wilfrid d'Indy, who, however, continued to compose in the vein of traditional French comic opera.

Franck was born at Liége in Belgium. Both he and his brother Joseph early showed musical talent, and their father took them to Paris when César was fourteen, for the sake of the larger field. Is Franck to be regarded as a French composer? The French themselves are not in agreement on the point. "French in heart and by choice," d'Indy says of him. French he certainly was by education, although the Paris Conservatory can hardly be congratulated on the grudging spirit with which it rewarded his gifts. The truth is that at an early age he was a better contrapuntist than his judges, and that he lacked the brilliancy and light charm then considered all-important. But we must recognize that some lack of sympathy was natural for one so non-French in temperament and outlook as Franck was. Long after Franck's major works had won world-wide fame academic France was unwilling to claim him for her own. In Lavignac's huge *Encyclopédie de la musique et Dictionnaire du Conservatoire* (1913 edition), there are two meagre paragraphs about Franck in the Belgian section and nothing at all in the hundreds of pages devoted to the French composers of Franck's time. And such a latter-day critic as G. Jean-Aubry scouts the idea of regarding Franck as a French master, saying:

"The man of genius who wrote 'The Beatitudes' is to be revered; but can this mysticism of his be called French, this obliviousness to irony, this metaphysical taste, this inclination to take everything so earnestly, this need of proving something, this absence of a critical sense, this insensibility to the strong sensuality of the Latin peoples, and, in his form, this fondness for developments in which we find the characteristics of the Germanic race?"

It might be interesting to speculate upon what would have happened to Franck if his father had taken him to Germany instead of Paris. He so obviously had the makings of a worthy German musician! But one's guess is that he might have remained undistinguished. As things were, his education was not classical, and the curious phenomenon resulted of a Germanically-minded musician who was brought up in Meyerbeer's Paris. He was a fine pianist, and his father's ambition for him was a virtuoso's career. The organ, however, claimed him. In d'Indy's words, Franck not so much "had" as "was" the genius of improvisation; and his pupil said that no other modern organist could be even distantly compared with him in this respect.

Cavaillé-Coll's fine organs gave him a scope no piano could afford. And his deep piety made the church organist's position wholly congenial to him. From 1858 he was organist and choir-master at the then new church of Sainte Clotilde, where a notable Cavaillé-Coll instrument was installed. Here, then, we have the elements of Franck's musicianship. To be remembered is the solidity of the French organ-playing tradition, which—with its demands for contrapuntal improvisation—encouraged more sub-stantial accomplishment* than the school of composition which had the opera-house as its goal; while, at the same time, the opera entered so much into the general social consciousness that not even a born church musician like Franck could remain untouched by it. If Franck had gone to Germany as a boy he would have made Bach's acquaintance much earlier than he did, and would have known much less about Méhul and Meyerbeer. May not some of the singularity of Franck's work come from the im-pingement upon an ecclesiastical and utterly non-dramatic mind of glaringly worldly, operatic music?

* Franck, competing for the organ prize at the Paris Conservatory at the age of nineteen, was required to improvise a fugue and a movement in sonata form.

Vincent d'Indy's book propagated a romantic legend about Franck, which has been accepted in England; and the newcomer to his work is often surprised by the disparity between the music he hears—rather Lisztian, he may think it seems in some respects —and the myth of an ethereal, other-worldly Franck, a kind of Fra Angelico, detached from his century. But, like every other good artist, Franck belonged to his age; and that excellent and stirring symphonic ballad 'Le Chasseur maudit' was the work of a man with more blood in his arteries than hagiologists like d'Indy wished to allow.

The famous question of Franck's 'cyclic system' must be touched upon. Here again d'Indy's exegesis must be read with caution. D'Indy preached that the three great men of music were Bach, Beethoven and Franck; and that Franck added to the sublimest achievements of human genius an incomparably logical musical form in the 'cyclic sonata,' that is to say, a sonata (symphony or quartet) in which the movements were not independent but were unified by the use throughout of the developments of a germ-idea. The proof of the pudding is in the eating; and cyclic form—which obtained such a vogue towards the end of the century that even Debussy, anti-Franckist though he was, adopted it in his string quartet—can be tested by its fruits. They have hardly justified the expectations of seventy years ago. Either the transformation of themes is so complete that the unifying intention escapes notice; or else (as in Debussy's quartet) the listener is inclined, by the time the finale comes, to say: "For heaven's sake, give us another tune!"

D'Indy saw hints of cyclic form in Beethoven, and allowed Franck no other forerunner. This may be questioned. The claim may be made for Schubert's 'Wanderer Fantasia'—composed in the year of Franck's birth—that, with its transformation of germ-idea and implied programme, it heralded both Liszt's symphonic poems and Franck's cyclic sonatas. The idea was in the air. Liszt obviously took a hint from Schubert (whose 'Wanderer' he arranged for piano and orchestra) and from Berlioz's Fantastic Symphony. The details of Franck's life have never been told fully, and we do not know how soon he made the acquaintance of Liszt's symphonic poems; but the relationship between those works and Franck's is unmistakable.

Our composer was fifty when he wrote the first of the pieces by which he is generally remembered, viz. 'Redemption' ('poem-symphony' for voices and orchestra, 1872). The oratorio 'The Beatitudes,' an unequal composition, containing some finely characteristic portions and others all too inferior, took him ten years to complete (1869–1879). 'Le Chasseur maudit' and 'Les Djinns,' two symphonic poems, came in 1882 and 1884, the latter being also the year of the famous 'Prelude, Chorale and Fugue' for piano. The Symphonic Variations of 1885, the violin sonata (dedicated to Ysaye) of 1886, the D minor symphony of 1886–88, the string quartet of 1889, and 'Three Chorales' for organ of 1890 are all famous compositions representing Franck at or near his best.

XVIII

FRANCK'S SYMPHONY

D'INDY, in an eloquent chapter on Franck's organ-playing, tells of a visit Liszt paid to Sainte-Clotilde. Franck improvised for him alone in an empty church, and afterwards Liszt, marvelling, uttered the name of Bach. Listening to Franck's symphony, while we do not think of Bach, we cannot help calling to mind the great organist, a man so obscure in the outer world but the master of the mighty instrument—Franck, who said, "My organ, why, it is an orchestra!" How impressive are the improvisations of leading French organists—men who are of little or no account as actual composers—the English public knows well. And those who heard Franck say that Dupré and the rest are children compared with him!

Listening to Franck's symphony, we cannot dissociate it from the thought of the organ-loft at Sainte-Clotilde. It would be less than fair to call the work a masterpiece of extemporization, but that the source of the music is the organist's extemporization is unquestionable. An organist's symphony! Yes, but the work of an organist who was also a poet. A great deal of the symphony would sound superbly effective on an appropriate organ. The score abounds in suggestions of Franck's beloved instrument. His use of the English horn, for instance, is almost certainly due to a fondness for a colour an organ-stop can produce. The great climaxes, with their sonority and sustained depth, are all organ-like rather than characteristic of the orchestra's brilliant activity, while Franck's habit of uttering a two-bar or four-bar phrase, then pausing and repeating it with slightly different harmonization, is characteristic of organ technique.

There he is at the console, playing a phrase on the choir organ (strings); then with loving touch he pulls out another stop and the phrase is uttered by another voice. He pauses an instant and changes his hands to the great organ (brass); finally, pulling out a favourite combination of stops on the swell (woodwind), he gives just a touch with the swell-pedal, slightly opening the swell-box, for his last version.

The symphony is in three movements, the middle one of which combines a slow (or slower) movement and scherzo. It is not a classical symphony. This is not said to Franck's disparagement. The first movement is a masterly piece of music; but the listener should not be led to expect a classical form. D'Indy (in his *Course of Composition*) defines the nature of the work as an "antagonism of tonalities" in which the key of D is finally victorious over that of F. Tovey (who admired the work) insisted that it was rather a symphonic poem or fantasia than symphony.

There is one generalization to be made about its performance: slow tempos are fatal here! Woe betide the orchestra under a conductor who has an exaggerated notion of Franck's solemnity and depth! The symphony then seems to have no end, and the immense amount of hated tremolando in the string parts exhausts the players physically—and exhausts their patience. The strings may be heard to groan when they find Franck's symphony on the desks at rehearsal. There are conductors who over-sentimentalize the work—this is easy!—and smother it in thick, glutinous colour. Tunes are pulled out of shape, Lentos and Allargandos stretched like elastic. The cornets blare and the string-tone wears thin by incessant forcing. The symphony needs a light hand, precise playing and strict observance of the expression marks. Great attention must, in particular, be paid to the pianissimos. It has sometimes been argued that the symphony should be rescored from start to finish; but two of its finest interpreters, Pierre Monteux in France and Adrian Boult in England, satisfy themselves with minor adjustments, generally to encourage an all too discreet soloist. The score includes English horn, bass clarinet, two cornets and harp.

The first movement has a double form of introduction, both parts being almost identical except that the first is in D minor and the second a third higher in F minor. The symphony opens in an

atmosphere of darkness and doubt. This mood is frequent in
Franck's openings—he begins in gloom and fear, and ends with
transcending gladness. The angular first theme recalls the opening
of Liszt's 'Faust.' In the depths of the pedals, as it were, darkly
coloured by violas, cellos, and basses, it is heard groping in the
shadows:

The first three notes are the germ from which a great deal of
the material of the symphony grows. The gloom is relieved by a
ray of subdued light in the 1st violins at the sixth bar:

But a dramatic, shivering tremolo in the violas and cellos shuts
out this light, and in gradual swells, as though operated by the
organist's foot on the swell pedal, a crescendo is built up, with the
tremolo bows of the strings becoming fierce. Then a sudden
cessation reveals the clarinets and bassoons with the main theme
in the grip of fear again, whilst 1st and 2nd violins carry on the
harmony, now chromatic, with more agitated tremolando. At
last the trumpet rings out on a splendid E, the tempo becomes
twice as quick, and a trial run of the Allegro begins.

This, the principal subject, is played with the utmost fire and
energy by the strings alone. Franck thoughtlessly gives the 1st
violins a problem. High up "in the rosin" they have to attack
that high A in the fifth bar with vicious force, and the composer

leaves them entirely unprotected. It is no easy task for twenty violins to leap up suddenly to an exposed height and be unanimous to a microscopic fraction of an inch.

Now a new chromatic motif on flutes and oboes wells up and down:

Fig.4

On the heels of this last theme a sudden fortissimo from the whole orchestra seems to express Franck's sudden dissatisfaction, and the cellos end this introduction on a questioning C.

In this eloquent introductory extemporization Franck turns over in his mind all the material he intends to use for the first movement and, as though to fix it firmly in his head, he tries it over again in another key, F minor. Monteux insists that the whole of this introduction be very restrained. He makes no great drama out of this introduction, as conductors of less insight are fond of doing. He asks: "It must be so simple and absolutely quiet! Jes' a crescendo vere it is marked, but absolutely pianissimo till then."

At the second allegro the movement begins in earnest. In place of a return to the opening adagio, Franck this time gently rounds his phrases off in characteristic manner, and after a new subsidiary tune (molto cantabile),

Fig.5

the music works up to its first big climax for the second principal theme in F major, fortissimo (if Elgar had written it, he would have directed 'nobilmente'). This is the celebrated tune known to Franck's disciples as the 'theme of Faith.'

Fig.6

It is typical of the composer in its rise and fall from one note.

The tune again is organ-like in its sonorous, smooth breadth, and its first two bars are used exhaustively through the movement. After the music has worked up to still greater power, the door is suddenly shut on its exuberance and Franck slips into one of his quiet, reflective moods again, where he softly plays with this 'theme of Faith' on a cherished stop—the French horn. A pause; and then the same phrase is tried on other stops, oboe and flute, in different keys. In danger of breaking the thread of the music, and to stop himself for ever dallying with these delightful colours, he begins to develop the whole movement, starting with the first bar only of the second theme (Fig. 6)—determinedly setting an energetic mood of strong rhythmic impulse:

Monteux, in this next episode, demands a marked contrast between the themes that are smooth and organ-like and those that are contrasted and strongly defined in rhythm:

New passages appear in the strings:

which build up quickly to a climax, down again to pianissimo with a lovely change of key; and the episode is concluded by a violent rushing passage in the key of D flat in the strings.

A chromatic theme, which has already been noted in the last bars of the introduction:

brings a more agitated mood, and the music is driven onwards by
the sharp rhythm in the wind:

Fig.11   Wood Wind

There are two great final efforts; this strenuous section subsides
at once, and the second tune is quietly heard all round the orchestra, over the initial two-bar pedal motif—this time in the
depths on the basses and tubas. Gradually Franck piles on the
sound, adding instrument to instrument; strings and woodwind
break into quavers for more power and brilliance, and at last the
strings are suddenly left to themselves for two bars of intense
bowing on a dominant seventh. Forthwith the great climax of
the movement crashes out on 'full organ,' the tempo returning
to the original lento. Basses, tubas and trombones blow the whole
of the opening theme of the symphony in canon with the trumpets
and cornets, while horns, woodwind and strings, playing tremolando, saw out the harmonies fortissimo. This focal point and
climax of the whole first movement is pure organ music, and for
that reason not loved by the orchestra.

At the end of this lento, which is sustained with all the orchestra's resources, there is a dramatic drop to pianissimo, and, as
before in the introduction, the organist pulls out his stops one by
one for a terrific crescendo, over four bars, and at the top bursts
out with the allegro again in the key of E flat minor. This is the
beginning of the recapitulation, which brings us eventually back
to the 'affirmation of Faith' again, now in the brighter key of
D major. This time Franck quietly plays over the first four bars of
the tune on the oboe and beautifully rounds off the whole theme
on the clarinets, ending with another pause. This final cadence
modulates exquisitely into the key of B flat.

Pianissimo, the strings whisper quiet harmonies. This mood,
however, does not last. Emotion again arises, movement is
speeded and the music builds up again for another effort. The
strings, with triple strokes of their bows to each note, drive the
movement on to the urging of the brass, and once again the full

organ peals out for the final lento. Quavers are substituted for the
crotchets of the initial theme, and Franck caps the whole movement with a wonderful final major chord. The violins seem to
leap up to this top F sharp as though it were the one note they
had been trying to find for the last quarter of an hour.

The second movement, in which we are sometimes reminded
of Schumann, is music that cannot fail to charm even those who
are not moved by Franck when he is grandiloquent. A lyrical
tune, given to the English horn, springs from the same germ as
the first subject of the symphony:

Fig.12 *Allegretto cantabile*

This is repeated; and the second part of the melody, on clarinet
and horn, is also played twice:

Fig.13 Clarinet & Horn

The second time, when the flute joins clarinet and horn, Franck
characteristically takes his soloists up to D natural instead of
D flat★, a celebrated instance of Franck's idiom.

The following theme, which at once succeeds the main one,
is broadly expanded, beginning on the 1st violins and taken up
by the woodwind:

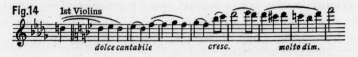

Fig.14 1st Violins *dolce cantabile* *cresc.* *molto dim.*

There is then a long scherzo-like section of much lighter

texture, composed of that lovely feathery material Franck was fond of using. He begins with a tentative string passage entirely unsupported:

This is like a question; and the answer comes from woodwind and horn:

The string passage (Fig. 15) then acts as a delicious accompaniment for the whole of the central section of the movement, in which we get a broken vision of the main theme (Fig. 12). A new melody is imposed on the music by the clarinet:

With the spider-web threads of Fig. 15 Franck eventually weaves together again all the principal themes of the movement. It comes to an end, after a lovely ascending phrase on violins and woodwind, closing softly on a held B flat chord picked out delicately by the harp.

The strings plunge straight into the last movement with tremendous vigour fortissimo, followed by the wind in sharp, heavy chords which, after a momentary hesitation, set the key in D major. The brilliant volume of sound suddenly vanishes to a thrumming, and cellos and bassoons in easy clothes and holiday humour announce the first subject:

7*

The violins take on the second part of the tune with excitement:

Happy and confident, the music speedily works to a climax. It subsides for the next important tune (or variant) on the trumpet, accompanied by organ-like accompaniment on the brass, in F sharp. Note how the second part of the tune is differently scored—again like the organist changing manuals:

Franck does not rest long, but modulates to B minor for the strings to creep about by themselves in a smooth, almost slippery passage of anxious, questioning doubt. Surreptitiously a triplet crotchet figure appears. This induces a change of tempo to 3/4:

and becomes a flowing accompaniment for a return of the main theme of the second movement in its entirety. It comes in its old English horn colours, but in a slightly more restless mood. After the last cadence of this haunting reminiscence Franck, with delicious, almost Schubertian, grace, makes the violins (with the tempo back to a quick two-in-a-bar) whisper the joyous theme, Fig. 18, as if fearing to intrude on dear and pensive memories, yet with the gentlest persuasion suggesting that the time for doubt and anxiety is over. The orchestra quickly becomes alive with fast-moving passages in the background, while Fig 13 is handed about from one instrument to another, generally in canon.

Extreme smoothness gives way to hard articulation, as the power increases, and after a slight drop in tone a big climax is reached for the trumpet theme again (Fig. 20), this time fortissimo from the whole orchestra. Twice the full power of the orchestra is exerted, and then a rapid diminuendo of both tone and tempo ends in a complete bar's silence.

The tempo is slowed to 'più lento.' The string quartet very softly plays a series of broken, doubting phrases answered by the woodwind on an ominous drum roll, the last notes of the wood-wind fading out to a whisper. The original tempo of the move-ment then returns, lifeless for the moment, though a chromatic figure for the cellos foretells coming excitement. The other parts are soon infected with urgent movement, and swiftly the orches-tral forces gather, the music quickens to three crotchets or a triplet to the beat, keys change to dominants of E flat, A major, G major, and the full energy and flowing jubilation of the main theme (Fig. 18) breaks out again in all instruments that can be spared from the harmony.

The English horn's tune (Fig. 12) peals out in joyous triumph on woodwind, cellos and brass, the violins embroidering it in brilliant colours. At the end of the tune there is a sudden hush, and the strings, suddenly abandoning their quick-moving modu-lations, break into the 'Faith' theme of the first movement, in the key of B flat. Becoming reflective, Franck looks back over the long course he has travelled. We hear the opening bars of the symphony return, now lit up by rich harp arpeggios. This is the beginning of the coda, in which Franck alternately uses Fig. 6 and Fig. 18. The close of the work is prepared by a dramatic pianissimo. Then comes a steadily increasing crescendo of excite-ment, and the symphony ends in ecstatic joy, with all the early doubt and questioning solved for good.

There are ultra-refined spirits who to-day dismiss Franck's symphony from the category of good music, just as a generation ago there were some who extolled it extravagantly. It is, we have said, not a work beloved by the orchestra. But the great public that delights in this music is not wrong. It sprang from a noble heart. The journey from anxiety to joy, from fear to rapturous deliverance from doubt, was Franck's innermost experience, and the telling of it was his message to the world of men.

XIX

TCHAIKOVSKY
1840–1893

THE second half of the nineteenth century was the great era of Russian music, and Tchaikovsky on the whole was, there can be hardly any disputing, the best composer of the young school. Time was when critical opinion ranked some of the men of the St. Petersburg party—Balakirev, Mussorgsky, Borodin—above him, but that was before there had been adequate opportunities of hearing their works. From Glinka to Stravinsky the Russian school has now been exhaustively performed, and everywhere its freshness, bright colouring and vivacity have made friends. From Glinka, the forerunner, still so pleasant to hear, to Stravinsky and Prokofiev—the principal representatives of the school in its twentieth-century decadence—many have had the talent to retain the world's interest.

With all his shortcomings Tchaikovsky stands head and shoulders above his compatriots. Refined persons may rail at his theatricality and crudeness and at the extravagance of his self-pity, but for sixty years this impulsive, melodious, superbly showy and genuinely expressive music has carried with it the mass of concert-goers. Each member of the nationalist school of St. Petersburg had, no doubt, some quality lacking in Tchaikovsky —an originality, a certain taste. If only Borodin had, instead of giving occasional half-hours to music, given his whole self, what a composer! And Mussorgsky, if only he had not drunk himself to death! And Balakirev, if only he had had more ideas and more impulse! And so with Rimsky-Korsakov and the rest. But the fact remains that Tchaikovsky, a composer of no intellectual eminence and often one of doubtful taste, possessed in abundance the creative faculty. If his music sprang less from his mind than his temperament, how it sprang! It leaped into life.

'From his temperament,' we say; and yet there is a striking disparity between the violence of Tchaikovsky's music, its gush of passionate confidences, its ignorance of all reticence in sorrow and in gaiety, and the nature of the thin-skinned, shrinking man as we find it depicted in his letters and in the biographies. In recent years Tchaikovskian literature has multiplied, and it has been made clear that he was a neurotic or some kind of psychopath. This "polished, cultivated gentleman and man of the world," as Ethel Smyth described him (Leipzig, 1888), "of all the composers I have known the most delightful as a personality," was a tortured creature, often on the verge of madness. Nature he loved, and he loved several members of his family; and composition, though it brought him disappointments, was a great resort. But existence he often felt to be a curse. His abnormal shyness and irritability blighted his days, and he seems to have enjoyed few of the compensations of the average man's life. To read Tchaikovsky's letters is to make the acquaintance of a deeply unhappy man, a sick man, indeed, whose sickness is not less real because it is one of the mind.

Yet he was by no means always the querulous invalid. We are made aware of a charmingly affectionate man, and also of a true artist. Whatever was ill-adjusted in him, his judgment was sane. He was modest but not unduly self-disparaging. There is something very attractive about the obvious honesty of his estimates both of his contemporaries and of his own compositions. When he says bluntly that he holds himself to be a better composer than Brahms or Saint-Saëns the assertion does not strike the reader as vain—it is so clearly unprejudiced. When Tchaikovsky could admire he did so with all his heart—for instance, on making the acquaintance of 'Carmen.' He was hopelessly out of sympathy with Wagner, and yet his drastic criticism of 'Tristan' and 'The Ring' can hardly offend the Wagnerian—it is so honestly the expression of an incompatibility.

Tchaikovsky came of a family of gentle breeding, and his early years were spent in comfortable circumstances. Later on his father, a mining engineer, suffered reverses of fortune. When Peter was fourteen his mother died of cholera, the disease that was to kill him when he was fifty-three. As a boy he showed excessive sensitiveness and a not strikingly exceptional disposition for music. He was twenty-two and had been for three years a clerk in the Ministry of Justice, before he went in seriously for music, and not till he was twenty-three did he give himself wholly to it. At the new St. Petersburg Conservatory his teachers were Zaremba and the great Anton Rubinstein. The latter's younger brother Nicholas, who was hardly less gifted than Anton, was principal of the Moscow Conservatory, also a new institution; and thither Tchaikovsky, when he was twenty-five, went as professor of harmony. At twenty-six he wrote his first symphony ('Winter Dreams'), Op. 13 in G minor; but the first of the works by which he is remembered, the fantasy-overture 'Romeo and Juliet,' did not come for another three years (1869–70). Tchaikovsky's other symphonies are the following:

No. 2, C minor ('Little Russian'), 1873.
No. 3, D ('Polish'), 1875.
No. 4, F minor, 1877–78.
No. 5, E minor, 1888.
No. 6, B minor ('Pathetic'), 1893.

To this list also belongs 'Manfred' (1885), sometimes called a symphonic poem but more properly a programme-symphony. One of Tchaikovsky's best works, it has failed to make its way because of its exorbitant length. Closely related to the six symphonies are several symphonic fantasies or fantasy-overtures, e.g. 'Romeo,' 'The Tempest,' 'Francesca da Rimini' and 'Hamlet.' Then there are the concertos—four for piano (if we include the Concert Fantasy, Op. 56), among which the first, in B flat minor, has been alone in winning the world's ear—and the famous Op. 35 for violin.

Ten operas were also written in the thirty years of Tchaikovsky's working life, not to speak of three full-length ballets, two considerable sets of incidental music (one being 'The Snow Maiden,' containing music that shows Tchaikovsky at his most Russian), three orchestral suites, some chamber music and an important number of songs and piano pieces. The list is, in fact, impressively long, and is enough to show that the moody and restless Tchaikovsky was a worker.

Another interesting thing about his life is the rapidity with which he became, when already in his twenties, a thoroughly professional musician. He seems to have had never a harmony lesson until he was twenty-one, and before he was twenty-six he was a professor of harmony at Moscow. Tchaikovsky was never a learned musician, but his technical foundations were as solid as those of the French and Italian composers of the day and much more so than those of most of the Petersburg men—men of genius, some of them, but often only amateurishly equipped and, moreover, handicapped by their principle of rejecting all non-Russian elements from their art. From the Petersburg point of view Tchaikovsky was academic and too often inclined to a cosmopolitan style. Tchaikovsky on his side was severe on the amateurishness of most of the northerners—Borodin, for instance, "whose technique is so poor that he cannot compose a single bar unaided." To Mussorgsky he allowed only "a flash of original talent now and then." He accused Balakirev of blighting Rimsky-Korsakov's career; and he summed up the whole group as "so many undeveloped, wrongly developed or prematurely decayed talents."

It is not to Tchaikovsky's credit that he saw so little in Mussorgsky. There is a rather painful passage in a letter to his brother Modest in which he sends 'Boris Godunov' "to the devil." In fairness one feels bound to say that certain pages in 'Boris' are stamped with an originality and genius beyond anything in Tchaikovsky. But it has to be remembered that the young professor who spoke so censoriously realized no doubt that he himself had only by luck escaped from the dilettantism which he—truly enough—saw as the bane of his Petersburg contemporaries.

When Tchaikovsky is censured by Russian nationalists for his Western or cosmopolitan tendencies we feel surprise, for Tchaikovsky's music has for so long been accepted among us as the very voice of Muscovy; there are obvious folk-tunes in the scores, and even when there are none the torrential emotionalism of the music is taken as being Slavonic. Then Tchaikovsky's own

passionate nationalism is on record. Yes; but what is the foundation of his music? A language that never had a literature may
produce one unaided, given favourable circumstances. But a
people that never had anything more of a music of its own than
folk-songs cannot expect suddenly to create a full-blown,
civilized music out of nothing but its own resources. Balakirev,
however, thought it could. And he was a sort of pope among the
Petersburg musicians.

Tchaikovsky went in for no such dogmatic exclusiveness. It is,
in fact, one of the signs of his creativeness that he was not afraid
of influences. It is the poor man, not the rich, who is afraid of
borrowing. At the same time he was as averse as any of the
Petersburgers to German influences. This was temperamental.
Extraordinary as it seems, he was never beguiled by Wagner, and
he genuinely disliked Brahms. He thought that the German
school was played out. One may be sure that this was a deeply
felt, congenital antipathy, and no mere reflection of national or
political prejudice. Curious is the absence of a German impression
on Russian music—on any of the Russian music, that is to say,
that counts. Racialism is a word with a bad name, but we cannot
shut our eyes to the existence of something only to be described
as racial (or national) temperament. But we have seen that
Tchaikovsky recognized the need of something more in the way
of a language for his purposes than mere folk-song. Where did
he find it? Like Glinka before him, he found it in Italian opera
and ballet music; that is to say, in the repertory (which included
Meyerbeer and some of the French composers of the day) of the
Petersburg Italian opera.

His brother tells us that Tchaikovsky considered that his introduction to music was by means of his father's mechanical organ
(orchestrion), which played melodies from Mozart, Bellini and
Donizetti, giving him rapturous pleasure. Later on, the best
musical performances by far at St. Petersburg were those at the
Italian Opera. And there Tchaikovsky acquired his life-long taste
for the ballet. Modest Tchaikovsky has a quaint anecdote to tell
of a manifestation of this taste, which he shared with Saint-Saëns.
The French composer was at Moscow in 1875, and Tchaikovsky

and he each confessed to the other that in his youth he had often tried to imitate ballet-dancing.

"This suggested the idea of dancing together, and they brought out a little ballet, 'Pygmalion and Galatea,' on the stage of the Moscow Conservatory. Saint-Saëns, aged forty, played the part of Galatea most conscientiously, while Tchaikovsky, aged thirty-five, appeared as Pygmalion. Nicholas Rubinstein formed the orchestra. Unfortunately no spectators witnessed this singular entertainment."

Russian folk-song enters largely into certain compositions of Tchaikovsky but into others not at all. That is to say that it does not belong to the fundamentals of his musical thought. The spring of his art is the Franco-Italian stage, the operas of Rossini, Meyerbeer and Verdi, the pomp of theatrical processions, the profusion of emotional outpourings between operatic lovers, and then the grandiose frivolity of the ballet, in which a childish premise is elaborated with such magnificence that its make-believe world looks almost serious. Tchaikovsky loved all this factitiousness, and his music is its idealization. When he is in good vein bold and fiery tunes spring forth as they do in 'Rigoletto.' When he deals with a sublime subject, such as Francesca da Rimini, the result is a more or less sublimated ballet-music—music for dancers with superhuman legs and arms.

This is not to say that Tchaikovsky's symphonies are literally ballet-music. When in about 1930 it was a choreographic fashion to dance to symphonies the attempt was made in London by Leonid Massin to make such use of Tchaikovsky's Symphony No. 5. Ballet-like though this music is, the form of the work proved to be unmanageable—each movement had far too wide a span for the dancers' art. The suggestion of ballet is to be found in a certain enthusiastic make-believe in the music, a theatrical pretence—which by no means excludes beauty. It does not even exclude a measure of genuineness. Joy in life, love, despair—these were sentiments not foreign to Tchaikovsky. Only his theatrical spectacles made his rendering of them inflated, and hardly distinguishable from the mock despair of the court of the Sleeping Beauty's parents when she pricks her finger. The listening world, then, is divided into two parts, the one saying that so much furore about so little is an insult to its intelligence, while the other exclaims with delight over the gorgeous colouring and swaggering tunes.

Sometimes a mystery has been suspected in the disparity between Tchaikovsky's personal refinement and a certain garishness in his art, but perhaps there is after all no need for far-fetched explanations in this respect, whatever may be the other grounds Tchaikovsky offers for psychological investigation. The young composer accepted the Italian opera at St. Petersburg as the norm of music, and the rest followed. We have to remember that the Petersburg Conservatory was a new institution and that its principal, Anton Rubinstein, was no great academic luminary, though a pianist of genius. Tchaikovsky's schooling had a minimum of the classical element. His admiration for Mozart, verging on idolatry, is often referred to in his letters, yet there is no evidence that Tchaikovsky was a deep student of Mozart. That queer 'Mozartiana' suite, Op. 61, suggests no intimate understanding of Mozart's style. Indeed we are tempted to think of Tchaikovsky's reverence for Mozart as detached from practical musical experience. Mozart, the divine Mozart, belonged to the past; he seemed archaic to Tchaikovsky, who was the last of the great composers for whom (as had earlier been the common view in Western Europe) music meant in practice contemporary music—as it had meant to Handel.

How would a classical musical education have affected Tchaikovsky? It is better to be grateful for what he has left us, whatever may be its lack of substance, than to wish for him a culture, academic and historical, which might, under the name of acquisition of technique, have stifled his native impulse and charm. We live in a century bristling with composers who have more learning and technique than they know what to do with. Stiffness of form characterized Tchaikovsky from first to last, and he was totally inappreciative of Brahms's suppleness. The sensible thing is to be grateful for his positive achievement, and to suppose that he had as much learning as he could make use of.

One or two factors in his education have still to be mentioned.

Both the Rubinsteins, who were the dominating personalities in the musical world of his young days, were powerful virtuosi. Their attitude, the attitude of the executant whose task is to fascinate at once and browbeat a scatter-brained public, by means of genius, by means of pretentiousness, by all means, genuine and sham—this must have gone deep into his conception of what the artist was. We hear little about Tchaikovsky as an executant. Did he ever so much as touch a stringed instrument? He seems to have played the piano more or less by instinct. In his student days he joined the orchestra of the Petersburg Conservatory as a flautist. On the whole he may be said to have given hardly more time to instrumental execution than Berlioz. Certainly the physical source of his music was not the piano, as it was of Schumann's and Brahms's. The orchestra was his instrument, and his quick mastery of it was almost as surprising as had been that of Berlioz a generation before.

We must not suggest a parallel between the two composers, who were in many respects widely divergent. But there are points of resemblance between them, and it is interesting that there should have been a moment's actual contact. In 1867 Berlioz, then with only a year and a few months more to live, was paying his second visit to Russia, and at a dinner of musicians given in his honour at St. Petersburg Tchaikovsky screwed up his courage to pronounce a speech in French. Twenty years before Berlioz had been in Russia for the first time, and had made a lasting impression on Russian music. The clarity and brilliance of his orchestral style appealed to the Russian mind as the contemporary German style never did. Modest Tchaikovsky, in the famous biography, says that his brother "felt no enthusiasm for Berlioz's music." But Tchaikovsky's own letters are evidence of his enthusiasm at least for 'La Damnation de Faust'; and his scores abound in evidence of the lessons he had learnt from Berlioz's orchestration. To Ethel Smyth, in 1888, he passed on this preoccupation with orchestral sound. "Not one of them can instrumentate!" he said to her of the Leipzig school. "And he earnestly begged me to turn my attention at once to the orchestra and not be prudish about using the medium for all it is worth."

Ethel Smyth was then thirty, that is to say, four years older than Tchaikovsky had been at the time of the composition of his first symphony. His five years of musical study had been insufficient for this task; it brought upon him something like a nervous breakdown, and the work has not lived. But we may fairly wonder at the achievement it represented in 1866, and at the considerable expression of a personality there already in this prentice work. Eric Blom * declares his preference for the first movement:

"an attractive study in grey, conjuring up visions of a troïka gliding swiftly over a snowy plain under a leaden sky. The melancholy thoughts awakened by the desolate landscape are almost painfully real, and the whole piece has that definiteness of mood and that unity of construction which often make even the longest of Tchaikovsky's movements appear as if they were the result of one single thought."

The two middle movements were played at St. Petersburg in 1867, and the whole (with some success) the next year at Moscow. Then it was dropped, only to be revived at Moscow in 1883. Before the composition of the second symphony, Op. 17 in C minor, Tchaikovsky had produced one of his true masterpieces ('Romeo and Juliet'). Composed in 1872, the C minor was revised seven years later. It is one of those works in which Tchaikovsky nearly approaches the style of the Petersburg nationalists —not introspective or passionately expressive; it is a folk-song symphony, and it would always be welcome as a very likable example of its kind if it were not that the public, expecting emotional outbursts from Tchaikovsky, is not well disposed towards such objectivity in him. With the third symphony in D, Op. 29, in five movements, composed in 1875, we are getting near familiar ground. It is sometimes called the 'Polish Symphony,' from the polonaise movement of the finale (not the best part of the work). The work is inferior to the second symphony, but is at the same time more Tchaikovskian, and Beecham's fondness for it has resulted in marvellously fine performances.

The fourth symphony, in F minor, Op. 36, was composed in

* In *Stepchildren of Music*.

1877 and 1878—the former having been the year of Tchaikovsky's luckless marriage with Antonina Ivanovna Miliukov. This is one of the works by which Tchaikovsky stands or falls. In essentials he could hardly do better—or, at least, not in a large-scale work. It is Tchaikovsky's musical rendering of much the same programme as underlies Beethoven's C minor symphony—he confessed as much in a famous letter he wrote to his patroness, Nadezlida von Meck, a letter which clearly puts his views on programme music. (Tchaikovsky always or almost always composed to an inner programme, but at the same time did not set out to illustrate material happenings in the Straussian way.) The fanfare at the beginning of the F minor symphony is the motive of Fate. After expressions of despair, disappointed illusion, and so on, in the first three movements, Tchaikovsky finds escape from the imprisoning ego in the finale—"Rejoice in the joy of others, and you can still live!" Still better known is the fifth symphony in E minor, of 1888—again an intensely representative composition. Even a finale of disappointing weakness, after three superbly Tchaikovskian movements, has not seriously damaged the symphony in the world's opinion. Before this Tchaikovsky had composed (in 1885) his grand and neglected 'Manfred'—a programme-symphony that lasts an hour and more. Twenty minutes too long! Because of those excessive twenty minutes the world hardly knows one of the masterpieces of its darling Tchaikovsky. The sixth symphony in B minor, the 'Pathetic,' must be allowed a chapter to itself.

XX

TCHAIKOVSKY'S 'PATHETIC' SYMPHONY

ON February 16, 1893—which was to be the year of his death—Tchaikovsky began the composition of his B minor symphony, the idea of which had been in his mind for a couple of months. In the previous autumn he had been at work on another symphony, in E flat. He soon lost interest in this composition, which, however, he did not destroy, but turned into a piano concerto. This comes to us in Tchaikovsky's arrangement of the first movement (Op. 75) and Taneëv's of the second and third (Op. 79). "An empty pattern of sound, without inspiration," he said of this work, at the time when he was engrossed with the B minor— "A Programme Symphony," as he announced the latter to his brother:

> ". . . a programme of a sort that remains enigmatic to everyone—let them guess it who can! The programme is full of subjective emotion. While I was composing it I frequently shed tears."

In June of that year Tchaikovsky paid his famous visit to Cambridge to receive, with Bruch, Boito and Saint-Saëns, the degree of Doctor of Music. Back at home, in August, he scored the B minor symphony, and wrote to a friend: "I think that the symphony I am now orchestrating will turn out, if not the best, then one of the best of my compositions." And to his publisher Jurgenson: "Never in my life have I been so pleased with myself." The first public performance was given at St. Petersburg on October 28, the composer conducting. In spite of Tchaikovsky's fame and popularity—for a dozen years now he had been in full enjoyment of these—the reception was not wonderfully enthusiastic. The next day Modest Tchaikovsky suggested a title for the work—'Pathetic.' On November 2 the composer was taken ill with cholera, and he died on the 6th. The disaster directed the attention of the whole world to the new symphony; but if the coincidence of its appearance with the composer's premature death had something to do with the immediate notoriety of the work in the two hemispheres something more is wanted to explain the lasting appeal the music has made now for more than half a century, particularly in Russia, England and America.

What is the programme that lies hidden beneath this music? Many guesses have been made, and it is safe to say that the one to which James Huneker and Edwin Evans committed themselves was wrong—the guess, namely, that the programme was political and was intended to convey some sort of protest from liberal or democratic opinion against autocracy. Tchaikovsky was, in point of fact, a conservative and a devotedly loyal subject of the Romanov family. The clue is probably to be found in a memorandum of Tchaikovsky's to which Gerald Abraham draws attention in his essays, *On Russian Music* (1939).

Abraham ascribes this memorandum to the end of 1892 and gives us this version:

> "The ultimate essence of the plan of the symphony is LIFE. First part—all impulsive passion, confidence, thirst for activity. Must be short. (Finale, DEATH—result of collapse.) Second part, love; third, disappointments; fourth ends dying away (also short)."

Abraham remarks: "Admittedly this rough draft does not quite agree with the final version of the 'Pathetic,' but we can hardly doubt that it is the embryonic plan of it and that this is the solution of the enigma." The haunting of life by death is the subject, then, of the B minor symphony.

The symphony begins outside the main key, in a short adagio introduction of abysmal gloom. Not only does the opening phrase, which foretells the main theme, speak of desolation, but the hollow, rattling tones of the bassoons, in an ascending sequence of three bars, suggest the grave itself.

The double-basses add to the effect, and then the violas—who finish the whole statement on a G in which Tchaikovsky may have known that 'wolves' are apt to lurk. This entire opening is repeated, and the violas finish the introduction with an expressive descending scale, disappearing on their lowest C sharp. Some have seen in this gloomy introduction a pessimist's view of the birth (or the life in the womb) of the human animal. The key changes to B minor, and the allegro opens with the main theme, full of anxious questioning and agitation.

The Russians make much of the nuances in the first two phrases. Koussevitsky, one of the greatest exponents of this symphony, was dissatisfied for a long while before the right degrees of crescendo and diminuendo at last began to appear, and a crisp enough staccato in the semiquavers. This opening statement of twenty bars or so is extremely difficult to bring off faultlessly. A series of staccato scales from 1st and 2nd violins and violas leads to a new and important rhythmic figure on the strings.

Vassily Safonov, another great interpreter of this symphony, used to ask for this to be played with particularly short semiquavers and rigorously strict tempo. Safonov was noted for his driving power, and he never allowed undue sentimentality. Intense emotion was expressed, but always with virility.

These figures are heard all over the orchestra, culminating in a minor climax when the heavy brass enters with a peremptory and aggressive version of the main theme at an increased speed. The agitation then quietens to give place to a new mood altogether. The cellos, after being left to murmur to themselves, finally give the last word to the violas, who again end this episode on their own, this time on an upward curve to an F sharp. So ends all the first subject-matter, very softly, in a mood of wistful sadness.

A complete break cuts off this section from the next. The tempo is now slowed to andante, for the violins and cellos to play the immortal second subject:

Fig.4 *Andante (Teneramente, molto cantabile, con espansione)*
Violins & Cellos (con sordini)

softly supported by horn chords.

The composer's directions are worth noting. *Teneramente, molto cantabile, con espansione.* The conductor has clear instructions to perform this tune with the utmost artistry. A great man can still touch one's heart with this inspired melody; but it has become so familiar that it needs no common outlook to bring freshness to it again. It must be played as though it had *just come from the composer's pen,* and with the most glorious string tone. Safonov used to dwell slightly on the first note of the phrase, and then accelerate slightly to the dotted crotchet, the whole phrase being played with great tenderness and emotion, but never exaggerated.

An occasion comes to mind which gave an opportunity for the freshness vital to the performance of the symphony. During a Promenade season Sir Henry Wood was not able to touch it at rehearsal, and, paradoxically enough, the result was something that lives in one's memory. The orchestra, of course, knew the conductor intimately and also his particular interpretation of the work and, apart from slight raggedness in one or two difficult passages which will not go without preparation, the work lived anew and was played like a long-forgotten favourite that suddenly delighted us again. Few are the conductors who could succeed in such a feat; but that night the spirit of the work was recaptured. If the symphony had been rehearsed in the usual Promenade routine, that is exactly what would have been missing, and that precious freshness lost.

After the full statement of this melody the flute has a new motif in quicker tempo, again in scale form:

which is passed about between the various woodwind until all join in unison in a slow, drawn-out scale to another break. The andante returns; the second subject now on the three upper strings, embellished with richer scoring, works up to a passionate *ff* and eventually completely dies out, after a *ppp* restatement of the whole theme on the clarinet. Never has the clarinet been blessed with a more perfect gift for its lovely expressiveness than this final appeal, which is generally passed over to the bass clarinet, to disappear in the lower octave. (Tchaikovsky does not include a bass clarinet in his score, but the bassoon is so inadequate to take over from the clarinet that nowadays it is so arranged.) This join is difficult for the two players, since the tone of the bass clarinet is subtly different from that of its cousin—just as earlier in the movement the violas have to try to match their tone with that of the cellos in the last arpeggio before the entrance of the second subject.

Now comes the moment when Sir Henry Wood was in the habit of saying: "I want a crashing chord that will make all the old ladies jump!" This sforzando announces the development; and audiences, in the early days of the symphony, after being lulled by the seductive clarinet must indeed have felt a shock.

Angry chords from the brass and vicious jabs by the strings transform the orchestra into a raging giant. The first subject:

Fig.6 *Feroce*
Strings

returns again in a violent fugato. The strings rush furiously about in more scales, while woodwind shriek. Basses and cellos are presently left alone, and then the brass, with ominous solemnity—there is supposed to be a reference here to the Russian Requiem—build up a climax. A great peak appears for a second in the clouds, to fade away in uneasy, pulsing chords on the horns, and the first subject, anxiously played on the violas, is this time hushed to a frightened pianissimo.

From this point the material is all gathered urgently together and worked up for the great climax of the movement, which is marvellously sustained—not only in length, but in the passion that is unleashed in the suspended harmonies of the strings over a continuous F sharp pedal. The full brass clangs out great bells of doom.

The strings are nearly exhausted on arriving at the recapitulation, for the whole effect of the return to B minor has depended upon the vitality behind their tone. Here is another instance where the great conductor knows precisely the right tempo which the strings can sustain. Too often it is unduly drawn out, and the sonority fails. A great mind is needed to obtain the full effect of this magnificent climax.

When the second subject returns it is with a sense of desperate appeal, and the clarinet finishes it in exquisite sadness. The majestic coda, with its great passage for trombones over an accompaniment of a slow and constantly repeated scale on pizzicato strings, brings the movement to an end in an atmosphere of tragic resignation.

The second movement still remains the most convincing piece of music ever written in 5/4 time. The 5/4 signature is common in modern music, but no one has equalled Tchaikovsky in maintaining for so long a genuine 2/4 plus 3/4 metre. The modern 5/4 is nearly always cut up with other time-signatures, and one usually feels that the composer could have obtained his effect with a simpler manner of notation. Tchaikovsky's movement, from the first to the last bar, is genuine in its lilt.

The form of the movement is that of the classical minuet. The first section, in D major, is in two parts.

Fig. 7   *Allegro con grazia*

Conductors can spend hours playing with this tune and trying to obtain from the cellos the exact colour they want, to say nothing of scolding them for imperfect ensemble. Readings of the famous sixth and eighth bars are legion, and never are two conductors alike. Koussevitsky tore his hair because he could not get just that lift in the sixth bar that he wanted from every cello. Always one or two would hold a fraction too long on the first note or else leave it too soon. Then the difficult octave leap and the subtle rubato wanted for the downward scale are subjects for the despair of temperamental conductors at rehearsal.

The second half of the tune is of the same character, but is delightfully enhanced by the composer's dividing it into two lines, each in thirds—the 1st and 2nd violins moving one way and the violas and cellos in the opposite direction, though each has the same rhythm:

Fig. 8

In the Trio, in B minor, melancholy returns, and poignant longing:

especially in the second half of the tune:

Throughout the Trio a pedal D keeps throbbing with a funereal beat. The listener may make up his own mind about the programmatic significance of this bewitchingly graceful, amorous and wistful Scherzo. There is still less mystery about the next movement, the famous march, in which, along with incomparable brilliancy, go a certain feverishness and desperate excitement. From the first bar to the last the movement never flags, and Tchaikovsky piles up such a climax in the end that no orchestra can ever play it without exhaustion.

The first of two main themes is a light and sparkling 'perpetual motion' kind of subject:

Here is the march theme proper:

The triplet subject is almost incessant until the final stages. At first, round about this continual fluttering, broken phrases of the

march appear, bandied about between the various instruments. One of them:

Fig.13

has a particularly spirited impulse.

Conductors are usually so insistent in their demand for 'staccatissimo' from the strings that the sound has perforce to be at times too strong, and important tunes in the woodwind are lost. One recalls a particularly happy performance under Boult at which much less staccato bowing was asked of the strings, and a much softer tone than usual. Tchaikovsky's own design, in fact, was adhered to. But it is debatable whether the loss of that light and brilliant bowing by the strings, which sounds so fascinating when played to perfection, is too big a price to pay for a better orchestral balance.

The great moment in the march is approached after a bar that is silent except for a timpani roll and a held note in the basses. The strings now begin to climb up a chromatic scale in tremolando, and all over the orchestra, very softly at first, sounds the first figure of the march theme. One after the other they take it up—horns first, then clarinets and trombone, oboes and horns, flutes, more brass, piccolo, some strings, the bass begin to boil. When the tension becomes unbearable the orchestra turns the last two quavers of this figure back on itself, as it were, and a general mêlée takes place, until with a crash the whole orchestra, minus brass, seems to lose its head in a flurry of furious scales. At last—and it is as though an explosion had narrowly been averted by this safety-valve—the march proper breaks out in G major, to swing along with inexorable power and rhythm to the end.

This overwhelming break-out of the march is frequently interpreted by a change of tempo; many conductors suddenly pull up after the scales and hold the march back for three or four bars before getting into the stride again. But if strict tempo is kept the rhythmical effect is all the more telling. From the orchestra's point of view rhythm is everything in a movement like this, and it is distressing to be checked like a 'pulled' horse in a race. Rhythmic impulse is the internal spring of perfect movement, and it is dangerous to interfere with a natural impetus. Safonov used to swing this movement along from start to finish with a wonderful impulse and a power that was never checked. Boult, again, works the movement up to a terrific climax without the need of any change of tempo, and with him the scoring is made to sound brilliantly clear and balanced.

Donald Tovey, who might have been expected to have no kind word to say for Tchaikovsky, paid this tribute to the fourth movement:

> "The slow finale, with its complete simplicity of despair, is a stroke of genius which solves all the artistic problems that have proved most baffling to symphonic writers since Beethoven."

After intoxicating visions of the world in the middle movements—the bewitching dance, the dazzling military pageant—we are back to ultimate realities, the black river that flows at the confines of life, pitiless Charon. The idea was good. Is it effectively carried out? The last movement of the 'Pathetic' is a piteous elegy, deeply expressive in its Tchaikovskian way, if in no sense profound music. But the fact is that Tchaikovsky was almost as stiff in his handling of forms as Berlioz had been two generations before. If Berlioz set to work on a march it had to have a triumphant ending; and just so with Tchaikovsky. The kind of effect that would have been made by the final lament's growing out of the march was beyond him. What we get, then, is a climax of brilliance and glory at the end of the third movement and no transition at all to the suicidal gloom of the next page. The finale does not explain itself. The listener is left to supply for himself the missing links in the argument. Never mind! The hiatus may be awkward, but the passion in the elegy has soon seized upon the attention of all hearers.

The celebrated opening of the finale is curiously scored for the strings. Tchaikovsky, having made extensive use of scale material, seems to have grown self-conscious and wishful of disguising yet another scale subject. In performance, it sounds like:

Fig.14 *Adagio lamentoso*
Violins

Fig.15 *Adagio lamentoso*
1st Violin

2nd Violin

But in the score, he divides the tune (Fig. 15), note by note, between the 1st and 2nd violins. The 2nds play the top note, while the 1sts have a harmony. The next melody note is taken by 1sts, with the 2nds playing the harmony, and so on down the scale. The effect, to all intents and purposes, is the same as if the composer had written in the normal manner.

This opening phrase, always punctuated by a horn note, is the first of the two principal themes of the movement, and is one of the most desperately unhappy in Tchaikovsky's whole creation. After a climax the hollow notes of the bassoon reach down to nothingness, and the horns, in a pulsating rhythm which makes the framework of the music to come:

Fig.16 *Andante*
Horns

prepare for the great second tune of the movement. This opens on violins and violas:

Fig.17 Strings
con tenezza e devozione

Now is the time for the great conductor. Here is an abyss open for the not-great-enough to fall headlong into! Lavishly marked

FRANCK

TCHAIKOVSKY

with expression and tempo marks by the composer, this subject needs the utmost sincerity of feeling and absolute command of forces in hand for the climax. How Koussevitsky laboured at his string tone and to gain flexibility of nuance and tempo, conducting even the rehearsals with white-hot intensity! Under second-rate conductors even a slight exaggeration makes the tune unbearably sentimental. Mishandled, the last great peak of the work becomes tawdry stage-scenery instead of a blood-red mountain-top.

Tchaikovsky's metronome mark for this movement is ♩=76—quicker, perhaps, than it is ever heard to-day. Tradition has set a slower tempo altogether, even among Russian conductors; yet when we hear it at the composer's own pace the music sounds more fresh, provided there is adequate intensity of expression. Under Boult the quicker tempo was taken, but something of the emotional appeal was lost in spite of a wonderful climax.

The working-up of this tune to its highest degree of intensity is still among the most exciting things in symphonic music. The violins and other strings at their topmost pinnacle sustain, while the rest of the orchestra, with the significant pulsing figure, fills the harmonies for a chord of B minor. The strings climb down to the next point for a C major chord, and finally for B minor, and there is a great passage of scales, getting faster and faster. The whole orchestra crashes in on a short C major chord. Comes complete silence, which portends the final stages of the symphony.

Exhaustion appears now. The tune falls away by stages to the return of despair. The first theme, now prefaced by a passionate upward scale, takes hold of the music, and grief and despair wail with the full power of the orchestra. The theme disappears to the depths of hopelessness with the weird stroke of a gong, which reverberates over four bars. Nothing is left now save a return of the second tune, in minor form, bereft of its power and utterly woebegone. The end is approached as the symphony was begun—on the hollow notes of the bassoon and with a fateful pulsing figure on the double basses, panting like the breath of a dying man.

8

XXI

SIBELIUS

WHO thinks of Sibelius thinks of Finland. Among lovers of music he has done for his country what Grieg did for Norway, Smetana and Dvořák for Bohemia. There have been other Finnish composers, but Sibelius alone of them has won the ear of the world. In England and America he has become one of the truly beloved composers of the twentieth century, and his country has reason to be proud of him. Millions of people for whom the word Finland would otherwise have been a mere geographical term or a rather remote patch on the map of Europe, curiously studded with lakes, have made for themselves a mental image of the country on the strength of Sibelius's music. So characteristic is this music, so independent of contemporary schools and masters, that the world has made up its mind that peculiarities of the composer's remote homeland and racial traits of his unfamiliar people have entered into it. The world is wrong in thinking that Finnish folk-music is at the base of Sibelius's art. Finnish folk-song—said to be uninteresting—is not used by Sibelius. All his music is his own. But the world is right in taking Sibelius for a national composer. The creative artist is largely made by the landscapes that surround him in his formative years; and in Sibelius's independence from fashion we may fairly read a national characteristic and the result of his country's aloofness from Russia on the one hand and Germany on the other.

Jean Sibelius was born in 1865 at Tavastehus, north of the Finnish capital. The Finns are a small nation of two peoples, both of which are represented in Sibelius's ancestry—both Swedish and Finno-Ugrian blood flows in his veins. Cecil Gray has told us that the Swedish strain is predominant. Sibelius's career is that of an artist who has achieved the expression of a high individuality with no opposition by fate or circumstance. He had no difficulties of temperament, none of fortune. The grand-duchy of Finland in his youth was a reasonably prosperous country. Jean, the son of a doctor of medicine, grew up a hearty youth. He was fifteen before he took a serious interest in music. He worked hard at the violin and began to compose. At twenty he finished his first quartet and went up to the capital to read law at the University. The next year, however, music won; and with the help of a sympathetic uncle—his father had died when Jean was small—he entered the Helsinki Academy of Music, hoping to become a violin virtuoso. There the principal, Martin Wegelius, encouraged him to work at composition. Wegelius was a Wagnerian; but Sibelius never, from first to last, was in the least touched by Wagner.

After three years at the Academy he bade farewell with a suite for string trio which charmed everyone, even Busoni. A remarkable encounter this—for Helsinki was then rather out of the world and its musical academy a very modest institution! But Wegelius had persuaded the young Busoni to go there to teach the piano for a few months in 1888–9. Busoni (as Mahler later on failed to do) saw talent in Sibelius, and they were friends until Busoni died in 1924. But the Italian could not bear the northern winter or Helsinki's provincialism.

Sibelius went for a time to Berlin, and it was there that he decided that a virtuoso's career was not for him to aim at, and dedicated himself to composition. The Wagner-Brahms battles were still being fought, but Sibelius had no interest in either side. The artist in him was evolving an inner dream, while the young man himself enjoyed life, shone in society and won a bride of the Järnefelt family. In the winter of 1890–1 he studied at Vienna. He went back to Finland at a time of lively political feeling, with national passion at fever-heat over the Russifying plans of St. Petersburg.

So far there was nothing in Sibelius to suggest genius—nothing in his career to mark him off from the horde of aspirants, young men more or less gifted who would most likely drift into schoolmastering or journalism later on. Sibelius is that rarity, an *homme moyen sensuel*, burgess and sound citizen, who turns into a great artist.

Notoriety came soon—notoriety rather than serious recognition, for Sibelius's symphonic poem with chorus, 'Kullervo' (Helsinki, 1892), came in on the crest of a wave of Finnish nationalism. Finland had long been in but never of the Russian Empire. At St. Petersburg there was now a movement for something like absorption of the small country that lay so near the gates of the capital. In the west it was an age of romantic faith in the rights of small nations, and since all the imperial tyrannies of the time were, by twentieth-century standards, very mild, patriotic demonstrations could be indulged in more or less innocuously.

Sibelius's hero, Kullervo, is a character from the Finns' national epic (the Kalevala). The work—still unpublished—is a large composition. It made a national appeal, and from that moment onwards Sibelius held enthralled the affections of his fellow-countrymen. The orchestral tone-poem 'En Saga' belongs to the same year—the first of Sibelius's compositions to gain a European hearing, though the piece as we know it represents a revision of 1901. A few years later (1897) the Finnish government allowed the composer an annuity of £100. He could then cut down the teaching by which he lived and write the more copiously. The dates of the major compositions are the following:

1899, 'Finlandia.' 1898–9, E minor symphony, No. 1. 1901, D major symphony, No. 2. 1903, violin concerto. 1906, 'Pohjola's Daughter.' 1904–7, C major symphony, No. 3. 1909, 'Nightride and Sunrise.' 1909, string quartet, 'Voces intimae.' 1911, A minor symphony, No. 4. 1914–15, E flat symphony, No. 5. 1923, D minor symphony, No. 6. 1924, C major symphony, No. 7. 1925, 'Tapiola.'

Be it explained that between these large works Sibelius composed an immense quantity of small pieces, songs and incidental music for the theatre—none of it less than respectable, yet none of enthralling interest. It is as though the composer's poetic imagination was kindled only when he saw a large canvas before him. Sibelius's smaller compositions would entitle him to the name of no more than a minor musician, nicely written though they are and sometimes very pleasing. The E minor symphony is described by Karl Ekman, Sibelius's pupil and biographer, as the pinnacle of the work of the period inaugurated by 'Kullervo.' The completion of the D major symphony came at the end of the 'storm and stress' period of his life. This symphony Busoni produced at Berlin in 1905, at a performance which did much to make the composer's European reputation (though, as with Delius, the Germans, who had at first shown such a liking, turned cold later on). The third symphony was begun in September 1904. In October 1905 the violin concerto was produced at Berlin with Carl Halir as soloist and as conductor Richard Strauss, who had for long shown an interest in Sibelius.

The composer came for the first time to England—a country where later he was to be idolized—in 1905. He stayed with Granville Bantock at Birmingham and made friends in London with Henry Wood and Rosa Newmarch. On February 27, 1908, Sibelius conducted the first performance of his third symphony at a Philharmonic concert in London. The next period was overclouded by Sibelius's concern for his health, caused by what was (after long uncertainty) proved to be a non-malignant tumour of the throat. Another visit to England came in 1909, and the only string quartet of Sibelius's mature life—'Voces intimae' —was then composed. Mrs. Newmarch had found him rooms in a quiet street in Kensington, behind Church Street, in a house owned by three old ladies. One of the 'witches,' as he called them, took to practising Beethoven's C sharp minor sonata, and Mrs. Newmarch's tact was called into play to bring about quiet while Sibelius was working. During this stay he conducted again at Queen's Hall, made many English friends, and also became acquainted with Debussy and Vincent d'Indy.

The fourth symphony in A minor was composed in 1910-11, and first performed at Helsinki on April 3, 1911. In the next year Sibelius conducted the work at the Birmingham Festival. This symphony, much shorter than the earlier ones, has never become a popular favourite, but its terseness is tightly packed with a personality, and nothing of Sibelius's is more intensely characteristic. The fifth symphony in E flat began to shape itself in 1914 and was completed in 1915. It was first performed at a concert Sibelius gave on his fiftieth birthday (December 8, 1915). Then it was revised and played on December 14, 1916. But, says Ekman, not for three more years did it reach its definitive form.

There was civil war in Finland in January 1918—a backwash of the Russian upheaval. "The Reds are behaving like beasts," so he wrote in his diary,* while trying to concentrate on his sixth symphony. Sibelius's own words for his last three symphonies are: No. 5, "triumphal"; No. 6, "wild and impassioned"; No. 7, "joy of life and vitality, with appassionato passages." (This was said before the completion of the last two.)

In 1921 Sibelius was in London once again, and here he met Busoni for the last time. He was respected here and had admiring friends, but the mass of the public still did not respond. Ten years before there had been such a vogue for gorgeous colouring that Sibelius's sobriety seemed dowdy. Now in the restless 1920s new music was looked to for sharp and violently novel flavours. "Others bring you cocktails; I have only cold water to offer," said Sibelius (the phrase has been reported in various forms). Only towards the end of that decade did a reaction set in. Stravinsky, half-deified in 1920, had sadly disappointed the world by 1930. Atonal music, which had been looked upon as a profound mystery, had come to seem to most people a bore. The wrong-note school and Dadaism in general had been given a chance and been found wanting. Every country in Europe swarmed, as the I.S.C.M. Festivals showed, with clever composers, but the need was felt of a great composer once more. The movement which set in then in Sibelius's favour reached high-water mark with Beecham's superb Sibelius Festival in 1938. Meanwhile Sibelius's creative period had come to an end. The noble symphonic poem 'Tapiola' is dated 1925. After that came a few trifles and then silence. Rumour has spoken from time to time of an eighth symphony, but there is no reason to suppose that the world will ever hear a note of it.

* Ekman, p. 243.

The seven symphonies cannot well be briefly characterized, but it is obvious that No. 1 in E minor derives from the Russian school. (A prominent English composer, hearing it at Queen's Hall, declared: "It's a continuation of Tchaikovsky!") It is a large-scale work, abounding in good ideas, and is justifiably popular. What is Russian is not borrowed. The work is in many ways superior to the famous Russian symphonies, and immeasurably superior to Glazounov's. On No. 2 in D, more anon, in some detail. No. 3, in C—dedicated to Granville Bantock—is a beautiful work in which shadows of things to come in the later Sibelius are numerous. It is more reserved and less emphatic than the earlier symphonies, and not yet so gloomy as some of the composer's later music. No. 4, in A minor, is curiously laconic, and the rareness of a performance shows that it has failed to win the hearts of the mass of music-lovers. It is a pity that it should not be heard rather more often, for, wintry and cheerless though it is, the music is deeply characteristic.

Sibelius's later style was not so uncompromising, though there was no return to the expansiveness of his youth. The masterly Symphony No. 5, in E flat, is the most popular of the later ones. It is sanguine and heroic. No. 6, in D minor, is darker in moods and colours, and is a work which an unsympathetic conductor can easily make dull. But this brooding music is full of thoroughly Sibelian thoughts and processes, and the work is dear to the inner circle of the composer's admirers. The noble Symphony No. 7, in C, in one movement, was originally called a 'Symphonic Fantasia.' This and the famous symphonic poem 'Tapiola' of 1925 were the last of Sibelius's large-scale compositions. At sixty, his creative urge seems to have left him, but if this was his farewell he had the satisfaction that it took the form of two masterpieces.

The inevitable recurrence of the classics in their cycle entails a loss for the orchestral player of freshness of interest. There are days when the sound of the greatest of them seems a tale too often told, and an effort is required to make of one's playing something more than a matter of routine. In such moods there comes a craving for music of a different idiom—a longing to get away from hackneyed ways into a new country. Yes, but not to another planet! The shapelessness of the atonalists, the brutal uncouthness of other kinds of experimental music—these do not bring the longed-for relief.

In the 1920s Sibelius's music came to the orchestra as a gift straight from heaven. Here was a composer who seemed to have all to give to revive languishing spirits. How extraordinary Sibelius's charm is can be judged from his making this effect despite the absence from his scores of one of the prime factors that win the orchestra's response, viz. interesting part-writing. It must, indeed, be said, taking the seven symphonies together, that the part-writing is uninteresting, and a first glance at the string parts fills the heart with lead, containing as they do whole pages of loathly tremolando, the bugbear of all string players. And yet this music—with the exception of Symphony No. 4—is so powerful to grip that even scrubbing therein is a pleasure!

The weird Symphony No. 4 is almost unintelligible from the player's point of view. One seems to be groping in a strange place with a magician lurking in the shadows, who may or may not wreak us harm. The second symphony makes the best approach to Sibelius. It represents a great advance over the first, and is more expansive than the later Sibelius. Orchestras will all agree that the second is the most exciting of them all to play.

There is a fundamental difference between early Sibelius and Tchaikovsky. The Russian is invariably personal, in his grief and in his exultation. Sibelius, no matter what his vein, has a broader humanity, and in his big works we always have a feeling of a translation into music of some saga of a whole people. Not that his symphonies are written to a programme. National traditions and character and the influence of the Finnish landscape enter into his art in a hardly definable and yet unmistakable way—and probably quite unconsciously. No other composer has written a music as radically original as Sibelius's with means so non-revolutionary. None of his contemporaries resemble him in the slightest, and yet he is of his time. He retains a strong feeling for tonality, and if his harmony is sometimes strange it is never unintelligible.

The characteristics that make Sibelius's music so freshly different show first of all in his tunes. Appearing fragmentarily at first, motives and themes gradually become drawn together in coherent shapes. Peculiar to Sibelius is the nebulousness of the first showing of his ideas. They are like ghosts—ghosts of the unborn—waiting for their creator to endow them with flesh and blood. Berlioz may have given Sibelius the suggestion for his characteristic bareness, often reduced to a single strand without harmony or counterpoint. The sixteen bars of clarinet solo, unaccompanied, at the beginning of the first symphony is a case in point. When harmony enters, Sibelius's tendency is to keep it thinned out. His basses are striking, and often it seems that in his great pedal-points, sometimes sustained for many bars with a peculiar pulse, he had caught the bass of the works of Nature—forest, sea, wind and storm—and Nature's own rhythm. Characteristic, too, are the backgrounds of scales or of some ceaselessly repeated running figuration, with which he sets off some powerful theme. These are found from one end of his creations to the other, from 'En Saga' to 'Tapiola.'

The scoring stamps any page as Sibelius's own. The outlines stand out, rugged and stark. Mists gather and dissipate, but there is never an effect made by an overwhelming number of notes. The means are reduced to a minimum compatible with the vital utterance, and at the greatest climax the texture remains surprisingly simple. Instead of a thickening of the score as he approaches a peak there is a merging of the separate lines of the instrumentation into great-hewn lanes, where the utmost volume of sound is concentrated in a mighty declamation and every instrument is heard, concentrated in the most effective part of its range.

We are given the feeling that Sibelius's music makes its own form. There is no adaptation to a preconceived pattern, but exposition, development and recapitulation are subjugated to the poetic thought. Sibelius's strength lies in the sense he conveys of unflagging movement towards a great purpose. He does not hesitate or dally; he takes no inordinate liking to a phrase and falls to no temptation to digress. What is said is said for a purpose,

8*

and an alluring phrase may be discarded after one hearing, while a single ascending scale may be repeated for half a hundred bars. It is curious that such repetitions, at which the orchestra toils up and down on one unchanging motive, do not become tedious, as they would with any other composer. No one surpasses Sibelius in his ability to bring out the utmost expressiveness from the instruments. Though it is seldom that he dwells much on unmitigated sentiment, he is irresistible when he wants to make a touching appeal.

XXII

SIBELIUS'S SECOND SYMPHONY

THE second symphony, we have seen, came three years after the first, with which Sibelius may be said to have closed 'the book of conventions.' From now on the symphony was to be for him something between formal symphony and unshackled tone-poem. The second symphony contains certain elements of up-heaval, but also has some characteristics absent from its more purely Sibelian successors. There is a wonderful sense of freedom in the work and of emotion unleashed, and it is writing that is the delectation of the orchestra.

The classical exposition is here abandoned; instead, Sibelius introduces fragmentary ideas which do not begin to attain signi-ficant coherence until mid-way through the movement. The first movement (Allegretto, 6/4) may be said to consist of the follow-ing: three short episodes; full working-out section; short recapitulation of the three episodes; and coda.

The symphony opens with an expressive phrase on the strings:

Fig.1

This may look like no more than an accompaniment, but it is one of the principal ideas of the movement and much of the ensuing material springs from this germ. Three conductors, Toscanini, Koussevitsky and Beecham, are particularly associated with this symphony.

Koussevitsky has been known to spend about twenty minutes on the opening string phrase alone, saying: "You know, I don' like it! You play without expression, and there is no ensemble. It mus' be absolutely perfect in expression, and the crotchet rest—

some of you play it! Like a silent breath, meine Kinder! And then *singen, singen,* molto vibrato!"

Toscanini treats it in much the same way, so that this simple-looking phrase sets the whole mood of the symphony. The breath between the string phrases becomes a vital feature as the episodes unfold.

The first theme to appear is of pastoral nature, and the wood-wind's cheerful piping comes in direct contrast to the emotional mood of the sustained chords:

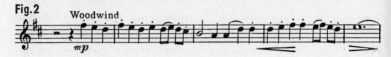

The horns echo its last bar at a slower tempo, dragging the quaver figure out to four crotchets against the 6/4 time:

This interpolation by the horn is only a fragment, but it becomes of great significance later, in a manner typical of Sibelius. This pastoral theme, with the horn's interpolation, is then repeated three times, and the first episode ends with the clarinet's taking the place of the horn. After a pause, the two bassoons boldly come into the picture, with an arresting upward passage in thirds, their hurrying call at the end making the flutes suddenly shiver into a tremolo:

Quite inconsequentially the violins now break into an impassioned recitative, entirely unaccompanied. They close on a pause, and then some more broken-up fragments of intensely expressive character well up on the strings and woodwind alternately.

The second episode is brought to a conclusion by a vehement

pizzicato passage for the strings, made all the more agitated by a
crotchet rest at the beginning of each bar. The passage gets quicker
and quicker till the tempo changes to poco allegro, and what may
be considered as the principal theme of the movement makes an
unpretentious entry on the woodwind, like a mere flourish after
a long sustained note, with the first phrase of the strings accompanying (Sibelius frequently introduces an important figure by
sustaining a long-drawn note):

Fig. 5 Woodwind

Three times the flutes insist on their tune, and now a new saw-
like apparition stalks on the scene, cutting across the top of the
score in the woodwind, fortissimo:

Fig. 6

This third agitated and final episode ends as the first began, with
the initial string phrase. From now, all these fragments begin to
draw together. The central working-out section of the movement
begins with the oboe timidly playing the principal subject, unaccompanied and changed into the minor key. Now the bassoons
further expand it to a long sustained tune, characteristic of
Sibelius. A particular feature is the group of four crotchets spreading over the 6/4 tempo, reminiscent of the horn interpolations at
the beginning.

The violas meanwhile have begun one of the composer's weird
backgrounds of running notes, as if in some dark forest the air
were crowded with unseen spirits. The music is eerie as the
strings in sudden crescendos and diminuendos become obsessed
with anxiety, while the sawing phrase (Fig. 5) appears from
behind the trees like an apparition. Then a sudden outburst
quickly subsides and the frightened strings fade out of sight. The
timpani are left alone with the steady rhythmic beats of six to the

bar, which serve as the rhythmic framework of the movement. Sibelius from this point gathers together all his spirits that have been haunting the orchestra, and imbues them with life and cohesion. The innocent pastoral figure of the beginning is now quickened and violently energized, and united to the early horn interpolations. The four spread crotchets which originally sounded like a natural cadence to the pastoral theme (Fig. 3) now attain great significance, as almost the entire orchestra attacks the 6/4 rhythmic foundations of the movement.

Disregarding all the composer's attempts to keep to his original rhythm, the orchestra, derided and led on by the shrill screams of the woodwind, bursts out with great strides, trampling the basic rhythm into the dust. The whole of this working-out, with its suggestion of tremendous warring forces, is wildly exciting to play. The prodigious effort of forcing this articulate utterance across the orchestra, in defiance of the composer himself, as it were, is like a thrilling "try" in rugby football. But, of a sudden, Sibelius brings in for one moment the principal theme, and instantly the strings are curbed, changing their tearing, single bows to each note, to long sustained strokes. The music, if repressed, is still extremely tense, and again Sibelius thunders out his principal theme, finally bringing up the trumpets to quell the turbulence. The strings are quickly out of hand again with the tearing bows, until the time is forced to change to 4/4, and the brass, with superb confidence, come into action with the original bassoon motive from the start of the second episode (Fig. 4).

Here is one of Sibelius's inimitable inspirations in the way of "articulate music-speech." Nothing grander than the sound of a great declamatory passage such as this hurled over the orchestra by a perfect department of brass! It is difficult, for not only is perfection of ensemble required but the tone must be rich and glowing with colour. Too often one hears it forced by a conductor and overblown. With the syllables of this declamation accentuated by the timpani, this is one of the great moments of the symphony, and indeed of all Sibelius. The brass continues with that inconsequential passage of the strings that we heard before, now transforming it to a glorious and shining figure of triumph.

If any are doubtful as to Sibelius, let them listen to this brass passage, which crowns the movement. No one else in the world would have thought of it! The fast and rising tremolo of the strings makes a radiantly shimmering background, and the gloomy forest, with its half-seen spirits, is swept away like Klingsor's magic garden.

With the last great cadence the time returns to 6/4, and excepting the strings' phrase which opened the movement (now omitted) we find ourselves back where we started. The recapitulation, which is short, goes back over much the same ground, but the sun lights up the fearsome trees and we are familiar with those ghostly shapes that now, in the light of day, prove to be only flesh and blood. The movement ends with the beautiful, expressive motive with which it began, the strings fading to pianissimo.

The opening of the second movement is a holiday for the rest of the orchestra to enjoy the spectacle of the double-basses climbing in pizzicato over the mountain crags of difficult intonation, just helped round one nasty corner by the cellos. It is curious that it should be more difficult to play in tune pizzicato than with the bow. We shall not forget the grooming and preparation that took place in the double bass department when Koussevitsky, that great master of the double bass, conducted this symphony for the first time at one of our concerts. When it came to the second movement at rehearsal, the orchestra awaited the double basses' fate with anxiety. So well we knew that 'beetling of brows' and gathering storm if everything was not quite as it should be. But, looking at his own 'children' with kindness in his eye, they more than satisfied.

The cellos have a more protracted task, for their lonely pilgrimage covers three pages of the score, until it becomes the background for a melancholy tune on the bassoons (not, as it is sometimes considered, a Finnish folk-song) :

Fig.7 *Tempo Andante, ma rubato*

The timpani intermittently rumble in the distance, while the warning calls of the horns prepare us for the oncoming of a time of stress. The tempo quickens, and we are soon caught up in a violent struggle. Many conflicting themes rush at us, and a sinister motive, shrieking in the flutes, is like the protagonist of the spirits of darkness:

These various themes fling their poisonous darts, until a vicious scale in the strings leaves the brass masters of the field. These thunder their threatening and forbidding harmonies, until everything eventually dissolves in air and nothing is heard save a rumble in timpani and basses. Taking the last, malignant chord of the brass, Sibelius resolves it into another one that sets a new atmosphere of supernatural calm. The violins, in a melting phrase—

with all the strings divided into eight parts, prepare the colours for as lovely a lyrical tune as Sibelius could invent, enhanced by a liquid woodwind accompaniment in thirds. It rises to a climax of emotion, though the whole melody is only six bars long:

But cellos and basses, over an angry buzzing in the violins, dispel this sense of refuge, and after a pause, while the timpani threaten and mutter, we return to the first part of the movement, for the melancholy tune (Fig. 7) to sound still more desolate on a solo trombone, in a curious dialogue with the flute. In words this sounds nothing, but Sibelius makes it extraordinarily impressive, with a most beautiful, rocking background on the upper strings, whilst the cellos remind us of their former pizzicato.

The conflict breaks out anew, now more intense, and the brass becomes more brutal than ever in its victory. The same course of events follows as before, but on a more sombre note and in darker keys. The strings have heartrending appeals, and here is an instance how Sibelius, when he is working up to an emotional climax, gives the impression that it is a whole people who are pleading for freedom and no merely personal grief. It is one of the great moments of the symphony, this grand united melody rising out of the two separate lyrical ideas (Fig. 9 and Fig. 10:)

But no answer is forthcoming. A diabolical buzzing, which again breaks out in violins and violas, shatters any illusion there may have been of relief. The barbarous cellos and basses trample down such thoughts fortissimo, and after a shriek of derision from the woodwind, in two bars of ghastly trills that no one but Sibelius could have invented, the movement ends with the unrelenting demands of the victors.

The third movement, an abnormal scherzo, presents violent contrasts. Instead of casting it in the usual way (scherzo-trio-scherzo-coda) Sibelius leads us by a bridge into the Finale. Moreover, the trio is in a completely different mood—it is a kind of enchanting nocturne.

The Scherzo sparkles with vitality. Only two quotations need be given, for the music is built up wholly from these two opposed ideas.

Fig.12 *Vivacissimo*
Violins

From this figure of only two bars a whole powerfully driving rhythmic creation springs. Sometimes it is violent with fury and then as suddenly soft, and always swift as Mercury himself. When it is marked fortissimo and hammered out on the timpani it seems full of the fury of the elements themselves.

The second theme—

Fig.13 Flutes

is a lovely lyrical strain of four bars, in direct contrast to the other's violence. Used with all kinds of scoring, it often takes precedence over the first motive which, except for vivid flashes of anger, whistles away like the wind in the roof-tops. Only when the door opens do we get the full blast of the gale. One of these moments occurs towards the end of the first section, when the wind rises to a tornado and then dies away into silence, except for single soft and intermittent knocks on the timpani.

The key is now darkened from B flat major to the minor, and out of a great stillness the oboe begins the Nocturne, with its single lovely theme:

Fig.14 *Lento and suave*
Oboe Solo

It is one of the Sibelian mysteries, how it comes about that these nine repeated notes sound perfectly natural, when on paper it looks as though the oboe would have to proceed with pumping operations before he could get enough wind for the rest of the tune. It is also curious that, with the orchestra's sometimes

irrepressible delight in guying certain effects grown too familiar,
the temptation to underline the resemblance to 'The Lost Chord'
is ignored. One rehearsal is remembered at which Koussevitsky
made the oboist play over the tune five times by himself, while
the orchestra joyously watched the unfortunate artist's face
changing first to brick red and then to purple, to explode at last
in unprintable asides to his partner.

It no doubt presents a problem in phrasing and expression, but
when played to perfection these reiterated notes grow into the
tune as naturally as thought becomes speech. Koussevitsky made
this little slow movement a particular object of care.

"You play each note der same! *Singen, meine Lieben!* Singen
from your hearts, each note with expression and molto vibrato!"

This Nocturne is only thirteen bars in length, and it rises to a
considerable emotional climax, when oboe, clarinet and strings
vie with one another in opening their very hearts. The flute ends
the movement with a half-questioning phrase.

Out bursts the Scherzo again, louder than before. Various
differences in scoring are made, but again, as the first time, the
storm, when at its height, suddenly dissolves and the calm and
stillness of the Nocturne returns. It is four bars shorter this time,
and now an upward accompanying phrase of the strings merges
into a new figure which forms part of the strong bridge to the
Finale.

Two phrases form the structure; this sweeping and powerful
phrase in the strings:

Fig.15 Strings

and a simple crotchet figure which punctuated the phrases in the
Nocturne:

Fig.16

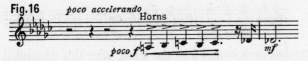

The bridge is powerfully built up until on the far side its span

eventually falls on the main, triumphant theme of the Finale,
which in its extreme simplicity looks on paper impossibly
inadequate for its task:

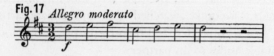

Fig.17 *Allegro moderato*

The scoring of this opening of the Finale is characteristic of
Sibelius's economy and stark outline. The strings have the theme
itself over bare harmonies sustained by horns and lower woodwind, which the trombones colour in each bar with a rhythmic
figure:

Fig.18 *Allegro moderato*

The basses and tuba support the whole structure on a reiterated
pedal note which continues uninterrupted for sixteen bars. This
is kept alive by a Sibelian pulse strongly marked on the last beat
of the bar. After the main theme has been announced two subsidiary tunes, the one a flourish on the trumpets and the other an
exulting phrase on the horns, come in their turn to be rounded
off by a great ascending scale on the strings, ending in a downward leap. This opening section is then repeated, but the stark
outlines are now filled in with brilliant colours and a new feature
enters into the theme, which has two more vitally important bars
added to it:

Fig.19 Strings

Another note comes into the music after this triumphal beginning. The flute, with a trace of sadness and longing, alters the

mood, infecting the rest of the orchestra, who discuss the new
line of thought almost passionately before a most expressive
cadence ends on a soft B minor chord. Sibelius thereupon bids us
remember the other side of the picture, with its strife for freedom, and paints one of his weirdly misty backgrounds on cellos
and violas by means of a continually ascending and descending
minor scale. Up and down they toil for thirty-five bars, while the
great second theme of the movement—a march in 3/2 time—
grows from a tentative fragment on the lowest notes of the oboe
to a climax for full orchestra:

Fig. 20

Sibelius asks for this great tune to be played as broadly as
possible and as pathetically. It is a great moment when the mode is
dramatically changed to the major and trumpets and trombones
call an end, on a new motive arising from the march itself:

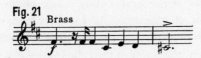

Fig. 21

An arresting passage follows, when the upper strings ascend
to the craggy heights, and cellos and basses, in pizzicato, to the
depths, on a chord of F sharp minor. The main triumphal theme
of the movement is now cloaked in gloom. It gropes about on the
lowest registers of woodwind, while the march is three times
lugubriously repeated. The composer—as he had done in the
first movement—from this point works out two of his principal
themes, the main one and the final motive of the march, adding
chromatic scales in double notes on the strings. The main theme
takes precedence, and a great rising scale piles up. Every instrument of the orchestra joins in, until the great song of triumph
(Fig. 18) overwhelms every other, and once again we are up-
lifted by the grand music of the opening of the Finale. There is a
brilliant addition to the scoring in the woodwind, which peals

over the orchestra like a multitude of bells. Higher and higher soars this song of exultation, until the basses suddenly change from a long dominant A to B flat, and the strings take the road the flute first showed them. But now the passionate discussion becomes an outburst of united feeling. For the last time Sibelius, to make the final scene yet more radiant, returns to the march and all its gloomy associations.

If Sibelius speaks for Finland, then this march may well represent his country's invincible courage. Imagine an indomitable people attaining, after fearful vicissitudes, to the ideal of their faith! Something like that is represented by the coming climax. Few are the masterpieces of art which equal it for exciting, superhuman effect. The players have the feeling of a huge, flooding river bursting all dams. Unlike the showy climaxes of inferior composers this one is superbly sustained at its height. The march in Tchaikovsky's Pathetic Symphony needs a great conductor to thrill the orchestra, but Sibelius's peroration here excites the players to peculiar efforts even though the conductor be an inferior artist. Unforgettable is Toscanini in this music. Koussevitsky has probably come near killing some of his players by his terrific demands at rehearsal. As for Beecham, those outflung arms and superb gestures never tell to greater effect than here.

As before, then, the scales of the cellos and violas form the background, but the key is altered to D minor, and the trumpet is the first to announce the fragment of the march theme. One may appreciate the increase of power that is coming when the length of this section is considered. It was exciting enough before, but now, instead of thirty-five bars of these scales, the passage is prolonged to eighty bars; but so superb is the scoring that this increase of power and tension never shows signs of breaking down. Whereas formerly the strings alone carried the weight of the scales, the entire woodwind are now called in, and the weird skirl of those pipes over the huge power of the brass is a sound never to be forgotten. Only the horns are out of it, having the sustained framework, or rather syncopated harmonies, to cope with.

The composer has firmly denied any programme to this work,

but it is impossible not to be carried away by the feeling of a spirited nation's liberation and triumph. The festive ending comes as with the resounding of great bells. No harsh clanging but a deep, reverberating booming of basses and tuba, and a hammering by timpani. Brass and woodwind declaim the main theme in a last noble pronouncement. The strings, after striving to get the utmost power from their instruments in repeated notes, join the horns at last in their ceaseless pulsing chords that have nobly borne the whole weight of the harmony in the march. So ends the movement and the whole great symphony, in grand rejoicing and thanksgiving.

PART IV

XXIII

ELGAR

1857–1934

THERE are no English symphonies of the classical period, and none that are remembered of the early romantic school. Musicology itself ignores Cipriani Potter, a principal of the Royal Academy of Music, one of whose symphonies was conducted in London by Wagner, in 1855. This was two years before the birth, at Broadheath, near Worcester, of Edward Elgar, thanks to whom England is represented in the tale of the great music of the romantic epoch.

The satisfaction that one feels in being able, with conviction, to make this last statement would have seemed eccentric to the average Englishman of the eighteenth century or even in a good part of the nineteenth. He would have said: "Provided we have good music, what matters it whence it comes—what has the composer's nationality to do with it?" That represented for many generations the English attitude towards music; and it is one of the reasons for the absence, over a long period, of distinguished names of English composers. Not that we shall maintain it to be the only reason. To analyse all would take us far afield; but there is so much misunderstanding of the subject that a short divagation is desirable.

By an accident of social history English life did not afford the native musician an economic foothold comparable with the court opera houses and ecclesiastical orchestras of the Continent. The English court never set up a musical establishment such as even a minor Italian or German princeling would have considered proper to his pomp and circumstance. And our cathedrals, great though their musical tradition is, great their heritage and beautiful and liturgically exemplary their performances, never regarded instruments other than the organ as required, let alone indispensable. The arts have their economic reason for being. Over a long period of modern English history, a period of her increasing power and wealth, music was anything but a promising career for an Englishman. The institutions and establishments were not there which would afford a living for more than a few of what may be called the class of musical artisans. By artisans I mean the rank and file of those who keep a musical civilization going. It is a mistake to imagine that musical genius occurs in isolation. The great men of music have had an economic as well as a cultural background. In generations of musical Bachs there was only one John Sebastian. Genius cannot be reckoned upon for sure. But where there will for sure be no genius is where there has been want of propitious soil and air.

While the economic prospect for the young native musician was unpromising, it was far other for the accomplished foreigner —and even, as time went on, for the not so very accomplished. The field was narrow for the artisans—for the providers of mere bread-and-butter music—but there were immense rewards for the bringer of exceptional gifts. Who did not want to come to England? From the beginning of the eighteenth century onwards London has been full of foreign musicians, some of them eminent and others who have had a pull with the public through merely being foreign, so great was the prestige won by the best of them. The movement began in earnest with the introduction of Italian opera and Italian violinists. Handel settled in England and became a British subject. Musical London was thenceforth cosmopolitan.

In how many histories of music has it not been said that in 1770, for instance, 'English music was at a low ebb'? Or in 1820? Or in 1860? The expression would have surprised the cultivated Londoner of any of those dates. He would have raised his eyebrows and have asked: "Have we not here the best that Europe can provide? What reason for wishing the names of acceptable composers to be English names?" The fact is that the London musical life of any of those dates was brilliant, while the segregation of European peoples into self-conscious nationalities seemed, then, to the enlightened man, not so much a tentative beginning of the rigours to come as the vestige of a barbarous past doomed to disappearance. We may see now that a more nationalist attitude on the part of our forefathers—the exclusion of all the second-raters who became more and more insipid and character-less in the London hot-pot—the cultivation of such small native shoots and sprouts as we could boast—might eventually have done more for our national glory. But nothing is more futile than to lecture the past. What is only just to realize is that our easygoing hospitality was considered by those who practised it —who still practise it—as enlightened. Was not music a uni-versal or at any rate a European language?

Well, not so universal as all that. Until such time as musicolo-gists condescend to turn up the works of Cipriani Potter I content myself with suggesting that the first protest against cosmopo-litanism was the foundation in the 1830s of the Society of British Musicians, which had J. W. Davison for its spokesman in the *Musical Magazine*. Sterndale Bennett, Macfarren, Henry Smart, Mudie and Loder were the rallying names. But it was the heyday of Mendelssohnianism and none of those names could shine in such a light. Still we have today no right to congratulate ourselves on a century's progress when we read of the numerous English opera productions of the time—in one season, for instance (1845-6), Wallace's 'Maritana,' Macfarren's 'Don Quixote,' Balfe's 'Bondman' and Loder's 'Night Dancers.'

Sterndale Bennett's music, even, and he was the best composer of the group, now seems pale, its charm inferior to Mendelssohn's, let alone Schumann's. But this ripple in a backwater meant some-thing. What? Certainly not, in that self-assured, prosperous, sanguine England, anything like the nationalism of a Balkan country—not the expression of the desperate vanity that we have come to know so well in our century, among frogs anxious to swell into bulls. It meant that, even in London, where Weber and Mendelssohn, Rossini and Verdi, and a hundred lesser lights from the Continent, were welcomed and acclaimed, the realiza-tion grew that the native voice may in its own plot of earth have something of an intimate interest to say, a chord to strike that is beyond the reach of an exotic hand. From that moment onwards, at any rate, home-made music was no longer as insignificant as it had been a generation before.

In the years when Mendelssohn had infatuated nearly all musical England there was born a stronger brood—first Sullivan (1842), then Mackenzie (1847), Parry in 1848, both Stanford and Cowen in 1852 and Edward German ten years later. All these, except Mackenzie, wrote symphonies—Stanford seven, Cowen six, Parry five, German two, Sullivan one—but none was primarily a symphonist. Sullivan, a brilliant and genial musician, won the hearts of his fellow-countrymen with something no Continental could have given them: a series of matchless operettas. Cowen's characteristic vein, too, was light, and so was German's. Parry and Stanford, both great pedagogues, were first-rate all-round musicians. The bulk of their work is enormous. Parry's massive choral music ranks high in the English heritage. Stanford was the more versatile and clever; he composed several operas; and, rarely though his music is heard now, admiration can never be denied his workmanship and a superior quality of mind. Like Parry and Stanford at the Royal College of Music, Mackenzie at the Royal Academy played a great part in musical education. His music, too, had sturdy and attractive qualities.

It cannot be said of any one of these three that his British nationality favoured him in his career, save in so far as choral societies found their wants met by their work. Down to the end of the nineteenth century England felt no need of national musical glory. If we had had no poets of our own that would have been different. It would have been something serious, a real lack as well as a reflection on native talent, to have depended upon translations from a foreign tongue. But as for music, everyone was satisfied with the best that could be got from elsewhere. Sullivan was thought a hundred more of than Offenbach simply because he seemed to be a hundred times better. (And then there were Gilbert's local witticisms!) And Stanford set Tennyson to music for choral societies, and Parry set Milton and Shelley, as no one—Brahms or anyone else—could have done. But there was no mercy on their symphonies or chamber music, since Brahms's were better. The rage for Mendelssohn having died down, musical England was engaged in the last quarter of the century in assimilating Brahms and Wagner.

There is a different approach to the native composer, a different measure of appreciation, in the middle of the twentieth century. One reason for this, no doubt, is that the European sky shows no star of such dazzling magnitude as those of old. And no doubt we have to some extent fallen into line with the Continental practice of giving the native musician a favourable hearing. Then there is the fact that every sort of exoticism has been worked hard. And in an age of disillusionment there is less promise of delight in the making of foreign acquaintances. One falls back upon the more or less known—the nature of one's fellow-countrymen—as the lesser evil. The young Elgar, growing up in an England hypnotized by Wagner—Bernard Shaw's well-known volumes of musical criticism give us the measure of this—enjoyed no such advantage. Nor was he favoured by any of the academic support which did a good deal for Parry and Stanford, for he had been educated far from the academies and came upon the official world as an outsider. Yet by the end of the century he was recognized by a grudging country not only as the leading English composer but also as an eminent European.

As much had been allowed no other English composer of the nineteenth century. And it was properly allowed. By what in our present temper we gladly acknowledge as a stroke of luck, not only was a new contribution made to the major glories of the century—a contribution that was practically the last of the euphonious and romantic music whose epoch was so near its end —but also an English contribution. As the sun sets in the west, so did euphonious nineteenth-century music send forth its last splendid beams from the banks of Severn, in the form of Elgar's oratorios, symphonic variations, concertos and symphonies.

So much is said here to put Elgar's career into perspective. In a country more passionately nationalist than England, Elgar, the composer at thirty-three of the already characteristic 'Froissart' overture (Worcester Festival, 1890), would have at once been lionized. His way was not made so easy. But it was not, after all, so very hard. Elgar was self-taught and he did not develop early.

The cantatas of the 1890s were taken up by the big choral societies. The masterpieces that then came were acclaimed, though 'The Dream of Gerontius' (Birmingham, 1900) suffered a momentary setback. In 1904 a three-day Elgar Festival was given at Covent Garden—a tribute such as no other English composer had ever received. No doubt there was for a time some coldness to him at the academies, which is reflected in Ernest Walker's *History of Music in England*. The academies were Brahmsian. And it must be mentioned that not so much Brahms's sentiment as the purity of his writing, his learning and the sobriety of his instrumentation was appreciated there. Elgar, too, was Brahmsian. His love for the Third Symphony was unbounded, though he criticized the scoring. But he lived outside musical politics, and frankly admired anything that took his fancy—in Liszt as well as in Brahms, and even in Meyerbeer. Stanford was a clear and accomplished orchestrator, but somewhat conventional. He had the conductor's instinct, and might, if he had chosen, have become a great conductor of the Weingartner type. But temperamentally he was rather dry and he disliked lavishness of colour. Parry was no master of the orchestra. It was the last aspect of music to which he directed his active, purposeful, buoyant mind. The orchestra was Elgar's world. That he wrote so much for voices was accidental—the accident of his being a nineteenth-century English musician. He was a great orchestrator, a passionate colourist; and such passion was not congenial in South Kensington. No one is to be blamed. All these men were considerable characters, not to be expected to see eye to eye. Stanford brought over with him from Dublin a quick temper; Elgar was, behind his thoroughbred English gentlemanliness, extraordinarily thin-skinned. Too much has been made of their natural differences. After the Enigma Variations (London, under Richter, June 19, 1899, a famous day *) Elgar's career was triumphal, mitigated

* Plunket Greene, in his *Life* of Stanford, gives this story of the Enigma Variations: "Parry was sitting at home after dinner one evening at his house in Kensington Square, when the late A. J. Jaeger of Novello's turned up and asked to see him. He had the score of the Variations under his arm, and showed it to Parry. It was a terrible night, with a howling gale and sheets of rain, and any sensible man would have put off his good deeds until the morrow. But one

SIBELIUS

ELGAR

only by the disparagement of impatient young spirits in the 1920s, when the rich splendours of his style were out of tune with an uncomfortable generation's unrest and the vogue was for the new acidulated music.

The sound of Elgar's orchestra seems to speak of the luxury of a great metropolis; and yet it came from a smallish country town, set in a green valley where agricultural interests prevailed, with, for principal music, the cathedral choir and organ. But Worcester is one of the cities of the Three Choirs, and Elgar must be held to be in some sort a son of the Three Choirs' Festival. There he first made his name in 1890, and there his music has ever since been heard with the greatest effect, in the setting of Norman or Gothic arcades, with afternoon sunshine coming through the painted glass and seeming to blend with its chromatic harmonies, and with high vaulting where the ardent praise and prayer of his thoughts seem to linger after the sound has died away.

But the cathedral was not his spiritual home. This was the Roman Catholic church of St. George, where his father, who kept a music shop at Worcester, was organist. At sixteen Elgar became assistant organist there. But primarily the lad was a violinist (as Mackenzie had been), and this sets him apart from the typical English musician, who is an organist. At seven he was given his first piano lessons, and at nine he was, with evident aptitude, teaching himself to play various instruments in his father's shop—principally violin, viola, violoncello and bassoon. At twelve he was composing, and some of those boyish pieces were later revised and published ('Wand of Youth,' Op. 1). As a violinist he showed talent enough for Pollitzer in London to promise to turn him into a concert soloist, but composition was Elgar's ambition. From twenty-two to twenty-seven he was bandmaster at the Worcestershire County Lunatic Asylum. By this time he was a fairly accomplished bassoonist. The asylum band was an unusual ensemble of two cornets, euphonium, bombardon, flute, clarinet, two violins, double-bass and piano.

look at the score was good enough for Parry. He jumped straight into a hansom and drove off with them to Richter. Richter did them at his next concert. This was in 1899."

9

Elgar's duties included the technical instruction of the players, and he not only scored arrangements for this band, but also composed for it. In these strange circumstances, where he worked for five years, was founded his marvellous orchestral technique. It was an accomplishment in which Richard Strauss ran him close; but in one respect no composer has ever matched Elgar. None other has fully exploited all the orchestral instruments and at the same time written nothing impossible. In this latter respect Strauss frequently sins, and so did Wagner. Most latter-day composers set entirely unnecessary problems of execution, impossible or nearly impossible of solution, simply through never themselves having played both stringed and wind instruments enough.* Elgar was unerring. He knew precisely what could and could not be played; and is never found guilty of a "black patch" of notes (Henry Wood's expression) written simply for its look on paper. At eighteen his ambition had been to study at Leipzig; but his resources would not run to it. At twenty-five he enjoyed his first holiday in Germany, but he no longer thought of Leipzig. At thirty-two he married a pupil of his, Caroline Alice Roberts, daughter of Major-General Sir Henry Gee Roberts. This marriage was to be a devoted partnership of a sort rare enough in the lives of the great artists. It is significant that none of Elgar's major music is dated before his marriage or after Lady Elgar's death (1920).

The story has often been told of the choir's failure at the Birmingham Festival of 1900 to do justice to 'Gerontius' and the disappointment Elgar suffered. The next year the great work was rehabilitated at the Lower Rhine Festival at Düsseldorf; and it was performed there again in 1902. Strauss was present—Strauss, then at his meridian—and at a luncheon toasted Elgar: "I drink to the success and welfare of the first progressive English musician!" The words had a great repercussion. Elgar had for some years been considering a symphony. Gordon was one of Elgar's heroes, and the unborn work was for a time thought of as a 'Gordon' Symphony, or even simply as 'Gordon.' Jaeger, his

---

* Many years later, when he was writing 'Falstaff,' Elgar took trombone lessons from Lettington, bass trombonist of the London Symphony Orchestra.

friend at 160, Wardour Street, encouraged him in the project; but Elgar was fifty before he wrote his first symphony—which was not 'Gordon.' Composed in 1907–8, the A flat symphony was played at Manchester under Richter (to whom it was dedicated) on December 3, 1908, and in London on December 7. At Queen's Hall Richter at rehearsal introduced it to the orchestra with these words: "Gentlemen, let us now rehearse the greatest symphony of modern times, written by the greatest modern composer." And he added: "And not only in this country!"

No symphony was ever so welcomed. By this time the Variations, 'Gerontius,' the masterly 'Introduction and Allegro' (1905) and other works were known throughout the country, and the symphony had been awaited with keen interest. It more than fulfilled expectations. Let us try to picture the time. A happy England—Britain at her meridian! It was not only that living was cheap and that every decade saw, with an enriched world, an ever wider social distribution of wealth and amelioration; it was, above all, the sanguine spirit of men and the universal belief, after a century of liberal progress, in the step-by-step betterment of man's condition and nature which made for a happiness—which, after the catastrophic vicissitudes we have lived to see, is hard for the imagination to recapture. A generation has grown up which—"hungry sheep . . . swol'n with wind"—professes to despise the Edwardian period and its opulence. There is talk of "post-Victorian complacency" and "Elgar's celebration of the over-fed sumptuousness of the Edwardian era."

George Sampson had a word for this: "journalistic nonsense." * He says: "The plain, simple truth about Elgar is that he is neither Victorian nor Edwardian, but Elgarian, and always was, from first to last. That is why people either like or loathe him."

It is also a fact that Elgar was a man of his day, aspiring and hopeful; and along with the splendours of the A flat symphony its optimism was that of his generation. The great tune to which we are briefly introduced at the beginning is obscured by doubts and strife, but is not defeated, and at the end it returns with

* *Music and Letters*, July 1946.

superb pageantry, like a hero who has done well by his country
and his conscience. To have been young in 1908 and to have heard
this symphony as a novelty is an experience for which to be
grateful. All England, for that matter, was grateful. A hundred
performances were called for in its first year of life. We may,
when we read of Elgar's poorish financial position, which, when
he was already middle-aged and famous, postponed his applying
himself to major instrumental works, deplore the necessity in
which he found himself of writing in more ephemeral forms.
But it is a mistake of historical outlook to fail to see what his
era gave him spiritually, small though his material rewards were,
down to the time of the coming of the gramophone.

This is not the place to speak of 'The Apostles' (1903) and
'The Kingdom' (1906), two large-scale choral works, containing many beauties but inferior in design to 'Gerontius.'
With the A flat symphony Elgar was fairly launched on the tide
of instrumental music. The year 1910 saw the glorious violin
concerto, dedicated to Kreisler and played by him; and 1911 the
second symphony in E flat, with which the next chapter deals.
Another major work—the richest of all, perhaps, in invention and
colour, although now out of favour with the passing of the
vogue of programme-music—was 'Falstaff' (1913). This represents Elgar's high summer. War came in 1914, and Elgar's compositions were occasional, though numerous. Three chamber
works were brought out in 1919, and later in the year the beautiful little autumnal violoncello concerto, the finest violoncello concerto of this century. Lady Elgar died in 1920, and it was as
though his life were blasted. For years he wrote hardly anything.
Then two large projects formed in his mind—an opera ('The
Spanish Lady') and a third symphony. A revived creativeness
seemed promised. He sketched copiously. But in 1933 a cruel
disease seized him, and on February 23, 1934, at Worcester, he
died.

Elgar as a conductor was sound but not always inspiring. He
obtained fine performances of his own works, since what he had
principally to do was to give a clear rhythmic beat, every detail
being accounted for in the score. His stick was fairly clear, but

curiously unimaginative in its movement. It was his face and certain expressive gestures of his left hand that would sometimes lighten up a page. One sometimes felt sorry for the soloist in a concerto, for Elgar gave the impression of feeling no great sympathy for his point of view. But in those days when he was growing into old age the orchestra loved him. His manners and quiet dignity, the quick, nervous gestures of his expressive hands, the twinkle in his eye when he cracked some old chestnut we were supposed never to have heard before; above all the sheer sight of the grand old man, looking the picture of a beloved country squire—this always charmed the players, and they were conscious of contact with a great man.

The B.B.C.'s Elgar Festival of 1933 will ever be unforgettable by those who took part. The great works seemed to unfold themselves in his hands. Born and bred to his music, the orchestra gave him everything it had, and Elgar had no worry—in return for a simple, clear beat his music played itself to him. Rehearsals were a joy. Every player was out to give him pleasure, and he could rely on the orchestra's knowledge and skill, assured that no detail would be overlooked. So great was the admiration we all felt for him that any small discrepancy in his conducting of a performance was invariably made up by immediate understanding and goodwill. Such a bond is rare. It was something like the attachment felt by passionately loyal subjects to a monarch. Elgar himself had a strong feeling for kingship; his devotion to the British Throne was almost mystical. In his later years the orchestra venerated him much as he and the country did George V. Elgar stood for so much! He gave us music to touch our hearts and exploit our skill.

Glorious are the masterpieces he has left us in three fields—in choral, in orchestral and in chamber music. Pieces that I have not even mentioned—the buoyant, brilliant overture 'In the South,' for instance—are satisfying and exciting for the player. The first symphony is at once intensely emotional and of great length, and the physical strain on the orchestra is exhausting. The violin concerto is a bridge to the E flat symphony; the more mature of the symphonies, less ardent, no less masterly but more serene. An orchestra that has been well prepared for the E flat symphony feels itself part of a wonderful organism of mind and sensibility, a glorious being whose each least sound is a living cell necessary to the full existence of the whole.

'Falstaff' is Elgar's most difficult score. Not that on the surface it appears to present such problems as Strauss's 'Don Quixote.' The difficulty lies in the accurate fitting together of the complex bits, and in attaining perfection of phrasing and balance. Elgar used to take immense pains in rehearsing 'Falstaff.' Not generally difficult to please, he occasionally became fidgety here over some detail. The side-drum one day was slow in obeying him at the moment of Falstaff's death. At the performance itself, which seemed a good one, the player was caught out again, and we were horrified to see a spasm of anger on Elgar's face. He stopped conducting and made no attempt to control things again. Somehow we got to the end together, but it was a shaking experience. I rate Elgar's chamber music higher than some do. The quartet, a reflection of his earlier religious background, is strangely moving in its sincerity and twilight beauty. The violin sonata has music of wonderful warmth of emotion, contrasted with deep tranquillity. I would maintain that the quintet stands as a peer of the great piano quintets of the nineteenth century. The slow movement has one of the greatest melodies ever written for the viola.

In what was to be virtually his last work, the violoncello concerto, Elgar remained in the zone of chamber music. The violoncello is not called on here for incredible feats of execution, but is given a wonderful opportunity to express itself within the natural compass of its voice; and the scoring is perfection. Lionel Tertis has transcribed the solo for viola. True, the viola cannot match the violoncello's sonority and depth, but, whatever cellists have said, Elgar was delighted; and the scherzo at least suits the viola better. Pathetic past words is the last movement of the concerto when, in the midst of cheerful activity, all happiness is suddenly wrecked by a memory—or the illusion of happiness is torn aside like a veil. "The days that are no more!" The music utters a heart-broken lament, and we know that never again will a dawn rise like the dawns of old.

XXIV

ELGAR'S SECOND SYMPHONY

THE symphony in E flat, Op. 63, "dedicated to the memory of his late Majesty King Edward VII," was first performed at the third concert of the 1911 London Musical Festival, at Queen's Hall, on May 24. There were two other new works, Walford Davies's 'Parthenia' suite and Granville Bantock's 'Dante and Beatrice.' The three composers conducted. The prices for the festival were, for those days, very high, and the audience, though large, did not quite fill the hall. Elgar had been used, by the success of 'Gerontius,' the A flat symphony and the violin concerto, to endless ovations, and he was disappointed at the lack of ecstasy in the applause. The fact is, of course, that the serene finale was not likely to stir people to frenzied hand-clapping. "The symphony was received with unhesitating and most cordial warmth." So said one of the papers (*Daily Mail*), the next morning. The glowing notice in this paper extended to a full column of 1,000 words. Such was musical criticism in the popular press of those days!

A note in the score says: "This Symphony, designed early in 1910 to be a loyal tribute, bears its present dedication with the gracious approval of His Majesty the King" (i.e. George V). The elegiac slow movement was written after Edward VII's death. There is an epigraph from Shelley on the symphony: "Rarely, rarely comest thou, spirit of delight!" An ambiguous epigraph! It would seem to imply a regret, but the music is rather a celebration of the spirit's coming and at the end a thanksgiving for the joy vouchsafed.

The symphony begins with a wonderful expression of a mood of nervous exhilaration. To the unprepared listener the sound that bursts upon his ears is marvellous. For the orchestra no symphonic opening is more exciting than this. It is the equivalent of a dive from an immensely high springboard. The audience should look as well as listen, to catch the flash of all the violin and cello bows on the first note, a repeated B flat, and then the upward swoop of a sixth. If these opening bars burst into the listener's mind and flood it, then half the battle has been won. It is the conductor's business to charge the air with electricity before a beginning is made. Indispensable the next moment is the utmost brilliance in the orchestral playing.

Elgar knew perhaps better than anyone else what the orchestra wants. Each player would like a fair share of interest and the opportunity of showing his instrument to the best advantage. Elgar allows him all this, handsomely. An Elgarian score is crowded with detail; the slightest nuance is marked. And everything is as vital and considered as the notes of a Mozart symphony. Elgar had infinitely studied both the art of balancing his instruments and every shade of their colours. Exactly he knew the effect he required, and no orchestra ever resented his meticulous demands. Never does he miscalculate. Aware of the weak spot that lurks in every instrument, he avoids it. Brahms is sometimes a terrible sinner in his string-writing. Elgar would seem to have had a sixth sense for steering clear of the awkward and ineffective.

The conductor, then, is relieved of much that he is called on to do on behalf of composers less expertly technical. How often we have had the experience of grappling with ultra-modern scores, often of the Central European school, which are crowded with difficult detail and labelled in every bar with expression marks. Conductor and orchestra toil endlessly to give each one its value; and then, perhaps, one day comes along the composer to conduct —and to over-ride and ignore the lot! This is not to say that the conductor has nothing to do in Elgar. Jog-trot, humdrum conducting is the death of this emotional, highly-strung music— which, it must be said, is often a music of a certain rhythmical sameness, demanding a special flexibility and nervous quickness of mind. Elgar's own tempos were always fluctuating.

Beecham conducted Elgar a great deal in his younger days, and even took the A flat symphony on a provincial tour. Latterly he has inclined to leave Elgar to others, but when he has returned to

his old love the effect has been surpassingly brilliant. Landon
Ronald was a great Elgarian conductor, and in Edwardian days
his performances excelled the composer's own. Henry Wood
could bring off a grand show on the rare occasions when he had
not been restricted by the meagre rehearsal of a Promenade
season. But for the most satisfying picture of Elgar, year in and
year out, we turn to Adrian Boult.   In this E flat symphony
Boult made his name. It was very soon after the 1918 war, at one
of the London Symphony Orchestra's concerts. After the war-
time lapse there was a new public. Boult was but little known, and
the symphony, though less than ten years old, had been
rather lost to sight. It was a wonderful night. Boult's self-effacing
manner and rather quiet movements notwithstanding, he not
only presented the work in its true perspective but also made the
performance glow. This was the beginning of the post-war
appreciation of Elgar; a new public was won.

The characteristic features of Elgarian tunes are at once apparent. Notice at the beginning of the E flat symphony the wide
intervals, the upward leap, the expressiveness and the exhilaration.
The motto theme 'Spirit of Delight' is represented by the third
bar with its two preceding quavers.

Allied with this main theme are others, the first of which
appears in the ninth bar of this joyous music, played by the
violins and immediately repeated in the octave below:

Notice the detailed directions for quickening the tempo here—
♩.=104, whereas the opening was ♩.=92. This theme of two
bars in length is immediately followed by another important one

9*

—also of two bars and treated in a similar manner, as if the composer were revelling in the ideas:

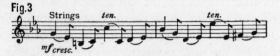

Last of this first group of tunes is this climbing figure:

Typically Elgarian is this queer phrase, with its wide intervals and sequence.

The complexities of the score are great. It is to be no straightforward affair of two main tunes and their symphonic treatment, but the interweaving of numerous themes like the above, in a brilliant, shining web of sound.

A queer bridging passage consisting of merely three notes in a series:

carries us to the main theme of the second subject. This lovely and wistful tune for the strings is marked as usual with lavish directions:

Elgar was insistent that this first entrance of the second subject should be absolutely pianissimo, and invariably warned the players: "Now, strings, you always want to take too much bow here! I only want the smallest movement at the tip of the bow. Give me all the expression I have marked, but on a tiny scale."

In this theme which looks like a sequence of two bars, notice that Elgar subtly makes a slight twist. The rhythm and shape of the two-bar phrase are the same, but the alteration of a semitone just brightens the colour. The tune is then built up from pianissimo to fortissimo in about eighteen bars, and subsides again to another theme for the cellos—of slow, lyrical character, very sustained. This also belongs to the second subject group, in or about G minor:

Notice particularly the accompaniment (in the violas) which is to become important later on in the movement. These groups of tunes constitute the main features, which are developed with wonderful invention and complexity. The first climax of the movement—marked by Elgar's direction 'Impetuoso'—is an unmistakable outburst after a warm section on Fig. 6. It is a huge chromatic passage in contrary motion—the bass pounding up in giant strides and the rest of the orchestra descending in semitones.

This leads to another peak, where woodwind and strings in the most brilliant passage-work illuminate a new version of Fig. 3 from the middle of the orchestra:

The violas, bassoons and oboes have a desperately hard time to force this through the mass of glittering sound.

Elgar now shows us the real summit he is making for. He alters the fairly smooth character of the phrases to some hard, broken jabs; quickens the tempo as if rushing to a point; slows down for a bar; and then the full climax bursts over us in splendour:

The unimportant accompanying figure of Fig. 7 has now become a major part of this heroic episode, with a trumpet call bursting through like a signal of triumph. Gradually the great weight of sound subsides until another version of Fig. 2 quietly disappears into the broken accompanying figure of Fig. 7—now alone except for a sustained note on the woodwind. The sounds melt into one of the most mysterious pages ever written. The phrase is one of immense leaps:

After a few bars of this weird preparation the focal point of the movement is reached, and the music begins to glow with an unearthly light of such intensity that Elgar himself must have felt his heart quicken at the wonder of his own creation. Tovey takes

this as the start of the development section. The tempo is marked
'più lento' and there can be no doubt to the listener where this
uncanny picture begins to form out of a dark background. To
those who know the symphony it is the more significant as fore-
telling a terrifying recurrence in the rondo (third movement).

The timpani first give the cue by a regular throbbing on a
pedal C under the basses a third higher, who accentuate the
rhythm of this relentless sound—at the moment held in dead
pianissimo. Violins and violas, divided into eight parts, alternate
by playing either Fig. 10 or a shadowy form of Fig. 1:

Fig.12

Woodwind and horns sustain or slide quickly up ghostly chromatic scales. The strange form of the picture appears finally in the
cellos. It is an extraordinary tune—of immense range and in-
calculable feeling. It does not touch the emotions, it is too veiled
and intangible; but there is magic in its every line:

Fig.13 Più lento ♩.=76

All the time the cellos are straining in their higher registers for
the unattainable, with sinister throbbing in the mass of texture
behind them. As the weird light dims, the 'Spirit of Delight,'
after seeming to strive for entrance, at last appears—not in
brilliance but with the soft touch of friendly humanity after a
vision. The music, in spite of its power, has never risen above
forte in the cellos, and no better example is to be found of Elgar's
mastery of orchestral balance. But it is a test for conductor and
orchestra, for the cellos should be able to stand out in this picture
from their first entrance to the moment when they join hands

with 'Delight' again. A 'Tranquillo' section now gently clears
the atmosphere with a new theme derived from Fig. 6:

References to Fig. 6 and Fig. 4 keep the mood calm and expressive as before, but Elgar's extraordinary vision is too poignant,
and once more the cellos are drawn into their Fig. 13, and a
further apparition of the supernatural picture. The throbbing of
the timpani is at half the speed this time, and the strings elaborate
the texture of the background. Finally the sounds fade out,
clarinets and bassoons just remaining audible on sustained notes.

Elgar places a double bar here, rather as though he had at last
finished some huge exposition, and the ensuing music gives the
impression that he is setting out on a super-development section;
but it is to prepare for his greatest climax.

He sets out in the key of C sharp minor with a conjunction of
two ideas—Fig. 2 in the treble and Fig. 6 in the bass:

The mood is agitated as the new section opens, and Elgar quickly
calls on all his great orchestral resources; the score is thick with
crowded movement. Dynamic accents pound all over the orchestra as if a giant had broken loose; and in six concentrated bars
of huge strides like this—

the orchestra crashes into the main theme again in E flat.

Like all Elgar's outlines this peak is as clear to the entirely new
listener as the highest snowy cap in a mountain range. Shattering
blows from the timpani backed up by trombones set alight the
whole main theme (Fig. 1). Now the single note of the strings has
become a blazing chord of 6/4, the 'Spirit of Delight' is split in
two by a break in the score; the sharp pinnacle then shines forth
in blinding light on the ensuing chord. Somehow or other the
conductor must reserve something for this moment. A look at
the following example will show Elgar's explicit directions
for it.

|| signifies a 'break'

It was curious how the composer, when he conducted this
work, invariably clouded this very pinnacle. The silent break,
which should represent a sudden catching of breath before the
plunge into the full tune again, never came off to perfection.
Somehow the orchestra never felt confidence in him at this point,
particularly on those last two preceding quavers where the most
vital lead is required. His eye would fail to hold us and his usually
clear beat become fluffy. Landon Ronald knew all about this
climax and found no difficulty, though he sometimes made the
moment of silence unnecessarily long, which endangers the
effect. Boult invariably brings the whole great section, with its
immensely concentrated preparation, to its magnificently sharp
and clear point.

After this return to the main theme there is a recapitulation
with vastly elaborated orchestration; the triumphant episode is
heard again (Fig. 9) in the key of B flat, the dominant; but the
unearthly vision does not return, and, unwilling to call it up a
third time, Elgar quietly allows the music to subside on Fig. 2,
fading with the broken accompanying figure of Fig. 7 into

the coda. This begins with Fig. 14, only in very extended form:

Fig.18

There is a wonderful sense of calm and rest for a few moments, until an upsurging of youthful exuberance whirls us on to the last breathless shout of the motto, with the utmost power of the orchestra. Notice the break this time is *before* the two quavers—the 'Spirit of Delight' is in his full shape.

Fig.19

The last three bars of the movement give the strings a glorious chance of showing the meaning of virtuosity. Every note is playable; and the skirling rush should leave the listener spellbound. If the movement is played with youthful excitement and the orchestra is brilliant the listener will feel himself rejuvenated.

The slow movement is in the nature of a funeral march. It is not a personal lament; and at the same time it is anything but empty ceremony. No monarch ever received a tribute more beautiful, more splendid or more genuine in feeling than this. It is music that leaves us with the sense of having been present at the passing of a great figure, who had much in common with us and meant much to us.

The movement opens with an introduction of seven bars, in a deeply hushed atmosphere. It consists of the following phrase for strings in C minor, and is repeated in F minor in the usual Elgarian way:

Fig.20 *Larghetto* ♩.=60

The scoring is beautifully laid out for strings divided into seven parts. The cellos, playing in thirds, give a certain colour in the orchestra, as of light through stained-glass, with the harp further enhancing the effect by two most telling chords. The march then begins to sound, in extremely soft tones, on woodwind and brass, to the regular, slow, funereal tread of strings and drums:

Fig.21

Another strain grows in the middle of the march, a strangely contrasted welling-up of passion, before the full march-theme is brought to a close:

Fig.22

A short phrase like a recurring sigh appears on the woodwind, modulating through various keys:

Fig.23

The music then melts to an episode lovely in its simplicity and pathos, for strings alone:

Fig.24

Landon Ronald used to make a great deal of this exquisitely

peaceful moment, with its dark beauty enhanced by the violas in the fourth bar, which he always slightly expanded. If this passage is much subdued, the effect is extremely moving.

The music rises to a climax, in a quickening tempo, though still kept on simple lines, until there is a sudden and dramatic fall to pianissimo and change of key to D major. Elgar suddenly releases his restraint and plunges into imaginative scoring, where the main idea is this short phrase (already foreshadowed in the march):

The orchestra comes into its own, and it is one of those places where the conductor has to restrain rather than drive. This typical passage on the strings swirls with glorious freedom round and about Fig. 25:

The music builds up of its own volition to a bar of thrilling virtuosity for both strings and woodwind, and the full climax of the movement peals forth on the brass in the key of F major. Never did Elgar put his beloved term 'nobilmente' to better use than here. The triumphal outburst is intensely expressive, with another figure, mostly in the bass:

On the subsidence of this immense structure, the sigh of grief wells up again (Fig. 23), and the end of the phrase expands and ascends in diminuendo as a new figure in the bass enters, in slow descending steps:

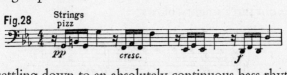

finally settling down to an absolutely continuous bass rhythm.

These last few bars are preparatory to a return of the march, in which Elgar creates one of the most impressive pictures ever to be made by music. When he conducted he always spoke of this to the orchestra, saying: "I want you to imagine a great crowd of silent people, watching the passing of a beloved sovereign. Strings, you must play those semiquaver figures of yours like the sigh of an immense crowd.

"You must slightly push your bow for the first stroke and then let it fall right away. Oboe, I want you to play your lament entirely free, with all the expression you can get into it. Don't worry about me or the rest of the orchestra. It must sound as if it belonged outside somewhere."

The oboe lament is this moving melody:

which weaves above the score, indifferent to the great march and everything else. The march, with the soft tang of the oboe improvising around the mass of sound, is, once heard, never to be forgotten. At the end of the march Elgar returns to the intensely quiet and intimate Fig. 24 and once more gives us the huge build-up and climax of Fig. 27, which this time bursts out in the key of the symphony, E flat, and rises to even a further pitch of intensity.

Elgar knew what fervour meant, and in this long-held, almost ecstatic second climax, fervour burns like a torch. As in the first movement, there is one peak higher than any other. Here the violins and woodwind climb to the extreme summit, the timpani rapping out three mighty blows:

Elgar at the rehearsal made a rare alteration in the timpani in the first bar, shortening the original roll (a semi-breve) to enable the terrific strokes mentioned above to take fuller effect.

In the coda comes an unexpected reappearance of the main theme of the symphony, played with all possible warmth of expression on the clarinets, violas and then violins:

A mournful reflection of the march dissolves into the introductory phrase which opened the movement. A snarl from the trombones brings a sudden cry from violas and cellos—quickly stifled—and the music is at an end.

After the solemnity and sorrow in which the second movement closes, Elgar hurls himself into an orgy. He gives this movement the title of Rondo. The main theme is of intense vitality and youthfulness:

Immense play is made of the figure  throughout the movement, especially in its use across the initial 3/8 rhythm. This kind of thing is typical—

The first episode has a contrasted and swinging tune as its theme. It is full of the composer's favourite leaps—

Landon Ronald used to accent the crotchets heavily and was annoyed if the orchestra was too correct in observing the strict quaver values—in fact with him each bar was a separate entity. On the other hand, Boult always seeks to join the quavers to the next crotchet, giving the tune a grand continuity of rhythm. It is curious how different the two interpretations can sound. Elgar himself wanted a fine swinging movement and great vitality from the string tone. "Now, strings, enjoy this tune! Don't rock in your seats, but let it have some life!" he would say.

The rondo subject is suggested again by much play with its various figures. A new tune on the violins—

growing into this grand phrase—

soon brings a complete return of the subject, fortissimo, from full orchestra.

The second episode is introduced by a new figure, on woodwind, of wistful charm:

This constitutes the main subject of this episode, which is quieter in mood and is made thoughtful by soft and smooth playing in the strings, like some lovely piece of chamber music. The rondo tune comes back, this time very softly, with a significant motif beginning in 2nd violins—

and gradually becoming more insistent in the foreground, until the character of the whole music becomes suddenly diffused with pulsing chords on an E flat pedal, and the significance of Fig. 39 suddenly strikes us. It is the initial bar of the great cello tune (Fig. 13) already introduced in the first movement in the full glow of the vision:

Once again, as in the first movement, the timpani give the unmistakable signal for this colossal episode, which seems to many of us in the orchestra never to have been surpassed for terrifying power. Though one may have played most of the music under the Western sun this passage still remains for the orchestra a shattering experience if played as Elgar himself wished. It is the axis of the whole symphony.

After the significant warning, then the timpani are heard striking in regular beats, whilst the bass of the orchestra is sustaining an E flat pedal. The tune itself begins softly, but with suppressed excitement, on 1st and 2nd violins and cellos, while the incessant strokes on the timpani are reinforced by woodwind chords and harp.

The percussion department soon begins to get out of hand. Bass drum and tambourine join the timpani in this fearful hammering and the strings give up the unequal struggle and hand over the tune to the trombones and tuba, while they themselves try something else and join the woodwind in endeavouring to force through the main theme of the movement (Fig. 33). But inexorably the hammering increases, and it takes the entire brass —horns, trombones, trumpets and tuba, striding about fortissimo —to keep the tune audible, the strings having already quite disappeared, despite almost tearing their instruments in fruitless endeavour. The percussive din now overwhelms everything. Only when it becomes quite intolerable on the mighty crash of the cymbals does the percussion at last relax, and a long diminuendo fading into a quiet chord on the horns brings a miraculous quietness.

Elgar used to say to the orchestra about this passage: "I want you to imagine that this hammering is like that horrible throbbing in the head during some fever. It seems gradually to blot out every atom of thought in your brain, and nearly drives you mad. Timpani and percussion! You must steadily increase your power until you come to the triple forte. Then don't worry about us! See if you can completely overwhelm everything—that is what I want!"

This sudden peace and stillness is unspeakably moving. With no more preparation the second tune now returns in the original key with extraordinary simplicity, as if nothing untoward had been happening at all. I quote Donald Tovey here, for he so exactly describes the way in which Elgar slips into his normal music again. "Without any preaching or tub-thumping, the music resumes the first episode (Fig. 35) quietly . . . as any nice undergraduate might relight his pipe after he had allowed it to go out during an outburst of enthusiasm."

The music is then similar to that which went before, except that the climax built up from this tune again is more incisive. The figures of the main rondo theme reappear, while the lovely, graceful tune arising out of this episode (Fig. 37):

Fig. 41 Strings

returns again with a charming embellishment in the fourth bar. There remains the coda, which now, with still something left in reserve, rushes the movement impetuously to the end, in a maze of cross-rhythms and brilliant orchestration, with a sense of acute impatience.

Impatience, agitation and violent contrasts are now things of the past. A calm detachment prevails, and a feeling of quiet happiness. The main theme of the last movement has great breadth and conveys a mellow sense of enjoyment, as though in looking back on difficulties at last overcome:

Rhythmic accuracy in this tune is not as easy as it looks, especially for the cellos, and the least untidiness ruins its character. Each bar is precisely the same in rhythm, yet it never sounds stilted. The characteristic leap of a fifth that ends nearly every bar marks the tune with Elgar's private seal. This is always considered the cellos' special tune, though it is strongly reinforced by horns, clarinets and bassoons. It was the cellos' colour that Elgar himself wanted uppermost, and the cellos eventually have the most enjoyment of it throughout the movement.

The next important theme is on violins and cellos:

—a more vigorous and aggressive subject, though only four bars long. Notice the skips of, first, a fifth, then a sixth and, lastly, an octave; and also the very Elgarian 'tenuto' on the highest note of the tune. This tenuto misleads indifferent conductors. Elgar himself used merely to direct the note to be emphasized, and not actually prolonged as in the tune in the scherzo of the cello concerto, which he wished definitely prolonged out of tempo.

This theme is built up to a 'grandioso' climax, and the third big theme of majestic character sings out on horns and strings, marked with Elgar's favourite direction, 'Nobilmente.'

The heavier instruments take it up forthwith, and a glowing section fades into a quiet and more tranquil, if momentary, return of the main theme.

The development of the movement now sets out on the second important theme on 1st violins in the form of a fugue, with many new and exciting figures as counterpoints. Some of them, particularly this one (4th bar):

call for exceptional orchestral virtuosity.

The complex and brilliant scoring culminates in a climax, when heavy brass and percussion lay hold of one bar of the main theme with sharply hammered accents, and a glorious top B for trumpet peals out over the whole orchestra:

In the score it only lasts for one bar, but a brilliant virtuoso of the trumpet—Ernest Hall—so delighted Elgar one day by sustaining it over the next bar that this has now become traditional. No trumpet ever made a more thrilling effect with a single note.

The second theme relaxes the tension, and another new figure:

of most peaceful mood persuades the main theme to return again in quiet dialogue. The original key of E flat is reached and a recapitulation of most of the music takes place. Another gorgeous climax comes as before, only this time with a feeling of sunset. The colours now fade gradually, and the tempo becomes 'più tranquillo' as the main theme (Fig. 42), very quietly in the cellos, under a lovely ascending phrase in violins, leads to the reappearance of the motto from the first page of the symphony. It comes in very slow tempo on the woodwind—

This music is of ethereal loveliness. It gently wafts us onward, until in the final bars the violins reach up from the cellos' last cadence, as if to kiss the fleeting spirit farewell. After the immense range that has been covered, the tranquil end of the symphony is deeply moving. The youthful 'Spirit of Delight' is gone, but there remains a memory that is like a blessing.

XXV

VAUGHAN WILLIAMS

IN his seventy-fifth year Ralph Vaughan Williams is the dominating figure still in the musical life of England, as he has been for a quarter of a century. Never, indeed, did his stature seem so great as now. Compositions of his which in the past had not won a generous hearing have lately come back with a new impressiveness—'Sancta Civitas,' for instance, the a-cappella Mass in G minor, and the piano concerto, which has found its proper form in the new version for two pianos.

It is curious to compare Vaughan Williams's career and position with Elgar's. Both great men belong to the West Country—Elgar to Worcestershire, Vaughan Williams to Gloucestershire. Elgar came to musical eminence by an unconventional road, but as a composer he found he could expand his genius within the frame of the conventions. Vaughan Williams's long years of education (Charterhouse, Royal College of Music, Cambridge, then the R.C.M. again) might be thought of as calculated to turn out a typical academician, but one of the most unpredictable of musicians was the result. Elgar's music is euphonious, Vaughan Williams's goes far in adventurous dissonance. Elgar had practically said his say when he was fifty-six (with 'Falstaff,' in 1913). Vaughan Williams was fifty-six in 1928, and since then he has given the world all manner of things—operas, symphonies, vocal and instrumental pieces large and small—each of an unforeseeable shape and character. Within a narrow range Elgar was intense; Vaughan Williams has a great open-mindedness, an intellectual curiosity that is never sated. Elgar was the more spontaneous musician; Vaughan Williams had not the same gift of facility. Vaughan Williams is more the musicians' musician—Elgar never had a following of disciples such as have sat at Vaughan Williams's feet during the latter half of his life. Both are counted among the greatest Englishmen of their time—not only great composers but also men of noble character, conscious of the high traditions of the race and of their responsibilities. While Elgar proudly sums up the glories of the Victorian century Vaughan Williams faces the doubts and portents of a tragic age. He has been honest enough at times to admit feeling its bleakness (see the fourth symphony). That is exceptional. He is supported as man and artist by a faith no less deep, although more given to questionings, than Elgar's own. These are the two great English composers of the twentieth century, and we may count ourselves thrice fortunate in claiming them. That the music of neither of them wins much of a hearing abroad is neither here nor there; it is music that expresses something of ourselves, music that has its roots in familiar places (to feel this to the full one must hear Elgar's 'Introduction and Allegro,' say, and Vaughan Williams's 'Tallis Fantasia' in Worcester or Gloucester cathedral).

Extraordinary is the range of Vaughan Williams's work, including as it does strictly liturgical compositions, operas of several different kinds, ballet music and chamber music, short lyrics, large choral pieces and concertos, as well as six symphonies. In the long list there are few or none without some representation of a facet of the great man's thought or personality. Certain ones, no doubt, do not fully carry out the prime intention and impulse. But the corpus of Vaughan Williams's work will speak to generations of Englishmen of a great Englishman's ranging thoughts, his love of the homely countryside, his piety, his inherited poetry, his adventurous mind and lofty ideals.

Thirty-seven years separate 'A Sea Symphony,' performed at the Leeds Festival of 1910, from the sixth symphony, in E minor, the work of Vaughan Williams's seventy-fifth year. Like Holst's later 'Choral Symphony' on poems by Keats and Stravinsky's still later 'Psalm Symphony' (1930), 'A Sea Symphony,' which is a large work for orchestra, chorus and soloists, is no symphony at all in the classical sense, but rather a choral fantasia. We shall speak in detail of the 'London Symphony' of 1914 in the next chapter, and here have only to say that it is an example of the symphony that has taken over some of the characteristics of the rhapsody and symphonic poem. 'A Pastoral Symphony' (1922) is again a work that departs far from any music that the nineteenth century would have recognized as symphonic. The 'Sea' and the 'London' are more active and eventful. The 'Pastoral' is more intimate, more the essential Vaughan Williams. Three of the four movements are slow, and these all express different moods of rapturous contemplation. Again nothing is here of the dramatic classical symphony, with its contrast and interplay of musical characters.

The fourth symphony, in F minor, came out in 1935. Here the composer returned to the world of action—and a violent world he found it. No one will ever call this a lovable symphony. It belongs to an unlovable age, which it interprets and criticizes implacably. The composer, who until the time he was forty had less readiness than many an inferior man, was by now a master, hitting every nail on the head. The matter and message of the fourth symphony may not be cheering, but no one is left in doubt that what was intended has been completely and finally said. With the fifth or 'Pilgrim's Progress Symphony,' in D, of 1945, the scene is once more changed entirely. The atmosphere is all a powerful radiance, such as had been hinted at before (e.g. in parts of 'Job'), but never with such assurance. Strong, concise and masterly, again, is the 1947 symphony in E minor, hugely energetic in its earlier movements and then mystically serene in the long farewell of the finale. From the 'Pastoral' onwards a high austerity of style characterizes these symphonies, and none of them has displaced the two earlier ones in the affections of the general public.

Everyone's introduction to Vaughan Williams should be through the 'Sea Symphony,' one of the most glorious works of English music of the century. The text is an American poet's (Whitman), but the symphony is full of pictures of England, our "sea-girt citadel." True, this is not what the work sets out to be; and it may be that the literal meaning of Whitman's words is to seek. Roughly it appears that the sea is a symbol of life and "the sailors, the unnamed heroes, whom fate can never surprise nor death dismay" are symbolic of the adventurous human soul, "steering for the deep waters only," ready for exploration "where mariner has not yet dared to go." But if some who have taken part in this splendid, exhilarating music have thought of it as philosophical it is fair to guess that a larger number have had in mind the seas of home and of our sea-faring forebears, who throughout the centuries cried, "Oh, farther, farther sail!"

XXVI

VAUGHAN WILLIAMS'S 'LONDON SYMPHONY'

IN 1900 Elgar composed his 'Cockaigne Overture' (produced by the Philharmonic Society in 1901), that vivid, rather Meistersingerish picture or series of pictures of London life, in which cheerfulness prevails. Vaughan Williams saw London in a different light. He is awestruck by the mysteriousness of its teeming life, by the immensity of the formidable city, by the tragedies implicit in its accumulated humanity. But—characteristically—not pathos and not melancholy prevails, but a sort of wonder with which mingles a barely formulated hope. In 1914, that last year of a brilliant old world, such a view of London struck many as unduly gloomy. Unimaginable then were the trials that London was to go through. In 1946 Vaughan Williams's music came back with something like prophetic force. It was as though the symphony had spoken for the tragic London that was to be.

The first performance was conducted at Queen's Hall by Geoffrey Toye at one of F. B. Ellis's concerts. Adrian Boult gave it in 1918 with the London Symphony Orchestra. Before the work was published (by the Carnegie Trust) the composer had made a considerable revision,* and in this form Albert Coates conducted it one memorable night at Queen's Hall (May 4, 1920), when Vaughan Williams became no longer the composer for a relatively few, but a great national figure. The scoring is for a large orchestra, including cornets; but Vaughan Williams, with his characteristic amenability, has also provided for performance by a reduced orchestra. Like Holst, he has always been free with orchestral cueing, so that here the third flute can be omitted, the

---

* " Cutting out the second trio of the scherzo and considerably condensing the finale."—*Grove's Dictionary*.

second oboe and English horn parts can be performed by the same player, the trumpet and cornet parts can be condensed, and so on. It is characteristic of him to envisage the general public of the land as his audience, and not the few who can attend the grandest metropolitan concerts.

The symphony is dedicated to the memory of George Butterworth (1885–1916), the rare composer of 'A Shropshire Lad' rhapsody, and other small and beautiful pieces of great promise, who was killed in the battle of the Somme. There are four movements: I, slow Introduction and Allegro; II, Lento; III, Scherzo (Nocturne); IV, Introduction, Finale and Epilogue.

The symphony begins:

Fig.1 *Lento*
Cellos & Basses con sordini

and of this brooding spirit is born the whole work. It is no formal introduction, but is a picture of the sleeping city, shrouded in mists. The slow majestic phrases, mainly on strings, but slightly coloured with woodwind, are deeply hushed, and just separated by little pauses. The effect is of slow regular breathing. The composer makes great use of divided strings, and the great range of their sounds, even in pianissimo, makes for an impression of enormous spaciousness. The harp, unobtrusively reinforced by the clarinet, is soon heard playing the first and second of the Westminster Chimes in harmonics:

Fig.2 Harp

—a queer, hollow sound.

Now the woodwind awakes clamorously; horns and brass take up the initial theme in a hurried crescendo. The orchestra takes a deep breath in silence, and the Allegro opens with a terrific crash.

It would be possible to describe this movement as though it were a classical symphony, but this would be artificial. All the features of a classical Allegro are here, but the nature of the music is something quite other. The movement belongs rather to the category of the rhapsody; and the listener will do well to take it on that footing. Some of the hesitation of the first audience in 1914 came from the shock of the disparity in the subject matter—themes of the sternest tragic drama and others picked straight from the gutter. We are worlds away from Brahms. The old consistency is sacrificed for the sake of a larger embrace of life. This does not mean in the 'London Symphony' a less lofty poetry; but what may be called the guttersnipe element of this first movement—which is in effect a tragic element, one of a kind of desperate gaiety on an infinitely murky background—has a picturesque realism not proper to classical music. In 1914 the audience was, in spite of Strauss, not yet ready to take Vaughan Williams on his own terms. No one should find that difficulty now.

The first subject is overbearingly harsh:

Fig.3 *Allegro risoluto molto pesante*

The mood is almost brutal. The lower strings squeak on their bridges (ponticelli) in nasty vicious sounds. But an irrepressible Cockney, in a typical remark whistled by flutes and woodwind, refuses to be daunted:

Fig.4

This is followed by another, more subdued idea:

Fig.5

The music has now subsided to quiet and uneasy movement, with this motif, of an accompanying nature, appearing again:

Fig.6 Basses & Double Bassoon

So far we have had the first subject and some short ideas belonging to it, but now the violas, clarinets and second horn morosely combine to prepare for the first full subsidiary tune. The music is sombrely minor, but there is the folk-song flavour characteristic of Vaughan Williams:

Fig.7 Violas, Horn & Clarinet — Brass

The composer lets in a little light with:

Fig.8 *Pochettino animato* — *p* Violins

And now comes the first theme of the second subject proper:

Fig.9 *Cantabile*

This 'subject,' so called, consists of a large group, a great feature of which is this powerful affirmation:

Fig.10 *Poco animato* W. Wind & Brass

On this the whole city seems to light up, and this cheerful, bank-holiday tune comes out:

Fig.11 *Poco animato* Strings

It is followed by another which suggests that some of these Londoners have come from homes deep in the country:

Fig.12 Woodwind

And finally this boisterous shout, which takes a central part later on:

Fig. 13

In this glorious merry-making we come to the first technical test of the orchestra. The string tune (Fig. 11) is scarcely ever played to perfection, and the reason is that the semiquaver nearly always disappears in the dancing sort of bowing Vaughan Williams requires. One can still hear Henry Wood tut-tutting here. "Not together! Not together! Careless, fluffy playing! Play it near the point! Clarity—clarity! Where's your spiccato, strings? I don't hear the semiquaver! And it's all too loud!"

The brass, not to be left out of this fun, now take up a tune of their own:

Fig. 14

and therefrom the entire orchestra combines in holiday-making. Is it factitious, all this show of high spirits? Vaughan Williams seems to say so, with the next feature, a return of the first subject of the Allegro, with which the exposition ends. It comes back with enormous power, rising to its climax from:

Fig. 15

Where else in music is such an expression of indignation and fury? All the orchestra seems suddenly seized with a hatred of life, or of the conditions of life. It is as though the composer had suddenly sensed the rancour, the exasperation and revolt of all the misfits in the cruel city, their feeling of society's injustice and of the unbearableness of their fate. Saucy before, the Cockney's remark—now uttered with a shriek and a yell by cornets, high woodwind and violins—is derisive and fierce.

This subsides and the development begins with quiet but restless talk all over the overture on a phrase derived from Figs. 1 and 9:

The whole of this section of the movement is strangely repressed, and it is as though sounds from the outside world impinged upon a dreamer so deep in thought that he is hardly aware of them. On a misty background of muted strings the flute, very softly and with the most enchanting effect of a distant street-cry, plays this expressive tune:

This, a perfect example of a Vaughan Williams tune, floats over the orchestra—a sudden thought transformed into song. Fig. 8 appears frequently, while the background becomes still more dim and vague. A solo cello begins the next episode, and its sound is most arresting in the empty air. We are approaching one of the great moments in the symphony. Admirable is the use the composer makes of his divided strings, which he splits up into a sextet of soloists playing with the accompaniment of strings and harp. The music in this shimmering passage grows from the most simple source:

The effect of the string soloists among their accompanying friends, with the harp spreading harmonies over them like a cloak, is pure poetry. Vaughan Williams's love of the strings and his frequent use of soloists make him one of their most valued friends. How they love the rare pleasure of hearing themselves play! Why did the classic masters never make use of the lovely device of an occasional string solo to set off the normal string-orchestra tone?

However we interpret the development, its effect has been chastening or placating. The recapitulation begins pianissimo, and although the 'Cockney remark' is fortissimo the anger has gone out of it. Everything is now a good deal shorter, until the holiday-making themes of the second subject group expand into music of solemn festivity in praise, after all, we cannot doubt, of London the glorious and inexhaustible. Before the short coda a broad singing tune for strings and horns starts to work up a protracted and immense climax. Tubas, trombones lead us up to the first peak in two terrific bars:

Fig.19

The first great peak is attained with a high unison passage for woodwind and strings:

Fig.20 *Poco animato*

Woodwind and strings glow to red-heat. The brass, after four bars, flings out the bank-holiday tune (Fig .10). A few more bars of 'general boiling up,' with the woodwind seizing on:

Fig.21 W. Wind

and the second and greatest peak is conquered with the same equipment as before, but in a suddenly arrested tempo, and in addition the brass thunders out the great initial theme of the symphony with a prodigious effect of solidity. Vaughan Williams marks the score with triple forte to sustain the gigantic effort for a few bars, and then quadruple forte for a final wave. Immediately there is a sudden dramatic drop to the coda. A shadow of the old

bitter first subject of the Allegro returns, but it is quickly over-
whelmed by the brass triumphantly sounding the grand affirmation of the second subject, as if the city's courage and purpose had
been sworn to a new effort of enlightenment.

The first movement has ended in the clear key of G major. The
Lento opens in the tonal vagueness and half-lights of the Introduction, and the air is cold with a shiver of the unknown. The
harmonic progression of the first two bars causes this coldness:

Fig.22 *Lento*
Strings con sordini

The orchestral strings frequently experience trouble with these
bars, for the tempo is extremely slow, and unless the conductor
gives an absolutely clear indication for the change of the harmonies a few stragglers will spoil the ensemble. This background is
set for a dark tune on the English horn, a tune remote and expression-
less in spite of its flavour of folk-song. It takes a prominent place
in the movement, particularly the bar which I underline:

Fig.23 Cor. Anglais

We are not long in this friendless atmosphere. The strings, in
a very different progression from their opening bars, are engaged
by a deeply intimate strain, the third and fourth bars of which
seem the very heart of the 'London Symphony' to some lovers
of the work:

Fig.24 Strings

It is hushed, and the sound of the strings, muted and divided, is ethereal. The suggestion is of a quiet and almost secret community of friendly souls. It may put some in mind of chanting heard in some dark old city church. For some time throbbing triplets form the background. A warm, comforting melody takes shape in front of it:

The scoring is for flutes and trumpets, warmed by a few horn notes. This dispels entirely the former mood, despite the return of the English horn's tune, which mounts to a climax and is then finally lost amongst the strings in a lovely passage of descending harmony. This section comes to an end in an ecstatic hush.

While the lovely sounds of the strings linger in the mind a solo viola lifts its voice. It is a precious moment, and the heart of the viola player quickens a beat as the last chanting of the strings fades and the player knows that for five bars his instrument, unbound by the orchestra or conductor, is free to express its individuality. Such a viola solo is almost peculiar to Vaughan Williams's scores. Not only is nothing of the sort known to the classics, but so much has Vaughan Williams made the effect his own that we think of him whenever another composer ventures to make use of it. Here is the viola's song—which springs from the old London street-cry of "Sweet lavender!"—

The clarinet echoes the melody, and some accompaniment grows while the viola, now joined by English horn, continues:

Thence, always in pianissimo, the music consists of fragments of tunes, such as this from the woodwind soloists:

A tremolando on the strings chills the air again, and a slightly sinister rhythm appears, hardened with timpani strokes:

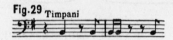

The strangeness and melancholy of the beginning return. But then an arresting and lovely up-reaching octave from strings, flute and English horn carries the orchestra into a mood of warm intimacy. Swirling harps and widely separated strings and wind reach up into a broad motif, richly coloured with high expression marks:

Magnificent is the climax, scored with all Vaughan Williams's love of vastly separated bass and treble—an opportunity for the most intense expression and fervour from the orchestra. The rest of the movement is a long subsidence. We hear again the familiar chanting and all the colours gradually become veiled. The music softly fades away. The last word is that of the solo viola—we are touched with a loving hand.

This movement, the greatest of the symphony, has nothing of sensuousness in its profound feeling. A wanderer's loneliness, then the welcome of friendly and devout souls, and above all a sense of divine compassion and protection—all this is in the great music.

'Scherzo (Nocturne)' is the title of the third movement, the spirit of which is a kind of ghostly animation. It opens with the peculiar misty colour of muted strings moving in pianissimo at great speed. It passes into the garish, gas-lighted scene of a

Cockney's Saturday night, and it ends in extreme softness, as though veil upon veil had come down, nothing at length remaining but a far-away echo of footsteps.

It is a most difficult piece. Any orchestra can play at breakneck speed provided that they play loud; but Vaughan Williams asks for velocity and at the same time tenuousness, and a rhythm so taut and lively that all the pieces fit and fall in together as if magnetized. If the conductor is a good magnet the speed will seem prodigious without an appearance of laborious exertion. But there are sometimes performances when the speed seems inadequate though the orchestra may be playing too fast for efficiency.

The form of this movement is of a scherzo with two trios. In the revised and published form a large cut was made, leaving out a third trio and reducing the length of the coda. The movement begins in D minor, but a D minor in which the woodwind insist on playing B natural—in other words, it is a modal D minor (Dorian mode), as, for that matter, the G minor of the first movement had often been modal.

The first main tune shows a very unobtrusive head in the clarinets:

Fig.31 *(Allegro vivace)*
Clarinet

A guide to the harmonic structure of this movement is given by these notes:

Fig.32

which frequently occur all over the orchestra, either in single notes or in chords.

Other ideas similar to Fig. 31 appear:

Fig.33 Violins   Fig.33a Oboe

10*

—some played smoothly, some short and staccato, but all formed from the original idea of Fig. 31. A flute solo leads into B flat minor, and cellos and bassoons begin a jig:

This provokes a scramble throughout the orchestra, some playing in 6/8 and others in 3/4 time, but only for a moment, for there comes an immediate diminuendo and the alert listener may notice this scrap of a ditty on bassoons and violas:

Two trombones and tuba, quaintly inebriate, hum with commendable delicacy this fragment:

The scherzo proper ends with this figure, a variant of the 6/8 rhythm on the bassoons:

The scherzo is repeated, and then comes the first trio in 9/8 time, with the pace faster than ever. For the first time in the movement we have a tune that is heavy and angular:

Running figures work against it in counterpoint, and Fig. 34 takes the stage, until the music dwindles to pianissimo. Now comes a modified recapitulation of the scherzo, which ends with a descent of bassoons and cellos to their bottom note C, which opens the door to a completely different scene, that of the second trio.

We now find ourselves in a cheerful and boisterous crowd with mouth-organ and accordeon preparing to back up a lusty chorus in C major:

Fig.39 *Poco animato*
Flutes & Oboes

As a representation of Cockney revelry this is matchless. The scherzo returns, working up to a climax that must have pleased the composer's friend Holst. Fig. 36 is heard fortissimo on lower strings and woodwind, while all the rest of the orchestra blaze away on a glittering background. In the coda the music disappears into the night, the bassoon having the last word. The whole movement is an extraordinarily successful combination of symphonic scherzo and symphonic poem. Musically it is self-subsistent; but the listener gains if he conjures up pictures of London by night, the glimmer of street-lamps, reflections in the pavement, and a momentary encounter with some late revellers, whose merriment seems somehow pathetic, set against the vast-ness of the city and of the night.

A slow introduction in G minor opens the last movement with two important features at once prominent—the harsh discord to which the opening bar proceeds, and an immediate answer with a richly warm phrase resolving on D major:

Fig.40 *Andante con moto*

The music has nostalgia and some bitterness in its chromatic harmonies, and the phrase with which the cellos finally bring the introduction to an end is like a memory of an intimate scene recalled over a long lapse of time:

Fig.41 Cello

A grand, impressive march then swings out on violas, cellos, clarinets and bassoons:

Fig.42 *Maestoso alla marcia (quasi lento)*

It is slow as a funeral march. No one but Vaughan Williams could have written this tune—a fine song for singers when the right men sing it, as English as the 'Meistersinger' march is German. This is the first time in the symphony that the composer has let himself go with a long serious tune. As it develops in power and scoring a heavy climax is built up with the horns and brass superbly ending the march at their full strength above a huge, widely spaced chord of G major.

The tempo changes to allegro, and the key is no longer G major but E minor. Excitement, stress and strain attack the orchestra, and the apparent unity and finality of the march is felt to have been only an illusion. There are typical harmonies:

Fig.43 Strings

This phrase:

Fig.44 Strings & Horns

played sharply with violent crescendo, provokes shouting from the wind. It drives forward to this vigorous tune:

in a blaze and clatter. Everybody, playing with the shortest and hardest staccato, presses this tune onward. It is thumped on the back, pushed from behind, belaboured into different keys. After a subsidence its gnomic message is uttered again, in much slower tempo:

The march returns, but it does not altogether take its previous steady course. A new mood, uneasy and violent, sets in. Strings with heavy tremolando bowing move in upward scales against the wind descending chromatically. Then the brass, breaking through the restless background, builds the march up to a climax for this phrase:

Twice it is repeated *ff*, and yet again; and this last time a gong clangs. Here is the summit of the movement, and this is the place where the true measure of the conductor can be taken. Has he—has the orchestra—reserves left? It is a greatly protracted crescendo, this. And the culmination is no triumphal blaze, but the bursting of a flood of human feeling. The string player should experience that rare moment when all the feeling he possesses is compressed into his fingertips, and by an intense vibrato and pressure on the bow the mass of sound around him seems to surge from his own instrument.

There is again a sense of oppression, as in the first subject of the first movement; but here it is all concentrated in a heavily sustained music. Words cannot say what it means; but if there is aspiration here a fear of frustration goes with it, and an apprehension of a tragic answer to the passionate question. A sinister ghost appears:

It is a shadow of the envy and hatred of the first movement. But it is time for the scene to change. It is done by a magician's touch. The air clears. Action ceases and the stage is suddenly empty. In the sudden stillness we hold our breath, to hear again the harp—only just audible—playing the three-quarters of the Westminster Chime.

The Epilogue to the symphony resembles the introduction to the first movement in matter and mood. Some have seen in it a representation of London's great river, flowing dark and inscrutable against the ephemeral life of its shores. Flutes and strings, quietly undulating, form a hazy atmosphere. The initial theme of the symphony appears again in the cellos and brass. It modulates, is extended to its full majestic breadth, and is held in the softer pianissimo:

The significance of the opening bar of the finale now appears:

Throughout the calm of the Epilogue its uneasy harmonies persist, to keep us in memory of the sadness inseparable from humanity.

The music moves onward until the strings, in rare serenity

and in extreme softness, pay their last contribution to the theme:

Fig.51 *Lento (molto largamente)*
Strings
PP molto sostenuto *ten.*

The scoring is of the widest, the double-basses playing with 1st violins four octaves apart. The end approaches. Under the quivering high D of a solo violin the brass again hints at old discontents. But this is more like a memory in a dream. Vaughan Williams is no cynic; he has no intention of ending on a pessimistic note. Gently and firmly he leads us to a long G major close. The serenity has not been easily won. Life's tragic aspect has been faced, its misery not discounted. At the end no blazing triumph is announced. But we feel that it is much—unspeakably much—that peace of mind should have been gained; and in this peace is to be read a great man's compassion and love for his fellow-men.

XXVII

HOLST
1874–1934

GUSTAV HOLST'S Life has been written once for all by his daughter Imogen, in a book that one feels the composer himself would have approved, so plain and unvarnished is the style, so candid the statement of the facts, suffused with affection but never distorted by it. Holst was the straightest of men. It is like a continuation of his own art that his daughter's biography should exemplify all his qualities of frankness and firmness, clean lines and a minimum—indeed an absence—of decorations.

English of the English he was, and an outstanding national composer of the generation that followed Parry and Stanford, Delius and Elgar, though he came, on his father's side, of foreign stock. The family was Swedish, and had arrived in England by way of the Baltic states. It was by tradition a family of professional musicians. Seventy years before Holst's birth his great-grandfather had made England his home, and Gustav was born at Cheltenham, where his father was a teacher of music. As a boy Holst learnt to play the piano and violin, and he composed almost as soon as he could read.

Early he was left motherless, and Imogen Holst has given us a saddening account of the discomforts of that Cheltenham home and of the lack of care which may have been a cause of Holst's insecure health. His life was, in fact, largely a fight against physical disabilities, as well as, for many years, against impecuniosity. His eyesight was poor, and when he was still young the curse of neuritis made writing a labour and the playing of most instruments almost impossible. He failed to win a scholarship at the Royal College, and when at length he arrived there, in an exceptionally brilliant period of the history of the College, his progress was slow and painful, while several of his contemporaries won rapid success.

This quiet and hard-up, insignificant-looking and rather sickly young musician had, however, a fund of character. Before the originality of his musical gift asserted itself he developed a genius for teaching and a genius for friendship. If he was not boisterous he was sanguine. He delighted in the English countryside and became a dogged if not tireless walker. In his musical progress he was guided by a profound instinct for what was genuine and sound. When he was twenty-one he made a great friend, Ralph Vaughan Williams; and he married happily. Success did not come soon. When at last it arrived there were a few years of brilliant notoriety, and then, too soon, life turned wintry for Holst. His arteries were old before their time, and he died when he should have been at the height of his productivity. But we must not think of Holst's as a sad life. He himself had a rewarding faith in mankind and in art. Toil—his teaching, for instance, at the famous school at Brook Green—which would have seemed a burden to many, he enjoyed. He believed in a social function of music; he worked to advance it and was rewarded by something like worship at such places as Morley College.

To balance his modest budget the young Holst took up (in about 1893) the trombone, and he played the noble instrument in circumstances where its nobility was at a discount—in theatre bands, and notably at the Drury Lane pantomime; and at seaside resorts, dressed in para-military uniform. It was not ill-spent time. A few years later, when Holst was writing for the orchestra, he had the backing of an experience all his own. No other major composer has been a trombonist; and when his thought had matured he had a peculiar technical resource—a knowledge of the capacity of the heavy brass which he used to unique effect. His knowledge of the entire orchestra was, for that matter, comprehensive. In those bare and direct scores of his each instrument speaks that which belongs to its nature. But while one feels that his principle of never writing two notes where one would do sprang from the integrity of his mind it was doubtless reinforced by his experience of trombone-playing. What a mighty sound does he produce from three or four instruments only! His harmony derives from a similar economy. It comes from a sense of responsibility in the least of utterances. Not a sound should be wasted; nothing half-hearted, nothing in the way of note-spinning could be tolerated. If a clash were wanted it should be a stunning clash. If simplicity served the purpose the simplicity was of the barest. He had no patience with complication for complication's sake. In all this we may detect the feeling of responsibility of one who had played the most responsible of instruments.

Holst, with his deep social sense, appreciated the orchestral player's life. "My boy," one can still hear him saying, "it's the grandest thing in the world to play in a first-rate orchestra, where you are part of the whole thing! The soloist never knows what he misses. He plays for his own ends and cannot understand the joy of being one of a grand team. But there's nothing else like it in the world; and if only I played the trombone well enough I should be doing it with you to-day!"

As a conductor he communicated this delight in the orchestra, and he was popular with the players—they felt he belonged to their guild. Before a rehearsal he would be seen climbing about the platform, discussing details with various players, gossiping with old friends and cultivating new ones—and leaving a trail of overturned stands as he short-sightedly made his way back to the rostrum. Though never a virtuoso of the baton, he knew how to obtain first-rate performances of his own music, for his cool head and unshakable sense of rhythm were enough. Such a master of effect was he in his writing that there was no need for him as a conductor to direct how to play this or that—it was all in the score.

When Holst was about twenty-five he embarked on a study that no other Western musician had thought of: he began to learn Sanskrit. The undertaking was characteristic of the man. He had no natural gift for languages, and he always laughed at the suggestion that he was a scholarly Orientalist. But the spirituality of the ancient Indian classics appealed to him irresistibly, and he doggedly worked at Sanskrit with grammar and lexicon to the point that he compiled his own versions of the 'Rig Veda' hymns, his settings of which were among the earliest compositions which made his name. Since Oriental lore commonly suggests vagueness and immaterial fancies, be it said that what Holst found in Sanskrit was nothing of that sort, but, first of all, the robust nature-worship of a simple pastoral people. At the time he was at work on his first Indian opera, 'Sita,' he also wrote his 'Cotswold Symphony' (performed at Bournemouth, 1902).

When Holst was forty he had still not won the ear of the public. Friends and admirers he indeed had; and at St. Paul's Girls' School he enjoyed a remarkable position, thanks to the enlightened High Mistress, Miss Gray, to whom English music owes more than is commonly realized. Two choral societies, viz. the Blackburn Ladies' Choir and the Edward Mason Choir in London, too, should always be remembered by Holst's admirers for their courage in performing this music, whose starkness was at the time antipathetic to the general run of concert-goers, in that period of lushness and opulence.

A noble friend was Balfour Gardiner, who introduced at his Queen's Hall concerts both 'Beni Mora'—of which Vaughan Williams has said, ". . . a work which if it had been played in Paris instead of London would have given its composer a European reputation" *—and the fine choral work, 'The Cloud Messenger,' the text of which Holst had translated from Kalidasa's Sanskrit. This was in 1912–13. But Holst's hour had still not struck, and then came war, blighting everything.

Everyone hearing 'The Planets' (1914–17) is inclined to imagine 'Mars' to be an outcome of the 1914 cataclysm, but Imogen Holst has told us that the movement was in fact sketched before that fatal August. 'Venus' and 'Jupiter' were written in the autumn of 1914, and 'Saturn,' 'Uranus' and 'Neptune' in 1915. 'Mercury' was the last; and the orchestration of the whole was finished in 1917. His daughter says that so bad was his neuritis at the time that much of the scoring of this and other works had to be dictated. The names of Nora Day, Vally Lasker and Jane Joseph are remembered by Holstians in this connection.

Holst would have given much to be able to lend some direct

* *Music and Letters*, Vol. I, No. 4.

aid to the war effort. His opportunity did not come until the autumn of 1918. It was, then, a great day when he burst in upon the young conductor Adrian Boult with the news: "Adrian, I'm going to Salonika in three weeks' time, and Balfour Gardiner has given me, as a parting present, the Queen's Hall full of the London Symphony Orchestra for the whole of a Sunday morning. We're going to play 'The Planets' and you are to conduct!"

Holst had been asked to go to Salonika as musical organizer to the Y.M.C.A. 'The Planets' was heard by an invited audience and made a great impression. In October Holst was off and away. Before he came home he had seen Constantinople—where he organized a competitive musical festival and coached a choir of soldiers to sing part of a Byrd Mass—and Athens. Meanwhile, Boult had given the first public performance of 'The Planets' (less 'Venus' and 'Neptune') at a Royal Philharmonic concert. (The first complete public performance was given under Albert Coates in 1920.)

With one more work Holst was established as a great composer. This was the choral 'Hymn of Jesus,' composed in 1917, published by the Carnegie Trust in 1919 and conducted by Holst himself at a Philharmonic concert on March 25, 1920, to such effect that the audience clamoured for a repetition, there and then, of the whole work. A pity that the demand was not complied with! Tovey wrote to Holst: "If anyone doesn't like it he doesn't like life!" * Holst was in America, enjoying new scenes and splendid hospitality, when his opera 'The Perfect Fool' was produced at Covent Garden (May 14, 1923), with Eugene Goossens conducting. A Maecenas, the late Claude Johnson, was enthusiastic and offered to pay the expenses of a Holst festival. But by then Holst's music was being performed everywhere, and what the composer most needed was a feeling of financial security to allow him to write more. In lieu of the festival, then, he accepted from Johnson the sum of £1,500. Holst was not in that year a hale man. In February, conducting a rehearsal at Reading, he had fallen from the platform, and suffered slight concussion. By the end of the year he was seriously unwell,

* Imogen Holst, *op. cit*, p. 80.

depressed and sleepless. The year 1924 he spent mostly at Thaxted in Essex, and there was written his Choral Symphony on poems by Keats (Leeds Festival, 1925). One remembers the London performance of this work from the orchestra. There had been a superb performance at Leeds, but at Queen's Hall the conductor was obviously not deeply interested, and perhaps from lack of rehearsal and still more of conviction the music failed to make an impression. The orchestra had been expecting some of the excitement of 'The Planets' or of the wonder of 'The Hymn of Jesus,' and in the lack of this we could not get going. It was felt that Holst was not taking us with him with that genial guidance and sympathy he had shown us on his earlier explorations. Yet the strangeness of the music might have yielded much if only we could have heard more performances. Of all Holst's major works the Keats Symphony is still the least known. It may yet become loved.

He composed another opera, the Shakespearian 'At the Boar's Head.' The earlier 'Savitri'—a pure masterpiece—had been a direct communication, distant and ethereal though its subject was. 'At the Boar's Head' was a setting of the great tavern scene from 'Henry IV,' but the music made the effect of leaving the listener behind a curtain. Paradoxically Holst, as he grew older, although commanding ever closer friends and a public that had been won over, wrote a music that became more aloof and cold.

'Egdon Heath'—overture for orchestra—represents his later phase. He was inspired by 'The Return of the Native' and a walk over the heath. The New York Symphony Orchestra asked him for a work. He toured Hardy's country by motor-car with Hardy himself, and 'Egdon Heath' was composed in 1927, just before Hardy's death. After the New York performance Talich conducted the work in London. The orchestra was nonplussed. We felt that Holst had dropped us from his thoughts; the music seemed a bare skeleton which we, in our ignorance, knew not how to clothe with flesh and blood. But on the tenth anniversary of Holst's death 'Egdon Heath' was again performed, Boult conducting; and a secret was disclosed. Perfect balance of tone, careful jointing of the orchestral pieces placed the picture clearly before the players, and the design came to life. Instead of the former sense of frustration and an atmosphere deathly cold there now came a glow, and the music held us fast with all Holst's magic. It was a lesson. Boult not only rehearsed the work carefully; he also spread the rehearsals over several days, until 'Egdon Heath' grew into our very bones. Not otherwise is Holst's later music to be entered into.

In the year before his death he carried out a long-cherished intention of writing a viola piece for Lionel Tertis, whose matchless art he had always greatly admired. This is the 'Lyric Movement' for viola and small orchestra, which he heard played in the nursing home where he was soon to die. It made on us the usual impression of the later Holst—bare, impersonal music, terribly aloof. It was as though the music was screened from us by thick glass. Tertis himself was mystified at first. But now, after these years, it is a lovely piece to study, and perhaps its long neglect will do it no harm. The lines are bare, yet Holst's gift was to evoke out of the slenderest material a mystical feeling and lovely sound. The demand that it makes is that soloist and orchestra shall allow it to take root in their minds. Holst said, after hearing it in his sick-room: "It looks as though I shall have to go on being an invalid if I am going to write music like that!" Words that were obscure at the time; but the 'Lyric Movement' is now appreciated as a cherished gift to the viola-player.

This is not the place to expatiate on Holst the teacher; enough to say that his memory will be beloved as long as there is a single pupil of his left on earth. How many have to thank him for a helping hand, a stimulating word! He was engrossed in each pupil. If he found any merit or original thought, what excitement! His criticism could be very searching. I remember writing to him on a day of discouragement, after playing a concerto badly. Back came a letter, asking awkward questions: "Do you think you were really concentrating? . . . Haydn is always the most difficult to play. I think you wanted far more study and hard technical practice."

As a conductor he came to us frequently at the B.B.C. studio under Waterloo Bridge, and very welcome his visits were, though some trepidation was felt, for he became very exacting in his later years and would suffer no imperfection. Always richly appreciative of fine playing, he would sometimes break off a rehearsal to congratulate a player. "I say, Mr. Hall, that was first class! I knew you could do it when I scored that bit, but I never thought it would come off like that! Sounds grand!"

Excessively short-sighted, he could not distinguish the players, but pointed his stick roughly in the direction of one or another. One remembers occasions when in 'Mercury' flutes, celesta or some other instrument failed to dovetail. Holst would look rather pained but went on quietly rehearsing until all fitted and the passage was safe. He felt a lively interest in contemporary music and often turned up to hear novelties at the B.B.C. studio. No audacity was too much for him, so long as he felt a genuine impulse in the music. But show without substance or mere freakish note-spinning—on that he would quietly but quickly turn his back. There is not another example in musical history of such a friendship as linked Holst and Vaughan Williams. Different as the two men were in many ways, they had a great fund of things in common—principally, perhaps, their rich humanity and their ideals. Each learnt from the other, but each had a strength of individuality that could absorb fruitfully what the other had to give without loss of original character. Both remained totally unspoilt by successes or reverses or any of the ups and downs of life. Holst, becoming lonely and apart, rejoiced in the rich unfolding of his friend's slower development. Too much of Holst's music is neglected. Those who have played and studied his work know that it is a part of our permanent heritage.

XXVIII

'THE PLANETS'

THE suite 'The Planets' was Holst's largest piece of orchestral composition. An exceptionally large orchestra is called for, and the seven movements take about fifty-five minutes in performance. The titles of the movements are: 'Mars the Bringer of War'; 'Venus the Bringer of Peace'; 'Mercury the Winged Messenger'; 'Jupiter the Bringer of Jollity'; 'Saturn the Bringer of Old Age'; 'Uranus the Magician'; 'Neptune the Mystic.' The scoring is for 4 flutes (including piccolo and bass flute), 3 oboes (including bass oboe), English horn, 3 clarinets, bass clarinet, 3 bassoons, double bassoon, 6 horns, 4 trumpets, 2 tenor trombones, bass trombone, tenor and bass tubas, 6 kettledrums (two players), and extra percussion for three players (triangle, side drum, tambourine, cymbals, bass drum, gong, bells, glockenspiel), celesta and xylophone, 2 harps, organ and strings —and in the final movement a hidden choir of women's voices in six parts.

Holst had composed beautiful things in the smallest of musical shapes, but he was naturally by no means a miniaturist, and in listening to 'The Planets' one is convinced of the zest with which he must have thrown himself into a vast undertaking. This time the frame was to be as big as he chose, and he would deny himself nothing he wanted in the way of material. Other men were demanding enormous orchestras. Strauss, Mahler and Schoenberg * went from luxury to luxury in numbers and extras. Since they were to be had Holst would demand them too—and justify the demand by proving them not extravagant but the proper outfit for his enterprise. One motive in his mind, it may be

---

* Strauss's 'Hero's Life,' 1899; Schoenberg's 'Gurrelieder,' 1900–10; Mahler's Eighth Symphony ('The Thousand'), 1908.

guessed, may have been the conviction that he knew a right way with orchestral numbers—he could show how multiplication need not lead to muddiness.

A case was made out for it all. The whole armoury was not too much for the composer's powerful technics; and the poetic motive had the appropriate grandeur. The subject, summed up in a title whose excellence is part of the excellence of the whole, is nothing less than the principia of life, in so far as it was given to the composer's gaze to survey them and to the method of his art to represent his vision. 'The Planets' are the elements of our humanity, or Holst's choice of the chief of them.

A halt has to be called here to look for a moment at the musical title in itself. Some have considered it a derogation to give a piece of instrumental music a literary name. On the other hand the popular inclination is towards labelling at all costs. The composer's will should surely be law here. Nothing could be more impertinent than the unwarranted naming of Bach's fugues and Beethoven's sonatas. The naming or not naming of a piece of music is clearly a part of the actual achieving of its composition. A title is likely to narrow the range of the music's import and at the same time to give vividness to some particular intention. The composer takes his choice, and to take the wrong choice is a fault of composition. You will not name your symphony 'Romeo and Juliet' simply because it was born in the shadow of love's young loss. That title is an invitation to the listener to find a dance, a duel, Queen Mab and Friar Lawrence; and (such are the mysteries of the 'meaning' of music) found they will be, no matter how little of the picturesque or narrative intention you had. It does not help that the artist and his audience should be at cross-purposes. Two modern English works occur to one as examples of titles tending that way: the 'Colour Symphony' by Arthur Bliss and 'The Song of Gwynn-ap-Nudd' by Joseph Holbrooke.

Some of the generic names, symphony, concerto and so on, stand for something so definite that with an opus-number and key ('Symphony in C minor, Op. 67') identity is established. Leave it at that and your music enjoys, for what it is worth, music's singular privilege of expressing a meaning independent of words and images. You add the title according as you want something of the effect of concentration and visual suggestion that lies in the power of words. But the other, less categorical terms for musical structures—overture, suite and the rest—are words so loose that a proper name is called for simply for its primary usefulness. The classical musical nomenclature has broken down under the variousness of modern practice. 'The Planets' is called a 'suite' inadequately. The proper term did not exist simply because there had never before been anything like this, Holst's set of symphonic movements or 'overtures'—a brood as diverse as can be in most respects, though at one in boasting a family look of proud young giants. 'Suite' is a puny and indefinite word. The proper name was wanted and the chosen one had every merit.

Not here or anywhere else did Holst depend on the development of the title into the 'programme.' He was young at the moment when Strauss's example was at its most bewitching, but he managed to avoid the confusion of musical with other argument. For all the amusing and brilliant turns of his art Strauss had to thank the stimulus of the external world. Narrative and visual impressions jogged his fancy, much to the relief of the expression of the inner Strauss, which would of itself have lacked interest. There was never a musician for whom the visible world meant more. No reproach is to be made of it—the musician has as much a right to all that is as the poet. But Strauss has often not half transmuted the outside elements. Inconsequential sounds occur in his music, and the excuse when offered professes no concern with musical logic, but takes the form of a legend in the score or in the concert programme to some such effect as, "Here someone has an accident with the soup tureen." Strauss has indulged in this musical form of practical joking in the course of some of his most splendid music. The aesthetic theory on which he banked was that a narrative told in the concert programme might serve much the same purpose as the dramatic action in an opera. It did not work because, in short, looking and listening is not the same thing as reading and listening. So far as his symphonic poems have

held the field it is because the author's sheer musical impulse has
sometimes managed to get clean away; there are times when the
music insists on telling its own tale, and the audience, giving up
trying to read and at the same time overhear, can gratefully
listen.

If the musical form of this composition of Holst's made a title
necessary, the breadth of the intention called for one that should
be no restriction on the imagination. Well, the title chosen could
hardly have been broader, the more since the planets were here
not to be thought of physically or even in their mythological
associations, but in their astrological signification. They are the
stars that shape our courses. Do not let us solemnly take Holst for
an astrologer. He would not make an orthodox one. He leaves
out some of the chief celestial forces and includes two planets not
known to classical astrology (Uranus and Neptune). His title
must, of course, be taken as a poetic value. Such symbolic terms
—like Dante's Moon, the heaven of the Inconstant, his Sun of the
Prudent—represent the most wondrous human ability, that of
fixing, amid the welter of physical things, on certain unchanging
truths of the spirit—the Platonic ideas, in fact. Though no one
may share Dante's view of the physical, his poetic truth remains.
Here is indeed one of the vital mysteries illustrated, in the modern
artist's resorting to the old symbols for the purposes of his
synthesis.

The planets, then, are the influences of destiny and the constituents of our spirit. The artist will isolate those constituents
and mould his separate images of them; and in the new-created
group is expressed the measure of his apprehension of God. The
artist is the critic of God, and the same general conditions apply
to his work as to the lesser criticism—it serves some practical
purpose, and it exposes the nature of the critic, while the subject
of the criticism remains unaffected. In Holst we certainly have a
man as little inclined to conscious self-exhibition as any artist
could well be. So far from his day's work consisting of a romantic
chase after his night's dreams, he sets about it like any plain
craftsman. He has undertaken a big job, the carving of this
great row of granite gods, but he feels cheerfully equal to it.

Self-expression is not in his conscious mind. He is as keen and concentrated on the scowl of Mars as on Venus's calm brow. It is as though by incident that the special vigour and mastery of this workman show up in the result.

Holst's well-known saying that "musicians express in sound what all men feel" tells us with simplicity what was to be guessed from his art—how little this composer deliberately concerns himself with the peculiarity of his experience and being. But however naturally the artist may assume that he is a plain type and that his outlook is the obvious and general one—however little subjective he may consciously be—his work must define him as surely as though he were the most subjective of them all. The very fact of his engaging in such an art as modern musical composition declares an individual enterprise and a radical sense of the seer's special gift. 'The Planets' was a scheme so large as to require, like any major work of art, all that the composer knew of "what all men feel." Holst was not a poet of the ivory tower. At a time when the arts had a way of taking themselves off to mysterious retreats he was so humble and so bold as to be interested in the general lot. He seems oblivious of himself in his earnest grasping at the real truth of things—in his portraying of the seven overlords of man. But in his very recognition of these he works his own analysis. The heavens are never the same. One wheel of influence seems to bless or ban a whole age, while another system shapes the personal lot. What does Holst see of the world at the converging of his star-beams?

He sees brutality, and does not underrate it. 'Mars' has been called the most ferocious piece of music in existence. He stared hard at Mars. What he saw induced him into no flattery, but neither was he wrung to complaining. We shall in fact find that Holst does not complain. He hews his image of Mars's bulk and merciless mask without love, certainly, but with a sort of appreciative recognition. It is no occasion—and nor, for that matter, is any of his works of music—for his private grievances. With something of the temper of a disciplined sportsman, sensibly stoical, Holst all along refrained from affecting moans. It was not in his nature, and as such could not be helped, even though a great array of nineteenth-century composers—Wagner and Schumann alike, and Brahms and Tchaikovsky—had worked to persuade that a personal wail was the very heart of music. Not by Venus was a wail to be wrung from Holst; nor yet by Saturn, bringing old age; nor yet by the unresolved mystery of the outermost of his planets, the suspended question that is the end of all things. There is something of antique piety in his observance of the gods, who, though they deal to man two evils for one good, are not to be charged with foolishness.

Holst seems to have been his own astrologer when he attributed to Venus the bringing of peace. Of the other Venus, *toute à sa proie attachée*, he admits no awareness. His Venus swims ineffably mild into the evening sky, and he counts from her nothing but blessings. After the frightfulness of Mars, her coming in this guise is an exquisite value. How, we ask ourselves, could the musical scheme have stood it if the second deity too had presented herself —as in unluckier horoscopes—hot with destructiveness, "the flame that made of Troy a ruinous thing"? Another artist might have hunted all round his mind for such a principle of repose. The admirable contrast between the first two of 'The Planets' cannot be passed over as a mere stroke of technical ingenuity. Such things spring only from the depths, and they suggest how much the artist is trustee rather than creator. A power beyond control has allotted his disposition. To him only to know, not to make, himself! How was implanted in our subject his special sense of the impersonal grimness of war and of the holy blandness of love? The honour to him comes from his having looked so straight to see what was within himself. The success depended simultaneously upon obscure co-operative forces within, of which his mind was not the chooser but the chosen. Such a success is not analogous to a result of the processes of physical evolution only because it is part of the same thing.

There is another point. For several generations—from Schubert to 'Salome'—nearly all harps had been tuned to tell of romantic love. The thing had been overdone. By the time of Strauss and Schreker there was a well-known procedure by which any technician could stir up what was conventionally taken to represent boiling passion. The agitated movement and pathetic harmonies of Schumann and Wagner were anybody's everyday tribute to Venus Pandemos. When a means of expression becomes so commonplace the artist naturally looks afresh into his heart to find a correspondence with reality. What is this love? Debussy would not have it that it was necessarily an affair of loud cries and tumult. Holst clearly does not allow that it is all a fever and a craving.

There is nothing of Venus Pandemos anywhere in Holst's music. In 'The Perfect Fool' the love-potion working on the princess brings not passion but a dreamy bliss. "All things have ended for me. I am at peace. No foe can hurt me. Hell cannot reach me. I am beyond the power of evil ones." Savitri's love, too, is blessed by the high Uranian Venus: "When thou art weary I am watching, when thou sleepest I am waking, when in sorrow I am near. . . ." In the pageant of the poets in the last movement of the Choral Symphony, the Passions, "a terrific band," evoked by Shakespeare are reflected in the music as merely active sprites, without a pang or a reproach.

Such airy and untroublesome influences were all along generous to our composer. The Mercury of 'The Planets' was one. Mercury, he has told us, is the astrological symbol of mind. And the music here flickers and plays in a state of disembodied joy. Mind, then, for him is not man's fearful burden of awareness, that lost us innocence and brought the capacity for regret and foreboding. It is, says Mercury, not that which sufferingly knows matter, but that which can overcome matter and make good its escape to a sphere of divine playfulness.

In the meantime, who so ungrateful as to deny the good things of material life? Not Holst, who is all for accepting the honest pleasures in their season. The splendid fourth movement of 'The Planets' might have been called an overture for an English country festival. On this holiday, on this green meadow, all men are friends. There is well-being, there are festal song and cheerful uproar. No supercilious or shrinking soul could have thought of this music. It declares a decided liking for crowds, it declares open house and a welcome for all. So far from setting himself above the common, Holst must have been aggrieved if any did not feel able to enter into the spirit of the thing, when he had been so ready to make it all plain: himself, as the music truculently sets down, being plain and proud of it, knowing how his fellows felt and what they liked.

The fifth planet, bringing old age—"that comes by night as a thief comes that has no heart by day"—is a trial of courage different from the first but as searching. This is the inevitable and the inevitably victorious enemy. Shall we desperately play at blindness at its approach? Shall we break down at the threat? Holst squares himself to look it in the face as steadily as at trampling Mars. He notes intently, and what he at first puts down is simply hard-observed description—the creaking advance, serious if not yet terrible. It is in fact not to become utterly terrible. Old age is seen as a dispensation too grave for a smile but also, precisely because inevitable, not to be dreaded—not to be allowed to be dreaded. Give way at this undermining of yourself, and what has become of your pride, your disciplined temper? It is no doubt the most difficult part of the whole game. The more reason, then, to play up strongly—so this music suggests, with its impassive and intent registration of Saturn's steps. The reward for standing out is that when the inexorable has invaded your soil to the last foothold, somehow the threat dissolves. Holst declares that he sees Saturn relent. The besieger and the obsessed soul patch up a mysterious agreement, celebrated by a solemn festival with a great clamour of bells.

Humour is the compensation for what has been supposed the want of passionateness in Holst. His downrightness, which might have been forbiddingly austere, is warmed by laughter. 'Jupiter' was full of it. After the stern business with Saturn he is ready for Uranus the magician. In magic the humorous eye cannot help seeing a joke. The magician turns things topsy-turvy, leaving simple nature puzzled. Holst's sixth god makes the mountains resound with his roaring fun. He might have been called the god of laughter if, after a point, the prodigiousness of the pranks did not pass a joke, turning laughter into a sacred wonder. He is a mighty if genial magician. The whirlwind is his plaything. This is he that made Behemoth.

The last planet swims in mystery, less seen than guessed at, on the far confines of our system. What is to be made of it, the ultimate unknown, by our peering into the dark? Holst is not able to proclaim a conventional apotheosis. The dark is dark, the question is left open. He, the downright, here affirms nothing. Only (says the music) in the light of what has gone before—since the sum of things has made for a balance of good—eternity shall not affright us. We stand at the brink of Neptune's flood that stretches away from the shore of time. For honour's sake we may not fear, nor yet foster unwarranted mortal hopes. We may only wonder at the wash of the unanswerable waves.

The general musical workmanship of this last movement, for all that, remained the same, as clean and direct as in the movements of war and festivity. The scheme required from first to last a bold and sculpturesque execution, making not so much for subtlety as high monumental effect. Granite and not sandstone, so to speak, was the chosen material, and the composer's genius was confidently adapted to it from the very opening strokes of 'Mars.'

Those strokes beat at a dominant pedal in a 5/4 metre. We shall find such fives and sevens very characteristic. The effects of these odd metres are two—an extension and a clipping short. We feel either an inserted beat making for languorousness, or the energetic suppression of one. The latter is much the more characteristic of Holst. The down beat comes cutting in an instant before its expected time, as though impatient with the easy-going way. In the pedal figure of 'Mars' it is like a lash on the movement, which each time springs into a quaver triplet. It is at first given out with a dry, rattling sound—

by timpani and mishandled bowsticks of the strings.

VAUGHAN WILLIAMS

HOLST

We hear the wind instruments awaking and assembling during some forty bars:

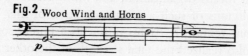

Fig.2 Wood Wind and Horns

Two punctuating chords which Holst knows how, without percussion, to imbue with a metallic clang appear (they recur again and again) with harsh and ominous effect:

Fig.3

Then, to an immense shout from all voices, the music moves to the tonic, C, under a clash of foreign harmony on the wind, and there continues louder its *arrière-ban*.

Holst has no mind to spare us. Thus things are; and nothing can mollify his obstinate presentation. He found in the repetition of an inflexible figure an effect corresponding to his sense of the forces of man's inhumanity. When first did music learn to create a collective spirit unknown to the individual? Song is man's personal music and sweet friend. Rhythm is communal and a tyrant to the individual, whether it throbs in a parade of Zulu warriors or in the workshops of Sheffield.

Of this subjugator of free life the Romantic Period cared to know little. Wagner, for instance, generally evaded it. One of his rare uses of a rhythm such as we have in mind is the 9/8 figure of the hammering of the enslaved Nibelungs. Romance is fain to escape into a world that the world's not. It dreams of indulgent passions and impractical wanderings, and prefers to shut its ears to sounds that compel obedience of the body in disregard of the soul's longings. In the middle romantic music of Wagner and Brahms rhythmical shapes were mitigated or subtly broken up, and in general denied their oppressiveness. At its extremity, as in Delius and Skriabin, they virtually disappeared. The rude facts of

II

existence and the social responsibilities were blotted out by clouds of hallucinatory beauty.

Rhythm means organization, and music clearly could not be always oblivious of such a prime condition of life. Holst came with a blunt reminder. At his moments a purely songful composer, he also realized the vital strength of the other music. The remarkable recognition that his work publicly received is to be put down in good part to the ideal presentation, felt in its rhythmic insistencies, of the masterful throbbing machinery of modern society. Correspondingly, the hostility it met with came from those who detested the very thought of the duress imposed by mass movements. Such may be the most pugnacious of spirits, but their fighting must all be in the form of the lonely encounters of knight-errantry, and they resist tooth and nail the intolerable coercion of the communal summons of 'Mars.' Instinctively and morally they abhorred the awful charm of the drum. Its recognition seemed a concession to barbarism. But what is, is. The artist shall not be forbidden any of his perceptions of the real, the very fuel of art; and it was Holst's strength to feel with intensity the barbaric in the modern state and the sudden appropriateness of a barbaric means in a new music.

Drum-taps, numbing to the self, stir an impersonal consciousness. In the clamour the ones succumb. It is the pitiless music of social cohesion and the defence of the racial life: a super-rational power that from the ages of pre-history has steeled the ranks and files of the tribes of men through innumerable marches and martyrdoms. It has throbbed in our contemporary air (to the words, "Who dies if England lives?" or the like)—if not physically audible not less vivid for that, and to our musician's ears one of the first of realities.

In the day when the civilized states had fallen into the trampling movement of fierce nameless hordes banded by rhythm to a common purpose, it was natural to think of the music of a country, Russia, where a brilliant cultivation of the arts had been in contact with a primitive populace. The Russian composers have never achieved much in the way of studious and melodic music, but they have had a fund of suggestions to draw upon in the susceptibility of their race to dancing and martial measures. Balakirev and his school, given the example of Liszt and Berlioz, attained to a Western technique, but not to the Western spirit of the time—which, in effect, meant the meditative and domestic music of the Germans. They had a different source of savage vitality. Their compositions, coming West, were taken as exotic curiosities or else, by the guardians of propriety, as a scandal. The West thought the individual safely free. It turned out that man was not to be so easily loosed from circumstance.

If the rhythmic figure of Holst's 'Mars' is here dwelt upon, the reason is that it is so significant and typical a feature of his art, which abounds in statements of the commands from without (Saturn's two grim syllables are another), which overrule the power of the self's will. The insistence is not to be put down to *parti pris* in Holst, but to his sheer faithfulness to his observation. What can the will count for when Saturn orders you into his stride? But the compulsions do not strike man as always or even often grim. Again and again Holst shows gaily how the dance takes possession of the feet. Mars is neither glorified nor denounced. Such is the god's summons, such the compulsion—that is all.

Between the savage's simple acceptance and the stoic's recognition of it as unrejectable there is a world of experience, but in practice such a resemblance that when it came to musical statement the world could not altogether dissociate Holst from the Russian example. Of course, as a practical musician, he was not going to rule out any serviceable example. The artists are a sort of priesthood of the Golden Bough—the precious emblem is there for anyone to take and uphold as his own. Plagiarism is an entirely different question. It does not enter here. There is no suggestion of plagiarism if 'Parsifal' is mentioned in connection with the chromaticism of Elgar and Delius. 'Mars' might quite well have happened without any of the Russians. Berlioz perhaps struck the spark. He made famous effects by compulsive reiteration, as in the last movement of the 'Te Deum.' The point is dwelt on because of the surprise Holst caused by a violence previously unknown in English music. But such connections are hardly more than technical. The spirit was new. Let this music be described as suggesting a system or control within inhuman forces. They press hard, but not to the point of the frenzy of Berlioz or Stravinsky. This god of Holst is brutal rather than mad.

We have followed him as far as the assembling of the brass. Trumpets and horns come out with the principal subject, which seems to lurch under the burden of its consecutive triads:

Fig.4

All must shoulder it in turn.

A change comes when the rhythm steadies to five crotchets in a bar:

Fig.5

The euphonium's hollow, unearthly howl—some monstrous commander yelling his orders—starts a clamour of fanfares. Panic seizes woodwind and strings (a series of horribly awkward passages!), and then there is a moment's silence—as if the world held its breath before the blast of an explosion—to be shattered by this thundering discord low in the bass:

Fig.6

Then the 'burden' (Fig. 4) is taken up anew. This time the voices are largely in unison, with the rhythm present but mitigated. The effect is of a gigantic groan. It swells intolerably until, once again, down comes the rhythmic lash, cutting sharper than ever, with the trumpets shrilling out on the dominant for bar after bar. The euphonium's fanfare recurs, but shortened. The 'burden' is piled on ruthlessly. The climax comes with a sort of hoarse roar and a terrific grinding of G's and A flats, helped out by a blast of the organ:

Fig.7

Once is not enough for the spirit of fury. There is a half-step back, as it were; then five times and six the monster barks to empty Heaven defiance or imprecation.

The admirable thing about 'Mars' is, of course, not the infernal noise in itself, for anyone can blast us out of our seats with his instrumentation, but the style that controls it. The whole is rigorously contained by art. 'Mars' is therefore different from other contemporary extensions of the dynamic range of music. It is severely, classically 'tidy,' without one futile note. The conception is altogether ideal, not realistic. Fanfares and all, it is martial poetry, not fact. In reality bugle-calls belong only to the camps of peace.

'Venus' opens with a soft horn-call rising a fourth:

Fig.8 *Adagio*
Horn

This is answered by flutes in their silvery high register. From the height where they have been awakened they float gently downward to meet the horn and form a delicate chord with the oboes. The general tone suggests a cool, clear air. The movement is adagio. Light chiming chords fall equably on the beats. For a little, virtually nothing is allowed to happen. Life's rare moments of equipoise are worth a jealous guarding. Only the dominant B flat of the last horn note seems to ask blissfully for something more. It is granted. The B flat becomes the A sharp of a new key, F sharp, which floods the scene with more light, and in the brightness

Fig.9

a violin solo comes out with a tender song. The syncopated harmonies here seem harsh only if roughly played: if the woodwind is exquisite, they merely bring a hint of bright frostiness into the air. The whole movement, for that matter, must be given with perfectly lovely and untroubled tone. If 'Venus' has ever seemed to interest less than other movements of the suite, the reason has been a want of the purity of sound on which this 'symphony in white' depends. If the woodwind chording is inaccurate the adagio may seem empty, and the andante is easily spoilt (whereas the other 'Planets' are rather hard to spoil) by anything less than steady tunefulness and suavity.

The falling fifths and fourths of the violins are like sighs of contentment. Then the oboe with its rising octave phrase brings a momentary sweetness

Fig.10 *Largo*

an element rather rare in Holst. Here it is admitted after due preparation, to delicious effect. It is not made much of. Holst does not expand the oboe phrase. Other instruments cannot refrain from repeating it once or twice on their own account, but the movement falls back into the trance-like state of the opening. There is a faintly heard repetition of the violin song. The ending of 'Venus' is a long series of delicate chimes, soft and softer still. Harp harmonics, a tinkle on the celesta, equable crotchet chords on flutes and horns, and high-held violin notes escort the Bringer of Peace as she passes out of earshot.

The whole movement is full of Holstian patterns and backgrounds which, often rocking on two alternating chords, may either suspend the music or give it an imperceptible momentum.

The following passage for harps, soon after the beginning, is an example:

Fig.11

Another characteristic patterned background is this, on the celesta, towards the end of the movement:

Fig.12

Of such lovely threads and colours is this music woven.

'Mercury' is an aerial frolic. The third Planet is of altogether slighter build than the rest. Any message it may bear is no burden. The messenger seems unaware of it. His life is a speeding, a darting, a rebounding. He knows no care and no feeling, nothing but the perpetual excitement of his travels. By the extent to which these are illustrated, and the extraordinary ingenuity, the piece properly has a place among the others, where it plays the function of the symphonic scherzo. The chief components of the music are a theme that darts forward in one key and back in another (B flat and A); a rhythmical flitting between 6/8 and 3/4; and an exploitation of all the lightest and driest tones of the orchestra. The middle theme, the one that starts with three crotchets followed by two quaver triplets, is of the sort that on a night journey the wheels passing over the rail-joints set going in a drowsy head. It is bandied about with regular Holstian persistence throughout the middle part of the movement. Then the frolic of the woodwind begins again. Shadowy revels! Among them the harp and celesta shed fitful gleams. But Mercury is due to be off and away. There is a rustling and a scamper of the woodwind— a glissando from the depth of the double bassoon to the top of the piccolo—a tinkling echo, and it is over.

Here is the first theme:

This, with an attendant falling figure—

flits all over the score, appearing as caustic comment on the bass oboe and high shrieks on the piccolo. The next idea consists of short, sharp descending chords, ending in a frothy splutter—

A high note on the violins and glockenspiel insists upon this rhythm:

which holds the threads together like an impish sprite. The trio is opened by a general clatter on the strings, which thins out to a peculiarly Holstian accompanying figure on the harps, this for the solo violin's tune:

At the end of the trio the woodwind makes two unsuccessful attempts to resume the scherzo. When eventually this starts again it does not proceed on its former course, for the second tune fails to arrive and the music dashes off on another tack—the famous string passage which is probably more rehearsed than any other in Holst's works (and still seldom comes off!). The idea here is almost Mendelssohnian—but most un-Mendelssohnianly harmonized.

It is marked with that most difficult direction, 'pianissimo e staccato.' Either the pianissimo or the staccato is achieved, but rarely both. Generally the music swells in a crescendo as the phrases rise, though the passage should be kept absolutely pianissimo except for the sudden fortes which occur when Holst changes the accent for the first time from 6/8 to 3/4. Shortly afterwards a crescendo is demanded, when the orchestra rushes up the score in a helter-skelter outburst. The effect then should be electrifying; but the point is often missed.

A perfect performance of this difficult 'Mercury' was a pleasure the composer rarely enjoyed. Even when the playing was note-perfect the effect could never be light and pianissimo enough for him. Not seldom one of poor Mercury's winged feet became entangled by a luckless woodwind player missing his cue. Holst must have chuckled when he wrote this scherzo, and the players even believe that he deliberately laid traps. Those bustling string passages that seem made for excitement and crescendos! How hard to keep them down to pianissimo! Then there are the cunningly overlapped passages for the wind, designed as it were to test their wits; and the punctuation of the 6/8 time by chords in 3/4. It all calls for players with cool heads. But Holst was a master, and this music seems to be like the very spirit of Mercury, given masterly playing. The movement should never be breathless, but must appear brilliantly clear, as shafts of sunlight through trees. Holst's flinging together of two of the most distant keys of the system is one of the factors that place it among the most striking and original of movements. Be it noted how the two harps are tuned in different keys as remote as the two poles.

II*

'Jupiter' is of course in C major. The horns come playing the first tune in, as they are later to do with the four others. This succession calls up the idea of a pageant. It is as though the horns were ushering in groups or guilds to the grand merry-making—which is not too grand to be from the outset thoroughly roysterous. 'Allegro giocoso' was never better said. Amid a great chattering of fiddles the first tune tumbles on the scene, boldly syncopated. This is clearly an invitation to no excessively polite party, as the kettledrums are glad to recognize. Their jovial entrance here, as they take up the tune along with the tubas, is enough to make laughter even at a symphony concert. Yet the music's mood is heroic. It is as grand as it is hearty. This is the holiday of a simple and jolly people without folly. There is nothing of the painful search for pleasure, but a straightforward enjoyment of the liberal hours this summer afternoon. The folk come streaming in to the fair, and Holst grasps the poetry of the scene. He is, like Hardy, impressed by the dignity of simple men. In his English villagers at play there is felt the force of the legend and history of the race.

Time is not to be lost on this holiday. In 'Jupiter' one's turn makes way for another's with the least possible formality. The second tune bounds up a seventh, G C F, G C F—spriteliness in hobnail boots. Woodwind and strings give back a syncopated answer in the manner of the first tune. The third one is more pompous but still extremely good-tempered. Very amusing is the way in which, after its important entry, it seems suddenly to decide for irresponsibility and takes itself off into the crowd. It plays this trick twice. But now a space must be cleared. The time, up till now 2/4, changes to 3/4, and a swinging dance-tune comes in loudly on the horns. It is something no one can resist. All join in to the best of their ability. This means a brilliant racket, coming to a head in a crashing F sharp chord (straight from C).

The music hereupon subsides. The next section of 'Jupiter,' andante maestoso, comes not to damp anyone's pleasure, but breathing serenity for a little over the scene. The festival is not to be given over altogether to high spirits. The song of the andante is a reminder of thought and feeling. By way of preparation for its entrance there are fewer than twenty very quick bars after the F sharp crash, but these are enough for the music's subsidence from excitement to a collected melodious effort. The composer has his boisterous crowd settled with extraordinarily little fuss. The passage is one of his characteristic short cuts—not too abrupt, but saving much ordinary meandering.

The andante comes sailing in triple time, in E flat. Eric Blom has well called it "exalted folksong." The clan is unmistakable, if it is difficult to name a close relation. Holst's thanksgiving song is a noble scion of the family of 'The Crystal Spring,' 'The Cuckoo' and 'Swansea Town.' The suggestion came from Vaughan Williams that its place in Jupiter was less than it deserved, and that it ought to be fitted with words for public singing. It certainly would have been a great find for one of the new European States in search of a national anthem. But in practice the idea did not work very well.★

The truce is over. Light hints are given by the woodwind that youth has not finished its fling. The hints are welcome. Everyone rushes back to the games. From now on 'Jupiter' is the most joyous jangle imaginable. The uproarious crowd is now full of old friends. Among them is the noble song. A little before the end it makes a brief reappearance on the bass wind and strings, with the lighter instruments eddying about it in scales and arpeggios. Then, presto! And the holiday is done.

Here is the characteristically Holstian pattern of the opening of the festival:

Fig.19 *Allegro giocoso*

f Strings

★ The melody has been published as a unison song with patriotic words ("I vow to thee, my Country, all earthly things above, entire and whole and perfect the service of my love"), by Cecil Spring Rice, sometime British Ambassador at Washington. Text and tune fit fairly well, but not quite to the point of pretending they were made for each other.

Over it this hilarious tune sets the mood and pace:

Fig.20 Violas, Cellos & Horns

f molto pesante

Lusty and rough-hewn though the tunes of 'Jupiter' are, they must be accurately and brilliantly played. Holst associates many varied instruments, and any laxity or raggedness in the execution takes off the edge, of rhythm and tone. The effect must be reckless but the playing disciplined. With a slipshod staccato the strength and virility of the movement is impaired. Holst had the art of getting about twice as much sound from a given combination of instruments as any other composer. Here, for instance, the racket set up by the violins in the opening bars and the manly strength of the tune played in unison by six horns, violas and cellos make up a prodigious volume. After a sudden break and a huge chord for all the orchestra on G sharp in the bass the tune is ushered off for the arrival of a newcomer:

Fig.21
Horns

The orchestra joins in exuberantly, but the master of ceremonies abruptly brings in a new guest. This is a very heavy, broad tune with a queer twist of false modulation in its tail:

Fig.22 Strings & Horns

f molto pesante

This is attacked first by strings and horns, raucously copied by the woodwind. When the horn subject (Fig. 21) returns it is altered to its definitive form, developing a characteristic Holstian pattern in its fifth bar:

Fig. 23   * Pattern
Trumpet

p

This subject is important, the pattern becoming later the main substance of the texture; but for the moment it serves as a link to a new tune in 3/4 time, which enters with tremendous swing:

A return to tempo primo, on a huge F sharp chord—

is a preparation for the central andante maestoso—the famous folk-song. It unfolds itself to the extent of forty bars, purely diatonic. The body of the melody lies in bars 9-24, as follows:

Bars 9-16(A) are answered by 17-24(B). Before this the second clause, B, an octave lower, has introduced the melody. A and B are then repeated an octave higher. The form, then, is: B, A, B, A, B, each recurrence being at a higher octave. The mood is of almost solemn happiness. Its character and mounting confidence are due in part to the crest-notes of the B clause which are higher than those of A, and to the ascent from octave to octave.

The carnival returns, more animated than ever. In the coda the noble song is heard again on basses, bass trombone and tuba under masses of arpeggios and running passages on wind and harps. The brass has the last word, turning the 'pattern' into the utterance of Jove himself:

Fig.27

Harps and flutes brought in Venus. Now they bring in Saturn, but the harmonies tell how changed the season and sere the leaf. This slow, pendulum-like reiteration of two syncopated chords, which keep up their succession of ninths for twenty-six bars, compares with any of Holst's most imaginative inventions.

Fig.28

"I begin to feel my own bones ache," said a susceptible listener. Beneath their impassive alternation a theme takes shape—

Fig.29

and it becomes, when transferred to the trombones, above a ground-bass on the lower strings, a solemn and, as it were, priestly march:

Fig.30

A dirge is intoned by four flutes:

Fig.31

It is the beginning of a long crescendo. The suggestions are bell-like long before the climax, in which the tolling of actual bells is added to the clamour and the syncopation is doubled. Here are typical patterns upon which the music is established:

and:

Be it noted how these patterns cross the bar-lines and continue irrespective of the main time-values. We are immersed in glorious sound, from the 32-ft. organ pedal to the highest register of the violins, while the initial theme of Old Age, transformed, over-arches all like a gigantic rainbow.

This music tells of a mysterious apocalypse, too strange for joy and yet beyond sorrow. The vision, if a vision it is, leaves behind it a profound peacefulness, and the movement ends with the long-reverberating chimes of flutes and horns, bells and harps, in a pianissimo of more than fifty bars. It is interesting to compare Saturn's peace with that of 'Venus.' If the colour of the tones is similar there is the difference of spirit between rapt bliss and illumined resignation.

Through trumpets and trombones Uranus utters four weighty words—G, E flat, A, then a drop to B—"a kind of magic formula."*

* Eric Blom.

A jest for the giants it must be, to judge from the instant appreciation of tubas and kettledrums, which go rolling off into the depths echoing it. For an instant a pause; then, as though answering the summons, there enters a queer dancing crowd of the magician's people. The bassoons lead the rout.

They are followed by all the whimsical woodwind tribe, and then the rest. The 'spell' is seldom absent for long. It takes on fantastic shapes:

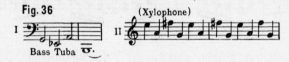

   The festival is a contrast with 'Jupiter,' which was all in broad daylight. There is something of the midnight sabbath about 'Uranus.' It is a revelry of the dark chthonic deities, uncanny if not sinister. The master's four-note command is uttered with a kind of rough good-nature. Every sort of strange beast, from xylophone to bass tuba, stirs at the bidding. Themes like these appear in the medley:

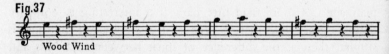

and this fugal subject:

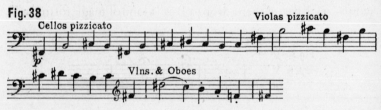

Droll and a little fearsome, they join in a wild round. In a lull after the first climax the 'formula' is enounced more vehemently, and in the rush to obey no one is before the kettledrums. 'Uranus' is of all Holst's movements the kettledrums' special turn, and here they come romping in like bears.

The droll entrance of bassoons in the seventh bar of 'Uranus' has sometimes been held to be reminiscent of Dukas's scherzo, 'The Wizard's Prentice,' a suggestion that the title of the piece may have reinforced. But there is no further likeness. Holst's evocation is of an altogether different scale and scope. This is not a picturesque anecdote. The power of the music seems to be inspired by some kind of ritual purpose. In the dance of the middle section the tempest of the Thyiades scares the loud night. It brings us again to an aspect of the mysticism that gives unity to Holst's various work, throughout his range from these warlocks in 'Uranus' and the gods of stormcloud and sunlight of the Vedic hymns, to the "spirit here that reignest" of Keats's religion of beauty.

The middle dance has this tune, of folk-song flavour:

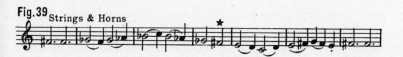

Fig.39 Strings & Horns

Be it observed how the tune is divided, the F sharp serving as a switch for the new key of the second half.

This tune is accompanied by resounding thumps from the rest of the orchestra not otherwise engaged. After a climax the music subsides and then Uranus's spell summons up another tribe of spirits, represented by the entire woodwind, who, with a gaseous hissing, scramble madly down the score to fall, as it were, upon the fortissimo 'formula' of the brass. This is the signal for the launching of a huge—a cosmic—motion:

Fig.40

ff Strings, Wood Wind & Timpani

As it gathers momentum the lower brass enter with a triumphant riding theme:

Fig.41

It is at first rather quietly uttered, as though the magician were a little awed at the potency of his spells and would fain keep the dangerous rhythm under control. The timpani, however, are impatient, and soon an orgy of all the warlocks is madly swirling. The magical master-stroke in 'Uranus' is the disappearance of the wild crew at the climax of the dance. It is a most amusing piece of orchestral craft. There is a mighty chord of C, helped out by a glissando for full organ. Follows a sudden drop from *ffff* to *pp*, leaving in the vacant air only a few faint strings quivering with a ghostly discord, while distant harp harmonics give a mocking echo of the 'formula.' But lest we should be tempted to dismiss the whole apparition as a trick of fancy the sound of the formula swells again, the kettledrums thunder it out, and back in an instant is the whole gang. A whoop and a shout—as if to leave no doubt how real and near at hand is their power—and this time they have gone for good. Only as night softly closes round in the last half-dozen bars the harps are still haunted by the magician's syllables.

The music changes from a sultry to a silvery fire. 'Neptune' is wholly a pianissimo movement. Its imaginative value in the scheme has been pointed to already. Musically its hushed interrogation comes as a beautiful relief, slackening the strain set up by the tremendous dynamic assertiveness that we have heard in the hour. The tubas and some other bold spirits have nothing at all to say here. The listener might fancy that bar-lines, of which he had been made so conscious in 'Mars,' 'Jupiter' and 'Uranus,' had been dispensed with too, so faint seems the emphasis and unfixed the metrical shape. As a matter of fact, there is a steady succession of a 3/4 and a 2/4 group.

Flutes breathe this phrase:

Fig.42 *Andante*
Flutes & Bass Flute
pp

Oboes and piccolos gently support it as it melts into the air. Remote harmonics shimmer on the harps. The mysterious character of 'Neptune' is rendered by vaporous orchestral colouring together with the setting side by side of unrelated keys. The flutes' phrase is—much as we noted of one in 'Mercury'—partly in E minor and partly in G sharp. As they come to rest on the latter, a further hint of homelessness is given by the A minor chord sighed by the trombones. A little later obscurity thickens with solemn chords on the brass in two keys simultaneously—trumpets in E minor against trombones in G sharp. It is no random shot, but perfectly serves a purpose and therefore sounds right—given, moreover, the extreme softness of the playing.

While upper strings sustain a quiet 'Neptune' chord the cellos begin an ascending phrase:

Fig.43 *Allegretto*
Cellos   Bass Oboe
pp

The second bar of this phrase, with its unequal rocking motion, brings the feeling of a lullaby. The woodwind take it up, until the clarinets sing an endless folk-melody, misty with Neptune's influence. The violins continue, to disappear faintly into the last and most moving section.

The time changes from andante to allegretto, and a hidden choir of women's voices sustain a high G, while clarinet and flute prompt them for their wordless song. It comes with magical effect, beautiful and lonely. The indeterminate tonality of the six-part writing (which generally becomes even more indeterminate than the composer has indicated) suggests an utterance beyond human ken, the more so as the music grows fainter and fainter. The violins leave off on a high B. The cadence of one choir is nominally in E, of the other in C sharp minor—nominally, since a door is slowly closed on the singers to leave the impression of a departing and not an ended song.

Fig.44

So is Holst enticed farther and farther from human ties. 'Neptune' is the last and most remote of the planets. Here Holst leaves his friends and, unguided, sets forth into the unknown by himself —and none sees him return.

XXIX

ARNOLD BAX

LESS is heard nowadays than forty or fifty years ago of 'Celtic
Twilight' and the 'Celtic fringe.' The green land of Eire—once
'John Bull's Other Island'—after exciting the sympathy of all
generous hearts with the shrieks of its sufferings under the
tyrant's heel, long since won independence and a comfortable
obscurity. It cannot be easy for the youth of to-day, faced with a
world of a very different grimness from that of the sanguine,
prosperous, essentially contented generation into which Arnold
Bax was born, to understand the intensity with which, in lieu of
anything more important, Irish affairs and Irish aspirations were
considered by the passionate few. In those days a good deal was
light-heartedly talked about races and racial characteristics, for it
was before the time when racial myths had shown all the ugly
consequences of wide-spread adoption; and it was believed
that England was inhabited by 'Saxons' and Ireland by 'Celts,'
and that those labels designated differences as remarkable as
those between totally dissimilar breeds of dogs. Celts, living
in the smaller and less prosperous island, were supposed to
be wistfully imaginative men; Saxons to be pedestrian, gross,
materialistic.

The Celtic Twilight was, in the arts, principally literary, and as
such it derived from the English Pre-Raphaelites and from the
Flemish Maeterlinck. If racial characteristics were what in those
innocent times they were supposed to be, the author of 'Pelléas
et Mélisande' and 'La Princesse Maleine' should have belonged to
the purest Goidelic strain instead of coming of the stolid burgessy
of Ghent. The word Celtic, which in these enlightened days is
known to be properly applicable only to the Goidelic and Bry-
thonic languages and to be inappropriate to present-day ethnology

(the Celts were long ago absorbed, and the Celtic-speaking peoples of Wales and Ireland are supposed to be principally of pre-Celtic origins), was romantically applied to almost any artistic manifestation that was in revolt against the complacency with which long prosperity had imbued a good many English minds.

The lively Irish political movement was accompanied by an interesting literary movement, which boasted one first-rate poet, but it had no musician. The young Arnold Bax, who was born of Surrey stock and was brought up in comfortable circumstances in London suburbs—first Streatham and then Hampstead—was a romantic lad. Looking about him for wild beauty, he found smugness. In effect, Hampstead failed to provide him with the matter of poetry, and under W. B. Yeats's spell he turned to Ireland. At a moment he nearly became one of the literary bards of the movement; but these were many, and Bax, though he won some compliments with the effusions he produced under the name of Dermot O'Byrne, was, after all, a musician—an outstanding one. There were any number of O'Byrnes but only one Arnold Bax, and he was to be the musical bard of the Twilight.

He has written a charming—charming, that is to say, when it is not waspish—autobiography, or fragment of an autobiography, called *Farewell, My Youth*, and therein is to be found an attractive picture of the "wide-eyed youth" he once was, "to whom Yeats had opened the gate of the Celtic wonderland," and of the good old days of the tyranny, before preaching had been rudely carried into practice and everything turned squalid. It seems that Ireland had no use for a first-rate musician, and Bax came home— but not empty-handed. He brought back with him a background for his music. One of Max Beerbohm's caricatures represents Yeats introducing George Moore to the Queen of the Fairies. Yeats did as much for the young Bax; and back at Hampstead— which had, after all, once been Keats's Hampstead—he always had this vision to draw upon for inspiration and for consolation in an unsympathetic world of machinery, commerce and brutal wars. In other words, Bax, coming at the end of the Romantic period, remained an impenitent romantic, utterly aloof from the cocktail-bar music whose vogue set in with the Armistice of 1918.

One Saxon trait in Bax's make-up the Queen of the Fairies did not exorcize, namely, his fondness for cricket. But this is a side of Bax that does not come out in his music, any more than does his witty and sarcastic side. It may be revealed that Sir Arnold Bax, the Master of the King's Music, is not so entirely hag-ridden —not so exclusively obsessed by the Shadowy Waters, Deirdre and her sorrows, and the mist-enshrouded career of Cuchulain— as those who listen to his music may have supposed. Though he has given to the world his own incomparable account of his young days a word or two must be said thereupon. He had to face none of the material difficulties that have handicapped many a creative artist. His well-to-do father put up the least possible opposition to the young Arnold's choice of a career. His vital and attractive mother one can recall to mind as she was in the later phase of her life—a wonderfully charming woman upon whom the years weighed lightly. She lived to see both Arnold and his brother Clifford, the playwright, fulfil her hopes.

We are told that Arnold never remembers having been unable to play the piano or to speak a certain amount of French; and to read music came to him as naturally as reading a book. His sight-reading became legendary when, after leaving the Hampstead Conservatoire at the age of seventeen, he went on to the Royal Academy of Music. There he was under Frederick Corder for composition and Tobias Matthay for piano. He admired the former greatly, and if there is an influence to be found in Bax's always remarkably personal and uninfluenced music, it is that of his professor, especially to be detected in the richness of his scoring. After fifteen and more years of Promenade Concerts only one of Corder's compositions comes to mind—an Elegy for organ and twenty-four violins, a piece which affords a small clue to his celebrated pupil's technique. The curious and beautiful work goes in for a rather extravagant use of divided strings (violins nos. 23 and 24 have to tune down their G strings); and the diffused sounds of the crowded harmonic scene fore-tell something of Bax. Corder was a great Wagnerian, so that Bax's natural interest in Wagner received encouragement.

It was a golden period at the royal schools of music. Bax's fellow students at the Academy, when he entered in 1900, included B. J. Dale, later to become Warden, Stanley Marchant, now the Principal, Adam Carse, Eric Coates, W. H. Reed, York Bowen, Theodore Holland, Myra Hess and Irene Scharrer. Lionel Tertis had not long left, to set out on his career as the prince of viola-players. At the College Vaughan Williams, Holst, John Ireland, Thomas Dunhill and Coleridge-Taylor were still students or else just starting out on their adventures. At the same time Elgar and Delius were writing their finest works. After two years Bax won the MacFarren scholarship, but he does not seem to have made a great impression outside the circle of his intimates. Diffidence has always characterized him, and the shy man we know him to be in the time of his fame must have been an extremely retiring youth. Shortly before he left the R.A.M., at twenty-two, he had a set of Symphonic Variations accepted for performance by the Patron's Fund. Stanford insisted on his attempting to conduct it, and the experience—quite unprepared as he was—was so distasteful that he would never conduct again. Henry Wood, in later years, multiplied efforts to persuade him to do so, but in vain. Many is the time Sir Henry, his hands full of new music, would hold forth in this vein to the orchestra: "Can't think why Bax won't direct his own works! Haven't I enough to do with nineteen new works to fit in, and no extra rehearsals? Always the same old story! And now I've got to sit up all night on this symphony of his, let alone correct all the parts. Never mind, don't be downhearted! Now, ladies and gentlemen, to work! Bax's Symphony No. 1, and start with the last movement!"

As his brother Clifford has said that, reading one day a poem of Keats's, he discovered that he was a poet himself, so did Arnold Bax alight, through reading Yeats's 'Wanderings of Usheen,' upon his congenial background and source of inspiration. A fragment or two will convey the spirit of the poetry which half-a-century ago young men found so heady.

. . . And kissed my eyes, and swaying her bright head
And her bright body, sang of faery and man
Before God was or my old line began;
Wars shadowy, vast, exultant; faeries of old
Who wedded men with rings of Druid gold;
And how those lovers never turn their eyes
Upon the life that fades and flickers and dies,
But love and kiss on dim shores far away
Rolled round with music of the sighing spray . . .

In the isles of the farthest seas where only the spirits come
Were the winds less soft than the breath of a pigeon who
    sleeps on her nest.
Nor lost in the star-fires and odours the sound of the sea's
    vague drum?
O flaming lion of the world, O when will you turn to your
    rest?

Let it be understood that the Celtic influence upon Bax's
music was general and not specifically musical. Folk-song and
primitive-looking harps which could in practice do little, and
that little out of tune, did not enter into it. As for folk-songs,
"I never use one!" he has said. What was Celtic or Irish was the
spark that fired his creative thought, out of which came, in his
twenties, two of his most lovely orchestral pieces, 'The Song of
the Faery Hills' and 'The Garden of Fand.' The sea-music of the
latter (composed in 1916) seems to spring from ocean's own surge
and swell. The garden of the title is a sort of Circean island. The
love-song with which the Irish Circe beguiles wandering sailors is
a strange and enchanting tune, very characteristic of Bax; but
the great moment of the piece is at the catastrophe when the
fairy's island is engulfed by the sea. The whole composition is
the best of introductions to Bax, whose later music, with its
elaborate harmonic scheme, heavy scoring and lack of contrast in
the movement (Bax has seldom, if ever, achieved a genuine
Allegro vivace), is sometimes found difficult to follow or
to assimilate. Already in the 'Fand' melody we find his

characteristic habit of diverging from the obvious path. Bax's harmonies, while based on normal foundations, are so generously embellished that their character is novel in effect. They may be compared with the last phase of Gothic architecture, the Flamboyant, whose underlying features, despite the elaboration and the audacious departures in the detail, are still those of austere Early English.

Bax had already established a position for himself in the world when he composed his first symphony, having then written the big Symphonic Variations of 1917, 'Tintagel' and 'November Woods' for orchestra; a quantity of piano music, including two sonatas; a number of choral pieces, among them the motet 'Mater ora Filium,' one of the works that will keep his name in long remembrance; and an important body of chamber music. The Variations, with a concertante piano part, will always be associated with the name of Harriet Cohen, who has done much to make Bax's music known. A comparatively early work into which Bax put all he knew and felt was the largely designed piano quintet in G minor, of 1914–15. It was followed a few years later by the more modest string quartet in G major, a work which won a warm welcome and an abiding place. Probably no other English string quartet has been so often played. The beautiful slow movement is a fine picture of the poet in quest of beauty. Bax did a great service to chamber music by composing for unusual combinations, for instance, a quintet of harp and strings, a sonata for viola and harp, and a trio for flute, harp and viola. He holds a leading place among the English composers who were inspired to write for the viola by Tertis's sovran art.

The first symphony was composed in 1921–2, by which date Bax had reached his full stature. One of the most exciting concerts that come to mind is that of his works given under Eugene Goossens at Queen's Hall on November 13, 1922. There was a picked orchestra, and Goossens was in wonderful form, brimming with vitality and feeling. The programme included 'The Garden of Fand,' some choral pieces and the then new Phantasy for Viola and Orchestra, with Tertis as soloist. The music was not typical of the 1920s, and for that very reason has lasted all the better. The Phantasy is still a grand work to play, though the scoring may be a shade too brilliant. The solo tends to be obscured unless the orchestra is very tactfully handled; but the music is spiritedly lively and youthful and the slow movement melting in its deep romanticism. A month after this concert came the first performance of the first (under Albert Coates, at Queen's Hall, December 2, 1922) of Bax's seven symphonies.

A few weeks before these lines were written one had an opportunity of hearing once again the third, played by the Hallé Orchestra under John Barbirolli to an audience of 3,000 in a large cinema. It was impressive to see how this great crowd was held fast by the music. There was every sign of rapt attentiveness, and the ovation afterwards was worthy of the beautiful music. Barbirolli is one of the finest exponents of Bax, who needs a conductor with an understanding of the players' technical problems, and able to respond fully to the emotion of the melodies. Bax often presents difficulties of his own to the orchestra; and players who come to him after being spoilt by the considerateness of Elgar's string-writing are sometimes tried by awkward passages entailing feverish manipulation and hard to bear in the mind. Audiences, however, are held by the power and beauty of the music, once they are acclimatized to the peculiar atmosphere.

In the years between the wars Bax stood aloof from fashion, and the experimentalism of the time was not his. Year by year he remained loyal to the ideal of beauty he had formed for himself in his youth, and the seven symphonies are like the cantos of some endless epic of ancient story, sorrow-haunted and darkly rich in colour and mood. Honours have fallen to him—he was knighted in 1937 and became the Master of the King's Music in 1942—but worldliness has never impinged upon his art. He has never played the Great Man, and the atmosphere of artists' rooms is hateful to him. Performances of his music leave him remarkably detached, unless they are catastrophically bad. He will turn up at rehearsal, but goes in for no fault-finding. If seriously annoyed he simply disappears from the scene. The extreme of his censure of an unfortunate performance is something like this: "I think old

So-and-so should be allowed to give only first performances. He is so much better then than later on, when he gets to know the work and has ideas about it." Bax's independence of mind, his aloofness from any sort of clap-trap and, above all, his great gift of realizing in masterly form his poet's dreams have given him a high place in the English musical renascence.

XXX

BAX'S THIRD SYMPHONY

THE orchestra, when faced with a new work of Bax's, has mixed feelings. Visions appear of troublesome passages, phrases with awkward twists and nasty problems of intonation. The strings, in particular, are apprehensive of harsh criticism from the conductor. While in Elgar and Holst every stroke of work at rehearsal is justified by immediate results the picture is not so clear in Bax's case, and the result is deferred. Part of the trouble lies in the difficulty the player often has, when sight-reading, of hearing a group of notes in the mind. Bax's peculiar use of accidentals is apt to put one's fingers off the mark, even though the passage be in reality not difficult at all. The average orchestral player, then, who is naturally concerned with his own part rather than the work as a whole, is apt to complain that he cannot see Bax's wood for the trees. "Why," some grumble at rehearsal, "does Bax have to write so many notes?"

It is true that his notes are many; he is characteristically fond of filling up his harmonic spaces. But that, after all, is part of his style, and as important to his idea as the observance of a rigid economy is to Holst. It is more true of him than of most of his contemporaries that mere acquaintance is not enough—appreciation comes with intimacy. The difficulty at first is to steer a clear course through the shoals of Baxiana. Let the newcomer be assured that these waters are of the loveliest to be found, once the ins and outs are mastered.

The first symphony is a grim and darkly coloured composition, more concise than is Bax's general way. It is full of anger and war. The music is exceptional in that it seems to represent no dream, but the composer's indignation at man's cruelty to man. The symphony is a powerful work, and hissing seas seem to whirl around jagged rocks. The final march, labelled by the composer

'trionfale,' is no joyous triumph but conveys bitter scorn. There
was a gap of three years between the production of the first and
the completion of the second symphony. The latter (not played
in England until after the production of the third) was dedicated
to Serge Koussevitsky. It is scored for a large orchestra, including
piano and organ. It is moody and powerful. A couple of passages
taken more or less at random from the last movement will
illustrate the reason why players grumble when reading Bax at
sight. The first is for the violins:

Fig.1

and this is for the cellos:

Fig.2

These examples are of the essence of Bax's style.

The third symphony, written in 1929 and dedicated to Sir
Henry Wood, shows the composer at the top of his form. A truly
great work it is, and one that makes an instant appeal to both the
orchestra and the listener. Every moment spent in rehearsal is
amply rewarded. One remembers the first performance of this
symphony under Sir Henry's direction as a landmark in Bax's
career. It was in the May of 1930, the year in which the B.B.C.
Symphony Orchestra began major operations. Wood was proud
of the dedication. He had long been an admirer of Bax's, and
Bax has remarked: "I would rather have Henry to conduct a
first performance of my work than anyone else. He has such an
amazing grasp of essentials, and does not mess the music about."
It is a work for the expert conductor, abounding in the details
that require a masterly hand and mind; and this first performance
showed all Wood's prodigious skill. As usual, he did not take
Bax's score for granted, but had everything worked out in his
mind before he came to rehearsal and had himself corrected all

the orchestral parts. Each change of tempo was heavily marked by his famous blue-pencil with the number of beats he intended to give, and when rehearsing began he would exclaim: "Bax, I'm beating six for this passage instead of two, although it's a bit fast. Otherwise we shall never get it together. And you mean B flat 'concert,' don't you, in the clarinet at bar five? It's B natural in the score!" So the symphony received no anxious and feverish performance but one that was clear, dynamic and inspiring.

Certain strong features stand out in the third symphony— the long bassoon solo with which it opens: the intense vigour of the first movement, which builds up to one of the greatest climaxes in modern music; the wonderfully impressive horn and trumpet solos in the slow movement, with their suggestions of a great military elegy; and finally the supreme beauty of the immortal Epilogue.

The symphony is scored for a large orchestra, but no out-of-the-way instruments. The theme upon which the first movement is based is a long bassoon solo of a very dark hue, and the first two bars are to have much significance. The bassoon has no support whatever, and the player must look upon this solo with some anxiety. It takes the instrument into its highest register, and the first bassoonist will have devoted all his care to selecting a reed, for an unfortunate squawk here would shatter the spell he has to weave over the audience.

Fig. 3 — Lento moderato. Bassoon Solo

It is an awesome beginning, and as other instruments join in, the atmosphere becomes fraught with unhappiness. This bassoon theme is extremely characteristic of Bax's idiom. The manner in which the expressive tune grows from the first two bars, to increase in strain and tension as the instrument climbs up to its topmost register, is typical of the composer in a sombre mood.

As the woodwind becomes more clamorous, urged on by the horns, cellos and basses appear for the first time to repeat a series of two-bar phrases which the English horn has already fore-shadowed:

Fig. 4
Cellos & Basses

Fig. 4 is the background for an impressive theme on trumpets and trombones, like a pronouncement in a saga:

Fig. 5 *Lento moderato*
Trumpets & Trombones

Note the queer Baxian twist of the A flat and E flat in the fifth bar at ★.

From this sinister utterance the orchestra is whipped into vigorous ascending passages, and the key which has been an indeterminate A minor is brightened to a clear F sharp minor and then immediately altered to B flat minor. At this point the wood-wind and horns launch out into a kind of 'witches' broomstick' rhythm. It is a clear landmark, for the tempo is speeded up to allegro moderato and this rhythm is at once established.

Fig. 6 *Allegro moderato*
Woodwind & Horns

A new aggressive theme stalks up from the bass:

Fig. 7 *Tempo giusto*
Cellos & Basses

The change of tempo at Fig. 6 is the opening of the first movement

ARNOLD BAX

WALTON

proper, the preceding music having been of the nature of an introduction. The principal subject, so-called, is made up of two tunes,
the first being Fig. 7 above, which is immediately answered by
the second on strings and wind—a brilliant and impetuous transformation of the opening bars of the bassoon solo:

The music gathers intensity, the tempo slightly quickens to
Allegro feroce, and with full brass adding their punches to Fig. 8,
violins and oboes break out with a new tune made from the
rhythm of Fig. 6, which settles down to this form on a sudden
damping of sound:

The following counter-subject associates itself with the above,
but plays no great part in the movement.

The orchestra soon gets into an angry, tempestuous mood
again, arriving at a fortissimo climax when full woodwind and
upper strings, reinforced by the hard tapping of the tambourine,
attack the rhythm of Fig. 6; and the tune (Fig. 7) is now heavily
backed up by the trombones, and expanded to:

Reference is made by the brass to the saga-like tune Fig. 5, and this leads to a terrific outburst by the full orchestra on the initial theme of the symphony (Fig. 8). From this point Bax begins to smooth out the jagged sounds, which have been a feature of the music. The tempo is slowed down; the initial theme is reduced to:

and an entirely new mood is prepared.

Bax is given to violent contrasts, and frequently a long passage of angry strife will melt into a most romantic and tender mood.

The next enchanting episode for strings reminds us a little of the composer's Irish days, but the music is now no faery stuff but has the warmth of human tenderness in its expressive phrases. This quiet tranquil movement within a movement, so to speak, begins andante and is scored for five solo violins (note that the theme is still made from the ingredients of Fig. 3, but in more expressive character):

After a few bars of this preparation, the tempo is retarded to lento moderato, for a warm, song-like theme on the 1st violins:

Bax develops this theme harmonically, rather than expanding the theme itself, and another tune rises in the horns, taken up by the strings, and the mood becomes suffused with emotion. There is a lovely, almost abrupt, hush as Bax makes a modulation reminiscent of César Franck:

Fig. 15

A weird half-light steals over the orchestra at this moment, and the horn, who enters with a horribly dangerous top note, descends as well as he is able in an important solo of about fourteen bars. The accompaniment adds to the strangeness of the atmosphere, which is scored for cellos and basses in their lowest registers, the softest sustained chords from the lower woodwind, widely spaced notes from the harp and the flute's weaving around the horn. This twilight brightens to the sun's warmth again, and Fig. 12 returns with its tender mood enriched by the orchestration. It is for the two clarinets to bring this quiet section to an end with an enchanting passage in thirds over an undulating pedal-note in the strings:

Fig. 16

There is a breathless moment as the clarinets fade into utter stillness.

A growl from the orchestra and three hard knocks ("like the kick of a horse in its stable," as Wood helpfully suggested to the timpanist) shatter the peace, and the composer returns to the opening bars of the symphony, but, instead of the bassoon, the violas take over the theme. Here the difficulties of ensemble between fourteen players, and particularly that of intonation, gave Wood plenty to talk about in rehearsal.

Bax, having stated again the whole of the music associated with the long theme of the introduction, then takes a different path. The orchestration has been considerably increased, and instead

12*

of a clear change of tempo and the cello and bass theme of
Fig. 4, this two-bar phrase is expanded, and the celesta helps to
alter completely the nature of the music, which becomes appallingly
disturbed, as if by impending catastrophe. Instead of the stark
landmark of Fig. 6 with the 'broomstick rhythm,' a jagged sound
leaps from the timpani and tambourine and a new version of
Fig. 3 is roared out by the brass amidst a turmoil:

Fig.17 *Allegro moderato*

There is so much going on that it would be unwise to
quote further details—the listener's attention should be concentrated on the immense build-up for the major climax of the
movement, which is the most thrilling of any that Bax has
written. There is no mistaking the great moment as it approaches. First there is a violent ascending passage for the strings
alone to an outburst on the following themes, the tempo broadened out to largamente:

Then immediately the strings and woodwind grip this phrase
from Fig. 17 fortissimo:

and as each bar is either repeated or slightly altered, they attack it
the more fiercely, whilst the horns blare defiance; the whole
orchestra is gathered together in a giant heave and the peak is

reached. It is a veritable blaze of sound with this constantly repeated figure in the bass predominating:

After a few bars of this terrific and concentrated effort there is a
general falling away in sound and tension, with the above ceaselessly repeated figure becoming more smooth, until the strings
at length restore the tender mood of Fig. 14, here broadened
out to:

Fig. 5 appears again, and the two clarinets, whose tone is enriched by the addition of the bass clarinet, again make a most
moving effect, similar to Fig. 16 in feeling but now in this shape,
the horns and trombones quietly supporting them in velvety
chords:

Like the former outburst after the quiet section, there is a sudden
upsurge of sound on a broken form of Fig. 8, the coda opens with
the 'broomstick rhythm' of Fig. 6 and the tune made out of it,
and the orchestra rushes to the end of the movement.

   The second movement, likewise, begins with an unaccompanied solo, this time by the horn. In six beautifully poised bars
the horn gives the effect of some ethereal Last Post. One is conscious of a vast gathering stilled to utter silence, and the quiet
notes sound magical:

The phrase is answered by a dark murmur in the strings, the form of its theme shrouded in shimmering mist. The scoring is unusual, the solo viola playing the melodic line in tremolando:

The trumpet breaks across the gloom as with a ray of sunlight. Instead of repeating the horn's tune, as his first few notes suggest, he sets out on a line of his own, with a lovely sense of freedom, over a diffused background on strings and harps:

All this music which opens the slow movement is in the nature of preparation and the setting of a deeply tranquil mood. The main idea is at length announced by the trumpet, and is formed out of the horn solo at the beginning of the movement:

Violins, with the dark tang of the English horn, bring in a new strain. The harmonies here are so Baxian that the last two bars are quoted (the delicate ensuing modulation into a clear chord of F major sounds delicious):

This F major chord, scored very simply, with a delicate arpeggio figure on the flute and clarinet at the top, begins the great episode of this movement. The strings open it with a luscious but soft statement of the principal subject, which is rudely interrupted by a vehement insistence of Fig. 24 by the horns in particular (note the harmony again) :

Strings pizzicato with Horns

Once again the thick and dark harmonies dissolve into a clear chord, now of B flat, and Bax adds some entrancing scoring for harps and celesta, through which the horn, in an inspired solo, seems to shine with iridescent light :

This ecstatic theme leads to an impassioned development by the whole orchestra, after a few bars of quiet thought. The full power of the climax bursts out after the violins have striven to dominate the orchestra with this insistent motive :

but the wind makes such a din with a series of descending chromatic chords that the strings have to resort to every device to force the motive through the orchestra. It is to no avail; on a crashing chord the horns take over from them, and this idea now overwhelms everything else :

The next passage is an impressive build-up of three warring subjects: Fig. 31 above; the first notes of the principal subject, Fig. 24; and this grim series of hard, sinister ascending chords on the trombones:

The whole rising structure rests on a great pedal note G. The horn tune (Fig. 26) wins, ringing out on the trumpets, and thereafter the music becomes emptied of passion, returning to something of the quiet tranquillity of the earlier part of the movement.

As the horn once more repeats his opening bars, this time supported by woodwind and harps, the same music occurs as before, but the clarinet now takes the part of the solo viola. A moving reference by the violins to Fig. 27 is like a pale reflection of the shining horn tune, and as the bassoon softly blends into the picture the movement closes on a deep, pianissimo chord of C major. There is no longer the same magical feeling of the beginning of the movement and the closing bars sound peaceful and natural, like the passing of a soul in sleep.

With the composer's strong sense of contrast, he gives us now a movement of restlessness and strain. The orchestra is beset with heavy stabbing rhythms; and although there is buoyancy in the music, the vigour and fire expended lack fulfilment until, in a moment of inspiration, the composer finds the answer in the Epilogue.

The movement opens with a series of harsh, angry chords, which in different forms and rhythms are to play a vital part throughout:

A vigorous rhythm then sets the pace for one of the main

subjects, a war dance played on violas and clarinets (note the usual Baxian twist in the third and fifth bars) :

The orchestra reacts to this tune by a general attack on the basis of the opening bars, working up in heavier orchestration for a repetition of the war dance with this figure churning in the bass :

This does not last long, for a series of chords after the style of Fig. 33 interrupts the continuity of the rhythm and pulls back the tempo lever half a notch :

This is an important moment, for these chords are immediately succeeded by an exuberant phrase on the violins and both ideas are to have significance later on (note the stately tuba's unusual behaviour beneath the violins, and the composer's satirical hint 'leggiero') :

This solitary cantabile theme of the violins is at once swamped by a mass of brilliant orchestration, which sweeps the next section along with spirit and vigour on a basis of Fig. 36. The tempo suddenly accelerates, in a violently attacked series of broken chords, the horns at length forcing the music, in heavily brassed rhythm, back to the dance theme of Fig. 34, and the tempo is pulled back again to poco più lento. The dance does not develop, but turns into a sort of brilliant fanfare, suddenly reducing in speed to announce a completely different scene. The tempo is now to be più mosso, the short 2/4 beat lengthening to 4/4, and yet another form of Fig. 33 sets a new pulsating rhythm:

Fig. 38 *Più mosso*
Strings

for a warm tune played by clarinets and oboes:

Fig. 39
Clarinets & Oboes

p canto piangendo mf p

This tune has a queer feature in the first bar, horribly suggestive of a certain habit dear to organists of a secular fraternity. Nevertheless, the tune itself is anything but vulgar. It may be that the clarinet and oboe are merely envying their string friends' prerogative of portamento. The background to this rich tune is extraordinarily alive, with the attractive lilt of a dance measure. However, the whole movement is too restless for an idea to settle down for any length of time, and again the tempo is suddenly pulled back to più moderato. The lilt of the rhythm is broken, angrily hurried by the woodwind (ancora più vivo). Still faster becomes the tempo, as the horns tackle an awkward passage, until the brass steadies the orchestra with an authoritative restatement of Fig. 38 (tempo giusto) now in this form:

Fig. 40 *A tempo giusto*
(Brass)

f

Strings softly repeat the brass subject, oboes and clarinets return
to their Fig. 39, playing this time with still more feeling and
colour. This is followed by a charming variant of Fig. 38 which
smooths out to sustained wisps of sound.

The mood becomes utterly changed, with a lovely strain from
the English horn:

to which the bass clarinet and basses make an appreciative reply
on a reflection of Fig. 39. In this intimate and tranquil episode the
composer for the first time finds some respite, and allows himself
to reawaken tender and enchanting memories, which fade rather
than are disturbed by the return of Fig. 36 in pianissimo.

The music, however, soon hardens again and spiteful scoring
banishes any further quiet reflection. All the old restless spirit,
typified by the rhythmic chords and the forceful fragment at the
end (from Fig. 36):

becomes ever more fierce. A full climax is attained when the brass
concentrate on Fig. 36, the violins doing their utmost to sustain a
thrilling and expanded form of Fig. 37:

From the peak of this climax we are magically led by the violins
out of a world of battle into one of ineffable peace.

The hush over the orchestra at the beginning of the Epilogue
is the greatest moment in the whole symphony. It opens with the

strings and harps playing the final form of Fig. 36, on which the whole Epilogue is built:

(Note how the shape of Fig. 36 is now welded into a single mass, no longer caught up by restless tags of rhythm, but as regular as the steps of a march.)

In the hands of a fine conductor this march-like rhythm is like a giant pendulum. From this impressive background the noble theme of the Epilogue stands out on the clarinets and oboes, its character one of breadth and tranquillity:

The simplicity of the music speaks for itself, and we are aware that the composer has been inspired by one of those rare secrets, all too seldom revealed. We know from his works and his words that his life has been spent in search of beauty, and here it seems as though he has found his heart's desire—in no external form, but within his own mind—and has succeeded in disclosing it to us. The Epilogue earned its author a remarkable act of homage from Vaughan Williams, who in his piano concerto, written at about the same time, quoted from this principal theme.

After a repetition and expansion of the theme on clarinets and flutes, and a moving variant of it on the first violins, the second theme of the Epilogue—like a distant trumpet call, and strange, rather unearthly in feeling—is played on the woodwind and echoed by strings:

The celesta, with its fairy tinkling, reawakens a misty, elusive memory of the initial theme of the symphony; it is mingled betwixt brass and strings, and the effect is of a half-forgotten incident, vaguely recalled and strangely moving. The picture fades into the theme of the Epilogue again, on violas and horns. A violin solo, extemporizing in the mood rather than on the material of the Epilogue, brings back barely audibly the march of Fig. 43, for the horn to make a final reference to the initial theme of the work in the brass; and the music fades away on a chord of C major.

XXXI

WILLIAM WALTON

SOME time early in the 1920s there came to the Royal College of Music a pale and thin young man with a string quartet which the Director, Sir Hugh Allen, asked us to play through for him. Afterwards we were, I trust, reasonably polite; but when the composer had gone some biting remarks were made.

"After all, it's only like a Beethoven quartet with all the instruments playing in different keys!" observed second violin. To which, "And played backwards!" added first violin. Such was my introduction to William Walton, who was then not much more than twenty and who, after a schooling as a chorister of Christ Church, Oxford, had distinguished himself by passing the first part of the Mus. Bac. examination there at the age of sixteen.

Let a later, enlightened generation be not too scornful of us! Stravinsky was but little known in South Kensington in that faraway year. This same quartet of Walton's was soon afterwards chosen by the jury of the International Society for Contemporary Music for performance at the Salzburg Festival of 1923, whereby the young man won the first fruits of recognition. It is, however, not one of the works by which Walton is now known. More familiar to-day is an earlier composition, a piano quartet which, composed in 1918 and awarded a Carnegie prize in 1924, was first performed in public in 1929. This, if not exactly a masterpiece, is a likeable, not to say charming, work, and a highly remarkable one as the production of a boy of sixteen.

Walton comes of a musical Lancashire family (he was born at Oldham). Both his father and mother were teachers of singing, and William is said to have sung Handel as soon as he could talk. He entered the Christ Church choir at the age of ten. After his seventeenth year he had no teachers. Beryl de Zoete has told us that in his last year at the university he made friends with Ronald Firbank, Roy Campbell and Siegfried Sassoon, and was by the last-named introduced to Osbert and Sacheverell Sitwell. "This meeting was the most significant event of his Oxford life, the opening of a new world." Walton's name became associated with the Sitwells. Osbert compiled the libretto of his choral master-piece, 'Belshazzar's Feast,' of 1931; but long before that he had won the public ear with his 'Façade,' a work which, in its first form, was an accompaniment for the recitation of some of Edith Sitwell's poems. (It took on other shapes, becoming a ballet and also a symphonic suite.) Humorous, witty and charming, this 'Façade' is an untiring joy to play. It must also be said to have mis-led a good many people as to the composer's essential nature—his essential seriousness. Walton was for long regarded as a typical playboy of the 1920s, the more since his brilliantly clever overture 'Portsmouth Point' (1925)—pungent, satirical music—belonged more to the period than to the man's inner self.

Two concertos, however, composed before the end of the decade—one for piano ('Sinfonia concertante,' 1927) and the yet more famous one for viola (1928-9)—revealed much of the real Walton. This music also was in the nature of an admission that the war of 1914-18 had not entirely cut off the younger com-posers from their seniors. Walton's music began, indeed, to be beautiful. His viola concerto is the finest of all compositions of that form and combination and remains his best-loved work. The first performance, given at a Promenade Concert at Queen's Hall in 1929, comes back to mind. The composer conducted and Paul Hindemith played the solo. Feverish was the activity that went on behind the scenes to get the orchestral parts ready. Up till seven o'clock on the night, the artists' room was full of copyists, while an anxious Walton and an irritated Hindemith (who wanted more rehearsal) paced up and down, debating over the score and agreeing upon various vital code-signs. Wood, very indignant, was meanwhile heard to mutter: "These young com-posers! I can't even get into my own artists' room! What next?"

The culmination of the first part of Walton's career was the electrifying effect made at the Leeds Festival by his 'Belshazzar,' wherein the new harmonic and percussive inventions of the age were combined with a music of expressive beauty (notably the psalm, 'By the Waters of Babylon,' the interest of which, indeed, after fifteen years or so, exceeds that of the more sensational pages). Walton was never a prolific composer, and as the years went on he became less than ever in a hurry to finish a composition. The symphony of 1935 took him four years to write, and when Hamilton Harty first played it (in December 1934) the finale was still not ready. Again, years passed before the production of the violin concerto, written for Jascha Heifetz. An overture, 'Scapino,' showed a momentary return to the sparkling dryness of 'Portsmouth Point.' Then, in 1947, came another masterpiece, a string quartet in A, again the result of a long gestation. This glorious music represents Walton's full maturity.

A shy and fastidious man, Walton is not a figure familiar to the public, though he is a fairly capable conductor of his own music. It has sometimes occurred to one that this extraordinarily gifted musician, who was at one time regarded as a typical product of his age, is possibly a victim of it—an artist who would have been better suited by a time of less incoherency and more certain standards of art and life. Like all the lads of the 1920s, he was much impressed by Stravinsky—Stravinsky, that embodiment of the fashions of the time, with his quasi-scientific experimentalism, his super- (or sub-) human dryness, his withering pessimism. But Walton had it not in him—had too much humane feeling in him and too little of a purely intellectual ferocity—to be an English Stravinsky. At the same time he was antipathetic to Vaughan Williams—antipathetic to what may be called Vaughan Williams's humility in the presence of nature, the masses of his fellow-men and divine Providence. He has himself said that— little though there is of Elgar in him—he would rather be thought of as Elgarian.

Walton is now a middle-aged man, and it is possible that— contrary to what was expected fifteen years or so ago—he is not destined to be one of those composers whose very names stand in certain men's minds as representative of a certain position in life, an attitude, a belief, a complex of ideas which make up a national or a supra-national character; but rather as the author of a rather small number of finely distinguished compositions, each rather partially representing a mind that has not, as a whole, realized itself in art.

The symphony in B flat minor, of 1935, is the most ambitious and noblest of these compositions, though it has won for itself rather less prominence in the musical life of its time than the viola concerto or 'Belshazzar's Feast.' Many conductors have coped with it, and a regret of my life is that I have never heard Koussevitsky do so. Harty's performance was the most vividly emotional; and Boult has brought to it an intense appreciation of its structure— an attitude which, too, the music can well support. Walton himself has succeeded with it to no mean degree. He is not a great conductor, and he never attempts to bring out quantities of the inner details with which his score is crowded. But he has a cool head; and I recall a performance at which he revealed a driving power and intensity of expression which his usually cold exterior had seemed to belie. Gone was the nonchalance of his early years, when—seemingly indifferent—he had restricted himself to the bare rudiments of time-beating with his right hand. So inactive thenadays was his left that a candid friend suggested he might as well put it into his pocket—and Walton came near doing so. He still ignores about fifty per cent of his own detailed nuances, and about that percentage of his music is left unrealized when he conducts. But, wise in his understanding of the orchestra, he leaves much to the players, never fusses them unduly, but spends most of the time at rehearsal in achieving a perfect rhythm. But at the particular performance I now recall he effected an intensity which was nothing less than exciting.

He was criticized for too fast a tempo in the first movement and for allowing too little space for expression. But if the rhythms were as clear outside the orchestra as they were within, then that criticism was answered by the compensating verve and vitality of the playing. Several alterations were made in the score— nearly all of them to do with over-heavy accompaniments. Mercilessly he drove through the strings' difficult rhythmic problems. It is to be hoped that these came off! They all seemed to be taken considerably quicker than the similar passages in Schubert's C major symphony, which are quick enough. In the scherzo every accent was put into its place, again with some adjustments of the published scoring. Here the music requires the coolest of heads and a deadly precision; and Walton was at his best. The slow movement seemed too fast, particularly at rehearsal; but there are two ways of looking at this movement. The faster pace means a more restrained emotion, but possibly an increase in the strangeness of the atmosphere. Walton does not encourage rubato, but asks for intensely expressive colour and sound within the tempo. Boult, always a master of balance, makes the opening of this movement beautifully clear, while with the composer himself the rich background tends to become foreground and essential voices to be submerged. Harty made a ravishing effect with these lovely phrases, and the music, in his hands above all, seemed human and warm. His tempo was slower and he gave full freedom to the soloists.

In the last movement Walton let himself go. After the doubts and disappointments of the moody slow movement he plunged into the finale as though he had found the very key of life. The ensemble of the introduction is usually a nightmare of anxiety, especially when the conductor indulges in much rubato. Walton, instead, relied on supercharging the intensity of those grand, rising phrases, rather than giving them with a virtuoso's bravura. They were consequently not difficult to play, and three clear beats in a bar were ample for clarity. In the Allegro he asked for the sharpest, clearest accents obtainable in absolutely precise rhythm. The first notable change in the published scoring came at the second subject, which previously he had always wanted as powerful as possible. His direction for the second violins and violas, who, unaided, bear the weight on their shoulders, is 'Fortissimo, focosamente.' Meanwhile there are fortissimo and slashing accents all over the page. From the 1st violins came complaints of scratchiness and references to sandpaper; and Walton modified his demands, now asking only for forte, with no undue forcing. He obtained the utmost effect from the wonderful trumpet call before the peroration in the Epilogue. Here he allowed the soloist ample scope. Never had the orchestra seen him give so much of himself as in the coda. When the percussion came into action that aloof personality became as violently magnetized as a Beecham.

XXXII

WALTON'S SYMPHONY

THE symphony opens impressively. Walton plants B flat deep in virgin soil; it is a tree of a forest; and we are at once held by the strength of the roots. The tonality is immediately clear, and there is a grand feeling of space and power in the wide lay-out of the score, clear in its sustained harmony of a bare fifth, agitated by the strings.

In the following example of the opening bars there are four main ideas which make up most of the important material of the first movement. The timpani open the movement with a continuous roll of B flat, and the horns build up the bare and clear harmony, which is really the basis of all the later harmonic background. Next the rhythmic figure (Fig. 2), which the 2nd violins begin to worry, goes right through the movement. This is the rhythm it is so difficult, but vital, for the strings to keep incessantly up to the mark, for it supplies the generating force for the intense agitation that is of the essence of the first movement. The 2nd violins have no mean task at the very opening of the symphony, for everything depends on their perfect ensemble and unshakable rhythm.

Fig. 1

Fig. 2

The heavy footsteps of the cellos (Fig. 3), which now only open the door for the oboe, attain great significance. A long way farther on—almost in the last stages of the movement—this long-drawn-out oboe theme (Fig. 4) is the most important idea of all. It has two particular features: the change of note in the first half and the falling scale in the last two bars. These features are to become a burning obsession.

Fig. 3

Fig. 4

After these four chief ideas have been firmly established—harmonic background, rhythm, subsidiary motive and long-sustained melody—the cellos throw their weight on the orchestra by a series of long, heavy, sustained notes, marking a new harmony in which the horns become interested:

Fig. 5

This brings an angry outburst from the rest of the orchestra—the rhythmic figure of the opening becoming more and more furious on the strings, with the woodwind yelling at the top. The brass, however, go over to the other side and back up the cellos, and the first scene comes to an end.

A new subject of an accompanying nature, derived from Fig. 3, now comes off at a tangent on the violas and cellos—accompanying

the woodwind who, fortissimo, play the chief melodic subject
(Fig. 4):

Fig. 6

and the chief rhythmic character shows signs of a new shape:

Fig. 7

This settles down eventually to a tearing, arm-aching bugbear
for the strings. Though assuming many melodic shapes, the
rhythm itself remains thus—fierce in its insistent urge to work up
the orchestra to a frenzy.

Walton himself is merciless to his strings, and drives the
orchestra at a tempo which can only just be borne. No good to tell
him that the players may come unstuck because of the impossi-
bility of the lower strings' sounding clear at such speed! "You
must do it! I don't like this movement any slower—it's too
emotional as it is, and it gets unbearable if that side of the picture
is drawn out. It must go *on*!"

Meanwhile the cellos begin a new, important tune:

Fig. 8 Cellos

Immensely sustained, it is one of those Sibelian melodies that
may lead to anything. Note the triplet and quintuplet in the last
two bars, spreading across the four normal beats. This will become
thrilling later on.

The music waxes thick with each one saying his own say—

those with the fierce rhythm having the loudest voices. The bassoons are at last clearly heard by themselves playing yet another subject, which begins with a leap of a seventh. It is the signal for a change of tempo:

Fig. 9

The insistent, brutal goading of the rhythm has at last succeeded in moving the great "tempo-lever" up a notch; *a tempo agitato* the rhythm, though just as fierce, has now become longer:

Fig. 10

and in a moment the woodwind, as at the beginning of the second scene, lay hold with all their force upon the first theme. The music, though made of the same ingredients of the opening bars of the symphony, is now violent. A landmark can be picked up, after a general turmoil in the orchestra boils up to a climax. The rhythm is suddenly beaten out by the strings alone on a grand unison, fortissimo. Walton led magnificently up to this point. It should be a grand clear-up of the whole first part of the movement; and the effect of this sudden concentration in one clear line is electric.

The next scene begins with the bassoon motive, the rhythm at last retiring into the background for a while. A new, slow but important fragment bursts out in the woodwind, and the first

bar—with its 𝅘𝅥𝅮𝅘𝅥𝅮𝅘𝅥 — might be well remarked as that of a

vital link, which appears in every movement of the symphony at some time or other, generally at the height of a climax:

Fig. 11

So, with these new ideas, and many references to the various themes, particularly the broad triplet which we noted a while ago at the end of the cello tune, we draw quickly on to the first major climax of the movement.

In a page taken from the book of Sibelius, woodwind, strings and trumpets suddenly concentrate on one note, and hammer out a terrific series of syllables, driving home that one change of note that the oboe makes in his opening phrase or first theme (Fig. 4):

To make no mistake about the significance of that one change of note, Walton crashes it, as it were, through the very bones of our heads. When our hearing becomes normal once more, Walton, with unwonted tenderness, suddenly soothes the agitated atmosphere and stifles that incessant worrying rhythm, with which he has been driving both his orchestra and audience crazy, to a mutter on the clarinets. In place of agitation, a gentle pulse calms the air:

The 1st violins, over this pulsation, play the first theme, stressing its two main features. A new scene opens with a very quiet passage for small orchestra, having this lovely expressive fragment as its chief idea on flutes and bassoons over a solo viola:

Then it takes us gently to an expressive, broad tune that has been imperceptibly growing in the music:

Fig.15

Full of Walton's most expressive writing, this melody eventually grows to splendid proportions. It is the kind of expansive phrase that warms the heart of a player, in which every note seems to need its own particular expression and the whole artist in one is roused. Before it is heard in its entirety, Walton, as if afraid to let himself go too soon, returns again to the quiet episode for the small orchestra—this time extraordinarily melancholy and unhappy in mood, with the sound thinned down to pianissimo.

At its close the violas launch out into the great cello tune again, now in its full form with an impassioned ending which, with the half of the 1st violins and woodwind, brings the whole tune to an intense glow of emotion:

Fig.16 Strings & Wind

The atmosphere becomes taut and strained again after these emotional episodes; hardness and brutality dominate the orchestra. In a terrific accumulation of sound and energy the orchestra bursts into an almost unbearable reiteration of that change of note in the original oboe phrase, with a savagely attacking rhythm:

Fig.17 Strings

For bar after bar Walton batters us with this brutally. When, as before, he lets us go at last the very instrument of torture he has been using becomes a sedative—it turns into the quick pulse which sets in for our blessed relief. The waters of oblivion gently close over our heads, a superb effect is made by the solo bass tuba. Giving sudden and immense significance to that fragment of the opening bars (Fig. 3), which we remember as heavy footsteps on the cellos, the tuba booms out like an enormous bass bell:

Fig.18

Four times this grand motive resounds, to be taken up in its original complete form and reiterated by the trombones. It is a signal for the concentration of Walton's forces again for the final and greatest climax of the movement. Great though the emotional intensity of the music has already been, what is coming is altogether surpassing. Wise is the conductor who can hold back his power and temperament for this last effort, which is not just a long crescendo of mere power of sound but also one of the intense inner feeling behind the music, which must now burst out in a continuous stream.

So, with the signal boomed out by the tuba, the 1st violins and cellos bravely fly the pennant of the final tune of all:

Fig. 19

With the clear simplicity of the beginning the harmony returns to a grand B flat in the bass, alternating with its fifth, F, but the rhythm, no longer having to work up the orchestra, remains in the form of a continuous pulse.

All the composer's resources now concentrate on this one huge tune, which has begun with the second tune proper of the

movement (Fig. 8). Certain bars are missing, but others—
especially that with the triplet—are expanded farther and farther
until an enormous Sibelian climax makes the whole orchestra
glow and blaze. Note the break at the comma at the height of the
climax:

Fig. 20

This violently cuts off everything short, but only to take breath.
Walton cannot leave this last idea alone, but, dropping the key a
semitone to A, continues to hammer at it with full woodwind
and strings, and all the force the orchestra can give him. For a
moment a queer passage for brass alone seems to find the composer himself perplexed; but, after a momentary hesitation and
two crashing chords, he suddenly plunges on again—lowering
the key a semitone farther down into A flat. The strings cling
with might and main to the first theme, once more in its original
form, over the bell motive of the opening bars, now pealed out
by the four horns. The key ascends again to B flat and, last of all,
back comes the rhythm of the opening bars, to end the movement
in fury.

'Presto, con malizia,' is the apt title of the Scherzo. If the
listeners' impression of this movement resembles the players', it
is one of being caught up in a whirlpool.

On the fringes of this vortex the first of the four main themes
grunts on the basses and bassoons—some twenty bars from the
harmonic and rhythmic preparations of the beginning. The key
opens and ends in E minor.

Presto, con malizia
Fig. 21 Cellos & Bassoons

The chief measures of the movement illustrate Walton's
particular, sharply accentuated rhythms. 'Portsmouth Point' is a

good rhythmical study for this Scherzo—though here is no flippancy but a succession of spiteful thrusts; whereas 'Portsmouth Point' was strongly flavoured with the hornpipe and the broad humour of old Pompey. As if out of perversity, the composer soon upsets the too easy flow of the basic 3/4 rhythm by throwing a 5/4 bar here and there into the works:

Fig. 22

The second theme soon comes into sight, easily recognizable by the new rhythm of its first bar (which is of great importance later) and the silent bar immediately following it:

Fig. 23

At first this theme seems quiet and harmless; but a noisy-voiced motive shoots it away, dinning itself into our ears and shrieking back at us as it passes on the woodwind:

Fig. 24

Then, with unexpected calm, we seem drawn away again to the edges of the whirlpool, and there is nothing but little disjointed figures which fade in and out of our consciousness—though occasional crashes warn us we are not far away from some demonic power. This respite is shortlived; the water quickly becomes confused once more, and we are drawn back into the rush and swirl. Round come the same shapes as before—some yelling, others whispering. A new voice sounds—not easy to pick out at first because of its similarity with part of the first theme. It

assumes a clearer shape as it hisses nearer, especially over a background of clear, static harmony in the strings:

Fig. 25 W. Wind

A great climax is piled up of all this material, and, just as a
catastrophe seems to be upon us, Walton, in characteristic fashion,
suddenly resolves all this swirling into a throbbing rhythm on one
chord over a buzzing in the violas.

Fierce crashes, as before, make this no lasting respite, and a
malicious scream from the woodwind pulls us inexorably into
the roaring mass again, now intensified. The movement, gathering a momentum that is thrilling to experience inside the orchestra, rushes to the end after another unusually merciful lull,
which is finally shattered by a terrifying unison shriek from the
entire orchestra. With Satanic humour, Walton thereupon bangs
down the lid of his gigantic cauldron.

After the orgy of the Scherzo, the atmosphere of the slow
movement is breath-taking in its stillness. We awaken on some
new planet, where everything seems spiritualized, detached and
wondering.

The soft C sharp on the strings, which is the first sound, has a
good deal more to it than a simple unison. It is the precious
thread on which everything is to hang. No other note in the
scale would have seemed so foreign—such worlds away from the
last crash of the Scherzo. The flute is the first voice to be heard, in
an intensely melancholy song, wayward and imaginative:

Fig. 26 *Andante con malincolia*
doloroso molto espress.

An intense sorrowing for humanity may well be the meaning this exiled spirit is expressing in its rhapsodical phrases. Many were the times this was played before one was able to feel in tune with its vagaries. Now it does more than touch one's sense of beauty. Softly the flute fades into the warmer tone of the clarinet, whose voice has less sorrow and more comfort:

Fig. 27

The two oboes enrich the accompaniment. The orchestra becomes more expressive, discussing the ideas suggested by the clarinet, who is encouraged to become more confident and takes on the most important subject of the movement. This is an intensely expressive theme, containing in its line a little figure

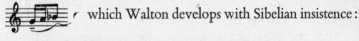 which Walton develops with Sibelian insistence:

Fig. 28 Clarinet

This clarinet tune is richly accompanied by pizzicato strings, while the harmony, until now moving above C sharp minor, falls to C, with an added B flat strongly marked in the texture. A lovely phrase of intense longing on solo viola and cello haunts one for days after playing it, though it is but part of the background and only one of many expressive phrases that now warm and colour the music after the cold simplicity of the opening. Conductors have great difficulty in keeping the full and complex background in true proportion. The music is so fraught with little, brilliant patches of colour and sudden intensity of feeling that the chief melodic line of, first, the flute and then the clarinet, tends to become obscured. The strings presently dominate the orchestra, suffused with dark colour and passion, but this is only the forerunner of greater things to come; for the orchestra is still, for a time, generally subdued, while the various solo instruments brood over the themes quoted, with much subtlety and range of expression.

The next landmark can be picked up on the violas and cellos, who passionately repeat the second tune of the movement (Fig. 27), over the basses and horns, who sustain a deep C sharp pedal, static as the opening bars. At this point Walton begins to gather his orchestra together, concentrating the department in blocks where he can obtain the utmost effect of sonority, and taking us through two and a half pages of the score to the greatest emotional climax of the whole symphony.

This wonderful passage ranks high in modern music. It is Sibelian in its sense of a bursting torrent of sound; but extremely original in content. The passage ranges over all the previous material and, with shattering power, Walton seizes all the quiet thoughts, mainly sorrowful and expressive, and with brutal force turns them into blazing fury. The C sharp here again sustains the whole fabric. Vicious scales on the basses attempt to rend it, but they always fall back upon this rock. When this anger subsides the calm of the opening bars prevails again and upon a background now utterly still the flute's unhappy voice of exile resumes its anxious and sorrowful questioning. The movement closes as it began, in the rarefied atmosphere of another planet.

It is a violent transition from C sharp minor to B flat, the key of the finale; and from a melancholy and contemplative mood we are plunged into one of bold, superb confidence. The composer seems to discover a new outlook on life and the clue to its problems.

The basis of the movement lies in the seventeen bars of introduction, marked 'Maestoso'; and, just as in the first movement, the germ is the opening phrase:

Fig. 29 *Maestoso*

The upward leaping figure in the first bar returns again and again throughout the movement, like the flaming up of sacred fires.

The bows of the strings tear the notes from the instruments with the effect of an almost frightening liberation of pent-up thought. The harmony is clear and bare, forming a rock-like foundation for the whole massive structure. It is the impassioned 'held' (tenuto) notes, as much as the furiously attacked passages, that charge the atmosphere with such electricity.

The allegro, the central section of this movement, opens with a number of short impetuous themes, strongly accented and cross-accented in typically Waltonian manner, and punctuated with exclamations from the brass and percussion. These scrappy, taut figures may be taken as a whole first subject; and the tension must be screwed up as far as the orchestra, and especially the strings, can stand:

Though the score is thickly dotted with this material, one must continually hark back to the introduction for the clue to this last movement. The music is seldom without some reference to the grand opening phrases of the introduction, and though this allegro, or working-out section of the movement proper, is extraordinarily ingenious and brilliant it is the noble introduction and final epilogue that lift the finale to its great height. This first subject-matter, then, is clear if these impetuous figures can be borne in mind, and it will only be needful to mention a few landmarks, such as the arrival of a second subject. This is easy to pick up. It is violently attacked by violas and 2nd violins:

Fig. 31 *focosamente*

Impetuous though the music is, the emotions are given a rest. New technical problems face the players, and in this fugue there is a feeling of relief, among the violas particularly, when other instruments join in with their own troubles, and the beam of the searchlight is directed elsewhere. At the height of the climax the whole orchestra is occupied with fugal engagements. The composer then completely breaks off the fugue, and a quiet section ensues. The oboe plays a climbing melody:

Fig. 32 *espress*

the significance of which does not appear until later on in the movement, during a second fugue. By dint of subsidiary phrases of expressive character, this relieving section is anything but dull, and it is not long before reference to the second subject (Fig. 31) wakes everyone up again, and a climax is built up, with a phrase from the introduction returning to round it off at its peak in double fortissimo. The tempo is now quickened to 3/8, 'Vivacissimo,' and fragments of the introduction mingle with the allegro material in the same vigorous, taut rhythm as before.

The oboe's tune of the quiet section (Fig. 32) is now pressed into its more vigorous and significant shape. It is made to form the subject of another fugue, culminating in a stretto in which the violas, again under the limelight, lead off with a bustling, hurrying passage of no less nasty a nature than the second subject, though this time in regular semiquavers. Marked fondly by Walton 'pianissimo,' it generally starts about mezzoforte in the excitement of performance, and the effect is spoilt:

Fig. 33

From this point, an important landmark, Walton begins to accumulate his forces, and we draw near to an immense concentration of sound and energy—a climax of the same prodigious dimensions as that in the slow movement. The force and rhythm with which this grand passage grows is awe-inspiring; the scoring, wasting nothing in over-much complexity, becomes more brilliant, until at last we hear those fiery progressions of the introduction flaming up again. We have now reached the epilogue, which is cast in the same mould as the introduction but is more brilliantly scored, and scorching now in its intensity. As in the beginning, 'Maestoso' is the tempo-direction, and from the first superb fanfare on the brass the orchestra is caught up as if in some mighty hand, and once again every instrument seems to burn with the passionate demand for articulate thought.

Yet Walton, before his peroration, has something more to say. Suddenly the tempo is slowed down and an unexpected diminuendo reveals a trumpet call, which sounds as from a great distance, extraordinarily moving in its calm and simplicity. This phrase, which at first only moves from its initial note to a fifth and then an octave, is like a magical echo of some dim Last Post:

Fig. 34

The melodic line grows and then fades away on one of the many expressive phrases of the introduction.

A violent rushing scale on the strings once more hurls us into the 'maestoso' of the epilogue, and the faint call that has just faded on the trumpet is taken up, echoed and re-echoed fortissimo on the strings and woodwind, amidst crashes from the percussion and brass. Now it is as though a colossal stairway were to appear before our eyes, its top disappearing in the clouds and its base resting on the dominant of the keynote, a great resounding pedal F.

The full percussion, with its reserves of extra timpani and gong called up, now crashes out at the top of each clamorous phrase, and the strings and woodwind surge up this shining stairway with a titanic heaving, as though dragging the very weight of the earth behind them:

A last shattering reiteration of the introduction theme (Fig. 30) brings the music to its final bars, when the whole orchestra combines to crash out seven chords that are like colossal shouts. The long silences between these chords are a test of nerves, and give one time to wonder whether the walls of the concert hall are made of tougher stuff than Jericho boasted. Thus does this splendid symphony end, on the seventh shout.